THE NOBEL CENTURY

THE NOBEL CENTURY

"To spread knowledge is to spread well-being"
ALFRED NOBEL

Preface by Stig Ramel

Executive Director of the Nobel Foundation

Introduction by Asa Briggs

Provost of Worcester College, Oxford

CHAPMANS

1991

Frontispiece
This false-colour bubble chamber photograph shows the
symmetrical production of matter and antimatter. For
his invention of the chamber, Donald A. Glaser (page 104)
was awarded the 1960 Physics Prize.

Where dates appear after
names in the text, they refer to the year
in which Nobel laureates were
awarded their Prize.

Chapmans Publishers Ltd
141–143 Drury Lane
London WC2B 5TB

BRITISH LIBRARY CATALOGUING IN PUBLICATION DATA
The Nobel Century.
001.44
ISBN 1-85592-516-8

First published by Chapmans 1991

© International Merchandising Corporation 1991

Developed by IMG Publishing,
a division of International Merchandising Corporation

Managing Editor: Campbell Geeslin
Picture Research: Meg McVey
Additional Writing: Ann Bayer and Martha Fay
Design: Andrew Shoolbred

Designed and produced by
The Albion Press Ltd, Princes Risborough

Photoset in 10/12 Palatino by
York House Typographic Ltd, London

Illustrations originated by
York House Graphics Ltd, London

Printed and bound in Great Britain by
BPCC Hazell Books, Paulton and Aylesbury

Publication of this volume was made possible
by the generous support of

PARKE-DAVIS,
DIVISION WARNER-LAMBERT COMPANY

Acknowledgements

This book has been assembled for all who want to be informed, entertained and exhilarated by stories of success, selfless dedication, and genius in the twentieth century.

An illustrated volume like *The Nobel Century* is made possible only because of many people and institutions. Most importantly, this publication would not have been possible without the Nobel Foundation's assistance. Not only did they welcome the use of their vast copyrighted resources, but Birgitta Lemmel, the Information Secretary at the Foundation, in concert with the prize-awarding institutions, patiently reviewed the factual details contained in the book. Stig Ramel, Executive Director of the Nobel Foundation, who retires this year, contributed the Preface. The distinguished historian Asa Briggs summed up Alfred Nobel's life and the awards in the sweeping, invigorating overview. Leading science journalists provided the introductions to the chapters on the science prizes; Emmanuel Le Roy Ladurie, the historian and Administrateur Général of the Bibliothèque Nationale in Paris, was asked to write the introduction to the Nobel Prize for Literature, since more Frenchmen have been awarded that prize than any other nationality; Irwin Abrams, unquestionably the world's expert on the Nobel Peace Prize, contributed the introduction to the chapter on that prize.

Throughout this book readers will find inspiring quotations, brilliant observations and predictions of the future by the Nobel laureates themselves. Many of them contributed specially to *The Nobel Century*, and for these personal insights we are most grateful.

Others who helped make this book possible include Ian and Marjory Chapman. The enthusiasm and dedication of the editorial and marketing staff at Chapmans Publishers, especially Mark Crean and Greg Hill, has brought this volume to a successful worldwide publication. Finally, Campbell Geeslin, who served as the Managing Editor for this project on behalf of IMG Publishing, tirelessly researched and compiled the supporting material and edited the diverse contributions into a coherent whole.

The cost of coordinating this worldwide effort during the past two years has been enormous, and we would not have been able successfully to bring this project to fruition without the generous support of the Parke-Davis division of the Warner-Lambert Company. Their worldwide sponsorship of *The Nobel Century* not only includes this volume but has provided funding for four one-hour television programmes being broadcast throughout the world prior to the Nobel Jubilee celebrations in Stockholm in December of this year. 1991 marks the ninetieth anniversary of the awarding of the first Nobel Prize. To celebrate this occasion, almost 200 Nobel laureates will be returning to Stockholm and Oslo to participate in a series of educational programmes and cultural events, as well as to experience, once again, the traditions of the Nobel Week as the 1991 laureates are honoured.

For fourteen years, International Management Group has worked with the Nobel Foundation to produce television programmes, books, educational curriculae and other materials in a continuing relationship designed to communicate the achievement of the Nobel laureates. Through these efforts, we are constantly reminded that Nobel laureates are the most interesting, original, and generally remarkable people of our era. We hope this story of *The Nobel Century* will inspire future generations to excel as we collectively face the challenges of the twenty-first century.

Todd H. McCormack,
Executive Editor, International Management Group

Contents

Preface

Stig Ramel

Alfred Nobel was a man of ideas. He once said, "If I have a thousand ideas and only one turns out to be good, I am satisfied." Of all the brilliant ideas he had during his lifespan of sixty-three years, none had a greater impact than his "invention" of the International Prize in Science, Literature, and Peace to those who have made the greatest contributions to the benefit of mankind without consideration of nationality, race, or creed. The idea, laid down in Nobel's will, signed in Paris on 27 November 1895, was born in a time of intense nationalism and with the dark shadow of the coming World War cast over Europe. At first, when Nobel's will was made public, it created a scandal: it was attacked from the Right as unpatriotic, and from the Left as a capitalist plot. Today, nearly 100 years later, we know how wrong they both were.

Through the Nobel Prizes in Physics, Chemistry, and Physiology or Medicine, starting in 1901, we can trace the path of modern science: at the beginning it was a narrow winding road; today it has become an express-way towards the future. At the turn of the century, the number of scientists could be counted in hundreds or thousands, and only in a few countries in Europe and North America. Today, they are in the millions and to be found all over the world. The Nobel Prizes have greatly stimulated international scientific contacts and helped to spread new ideas. Publish and publish quickly so you can get international recognition, and possibly a Nobel Prize, has become the credo of international science. Countries in which dictators and narrow-minded nationalism build walls against the outside world have slipped behind those who are partners in the international free-flow of ideas. The success of the Nobel Prizes has stimulated other men of fortune and goodwill to create their own form of recognition – there are now more than 2,000 international prizes. The prestige and glory of the Nobel Prizes have often made governments aware of the importance of science, helping to increase the flow of financial resources into the laboratories.

The young Nobel, a dreamer, wanted to become a writer; his passion for literature continued throughout his life. The Nobel Prize in Literature has helped to stimulate the reading of books written by authors of non-Western languages and environments. At the beginning of the century, the Prize was more or less confined to the world of European literature. The first non-European Nobel laureate, Rabindranath Tagore of India, was honoured in 1913; the first American, Sinclair Lewis, in 1930; the first Latin American in 1945, Gabriela Mistral; the first Japanese, Yasunari Kawabata, in 1968; the first Australian, Patrick White, in 1973; the first African, Wole Soyinka, in 1986; and the first writer in Arabic, Naguib Mahfouz, in 1988. Thus the Prize in Literature has helped to create a world literature: those writers who receive the prizes soon find their books translated into new languages and printed in millions of copies, and read by as many.

When Nobel wrote his will he feared the new, horrible kind of war he saw coming, a juggernaut built with industrial technology and fuelled by perverted science. He believed that if the world did not in twenty years adopt an international world order of peace, for which he himself drew the blueprint, mankind would commit suicide in a world catastrophe. And to Nobel, the scientist and poet, those horrors were easily imaginable. The world survived, however, and today the United Nations, which is very much the organization Nobel himself looked forward to, has helped to preserve peace – and so have the dreadful weapons Nobel imagined.

Nobel once wrote, "The day when two army corps can annihilate one another in one second, all civilized nations will recoil from war and discharge their troops." He was right and he was wrong. War is still with us, but not the world wars. The Peace Prize, the most well-known but also the most difficult and controversial of all the Prizes, has helped to establish a forum, and to give the limelight to those who believe in peace and the possibility of change without war, with the rights and dignity of man preserved.

Many of the Prizes have gone to the international organizations of which Nobel himself dreamed, and to people who are working in their spirit. The Peace Prize has gone to holy men and women, civil rights workers, and to preachers of peace – but also to hard-nosed politicians who at least once acted like statesmen, and for that moment they were honoured.

The Nobel Foundation, established in 1900 at the very threshold of the new century, was given the task of enacting Nobel's will, furthering his ideas and speaking in his name. The Foundation was also entrusted with his fortune in order to give financial backing to the Prizes he created.

As the new century draws towards its end, it is with pride that the Nobel Foundation can report that the Big Prize, as Nobel wanted it to be, is at least as big as it was in 1901. We have succeeded in weathering inflation, depression and wars, and other disasters of the financial markets. The Nobel fortune is today in real terms considerably larger than it was when Nobel left it to us. This helps the Prize-giving organizations – the Royal Swedish Academy of Sciences, the Nobel Assembly at the Karolinska Institute, the Swedish Academy and the Norwegian Nobel Commit-

tee – to continue the outstanding work they have done since 1901, work which has made Nobel a symbol of what is best in the twentieth century.

Not long before he died, after a full life of constant work, poor health, many sorrows, some fine moments but many more of shattered dreams, Alfred Nobel wrote a poem of which I shall permit myself to quote the following lines:

Thus are the realities of life laid bare,
leaving our dreams of happiness
as the ghosts of memory alone.

When on 10 December each year, the day of Alfred Nobel's death in San Remo in 1896, we celebrate his Prizes in Stockholm and Oslo, "the ghosts of memory" vanish, and "our dreams of happiness" are with us again.

Stig Ramel,
Stockholm

Introduction

Asa Briggs

It is not only historians who deal in centuries. For at least 300 years centuries have figured in the imagination, most recently in the popular imagination. So, too, have decades – and, above all, anniversaries, jubilees, and centenaries. All of these provide opportunities for reviewing the past, assessing the present, and scanning the future. This is not a centenary volume in that the centuries both of Alfred Nobel's death, 1896, and of the first Nobel Prizes, 1901, still lie ahead. Yet it is the right time to search for a perspective.

The story of the Nobel Prizes and of the people who have won them has a peculiar interest about it in our own time, not least because at the end of our own century – the century of the Nobel Prize-winners – the world will enter a new millennium. Such a conjunction 1,000 years ago created both interest and concern. How will our century be related not only to the next century, but to the next millennium? To what extent are the Nobel Prize-winners, outstanding in their own generation, pointing the way? Ours has been the only century when it has been possible for a book to appear with the title *Tomorrow is Already Here*.

Towards the end of the nineteenth century, an age of unprecedented material progress, there was much talk of drawing up an account of the century's gains and losses, talk that fascinated Nobel in his last years. It was two years after his death that the biologist A. R. Wallace, who had worked on a theory of evolution in parallel with Charles Darwin earlier in the century, had attempted such an account in his still-illuminating book *The Wonderful Century* (1898).

Wallace was a critic of his age, drawn to original ideas, who observed pertinently that "we men of the nineteenth century have not been slow to praise it". Nonetheless, he himself, as originator of the phrase "survival of the fittest", was proud of the fact that much had been accomplished during his century, and did not hesitate to conclude that it was not only superior to any century that had gone before, but might be compared with "the whole period of history" that preceded it.

Whatever the relationship between the twentieth and the twenty-first centuries may be – and we move out of our own century uncertainly – the nineteenth and the twentieth centuries remain intricately interconnected. Indeed, while in the twentieth century there have been many surprises, and we have been tempted to look back to the late Middle Ages for mirrors of our own time, it remains useful in historical interpretation to consider the nineteenth and the twentieth centuries together, in order to fathom where we are, and to forecast where we are moving.

This is not least true in discussing the evolution of the Nobel Prizes. If ours is the century of the Nobel Prize, the nineteenth century was the century of Alfred Nobel himself.

Born in Stockholm, Alfred Nobel was in many respects a typically successful man of his century – a talented inventor who created a prosperous business, and who in the process made an enormous fortune. Yet Nobel was exceptional, if not unique, in two respects. First, the geographical spread of his complex business pursuits, which were international in an age of active nationalism, made him care little about frontiers; second, there was irony in the fact that his fortune was made from the development of explosives for peaceful purposes, which in our own century are used for both peace and war.

Nobel considered the main use of his new explosives – including dynamite, which was discovered almost by accident and first patented in 1867 – to be not destructive, but constructive. His was an age of great civil engineering projects on both sides of the Atlantic, in new as well as old countries, and dynamite made many of them possible. It was also, however, an age when most politicians were prepared to resort to war, and when military establishments demanded more and more powerful armaments. It was against this background that perhaps the most well-known of all the Prizes which Nobel was to endow was the Peace Prize.

There was, therefore, a Shavian dimension to Nobel, who, because of the complexity of his motivations and deeds, might have figured not only in George Bernard

13

Shaw's *Arms and the Man*, first performed in 1894, but in "Socialism for Millionaires", a tract that appeared in 1901, the year of the first Nobel Prizes. "Never give the people everything they want" was Shaw's advice to "the millionaire class, a small but growing one". "Give them something they ought to want and don't." Nobel would have approved of two sections, in particular, in Shaw's Fabian Tract 107 – one headed "sorrows of the millionaire", the other "millionaires must not leave too much to their families".

As for Shaw, he was to win the Nobel Prize for Literature in 1925, but to refuse the money, asking for it to be used to endow an Anglo-Swedish Literary Foundation. Four years earlier, in *Back to Methuselah*, he had propounded a philosophy which again might have appealed to Nobel: "You imagine what you desire; you will what you imagine; and at last you create what you will."

"The history of the development of modern explosives," it was claimed on Nobel's death in 1896 – with no touch of imaginative rhetoric – was "practically the history of his life". Certainly the twentieth-century explosives industry – British as well as Swedish, French, German, or Russian – could not have been developed except on the basis of the science – including that of ballistics – that Nobel knew best. As a result, we can appreciate in retrospect the significance of Nobel's career in the light of our own fading century, in which there has been not one world war but two, and when there have been many smaller wars in places that Nobel, for all his restless travels, would never have placed on his own map.

For all its continuing, if increasingly precarious and ambivalent sense of "progress", particularly scientific progress, of which the Nobel Science Prizes provide a kind of barometer, our own experience has diverged sharply from many late-nineteenth-century expectations. When the British periodical *The Twentieth Century* produced a special issue *"Eighty Years of Progress?"* in 1977, it was the question mark that was most significant.

As Gilbert Murray put it rather too succinctly in that number, Nobel himself lived in an age when Europe "really became civilized and had a conscience". Yet Nobel was more aware than anyone else of the motivations of many politicians and soldiers, and put little trust in disarmament – one of the panaceas of the 1880s and 1890s – as a means of checking conflict. He once told Bertha von Suttner, "my factories may well put an end to war before your Congresses. For in the day that two armies are capable of destroying each other in a second, all civilized nations will surely recoil before a war and dismiss their troops."

Bertha von Suttner was an active organiser of the peace movement, formalized and developed like many other movements during the nineteenth century, and a founder of the League of Friends of Peace. She took part in the Fourth World Peace Conference in 1891, and was the author of an influential novel. The efforts of the Baroness interested Nobel. Indeed, he even hired a diplomat to draft a plan for peace, many of whose suggestions were used in setting up the League of Nations. However, he would probably not have been surprised that two governmental conferences on disarmament at the Hague in 1899 and 1907 both failed. Nor would he have been surprised that there were far more weapons in the world by 1914 than there had been in 1896, the year of his death, and there are now far more "sophisticated" weapons in the world than there were in 1914, or have ever been before. Fortunately for the Baroness, she died in June 1914 just before the Great War began. She won the Nobel Peace Prize, however, in 1905, the only woman to do so before 1931.

Unlike the Baroness, Nobel never wrote a book, but he wrote an enormous amount that was unpublished, not only about explosives but about life and death. At times, he argued simply, as scientists often do, "there is nothing in the world which cannot be misunderstood or abused". On at least one other occasion, however, he told Bertha that he would like to invent "a substance or a machine with such terrible power of mass destruction that war would thereby be made impossible for ever".

In the twentieth century there were to be others who

Right
Baroness Bertha von Suttner (page 46) was photographed as she left the London Peace Congress in 1908. The Austrian author and peace activist (on the left) was awarded the 1905 Prize.

Left
Alfred Nobel, who did not like to have his photograph taken, was described by a friend as "a thinker, a poet, a man bitter and good, unhappy and gay – given to superb flights of mind and to malicious suspicions . . ."

believed they had done this, including more than one Nobel Physics Prize-winner. It is of some interest, therefore, that during his last years Nobel was meditating on the atom. In a paper prepared around 1890 called "Philosophic Reflections to be Written", the first item Nobel listed was "interacting atoms", followed immediately by "the functions of the brain, thought and memory". "I have acquired a sublime contempt for the paltry dimensions of our globe," he also wrote, apparently a little later, "and take the most interest in a much smaller world body, namely the atom. Its form, movements and destinies, both as an individual and as a contributory cell in the life of the universe occupy my thoughts more than they decently ought to."

Nobel had another thought about the ways to peace, which remains topical in 1991: "I have come to the conclusion," he told a Belgian friend in 1892, "that the only real solution would be a treaty by which the governments bound themselves jointly to defend any country that was attacked. By degrees this would lead to partial disarmament, which is the only thing possible, since there must be an armed force for the maintenance of order." Nobel added a controversial footnote, however. "Formerly governments were even more shortsighted, narrow and quarrelsome than their subjects. In our day it looks as if the governments were at all event making an effort to quell such idiotic popular outbursts as are incited by a malicious press."

The dynamics both of "public opinion" and of governmental action have proved more complicated than Nobel suggested, however, and when war broke out in 1914, governments – the agencies that decided upon war and were prepared to wage it at high cost – were backed by sometimes frenzied opinion in their own countries. Nonetheless, the effect of a protracted war, "The Great War", was to bring down several of the proud governments of 1914, including the Hapsburg Empire, and the Tsarist

Empire, which had added greatly to the Nobel fortunes. Thereafter, the world was to be a very different place.

Nobel died in the middle of a remarkable decade, when Vienna was one of the great capital cities of Europe and when tsarist Russia was in a phase of rapid economic and social development. Everywhere new ideas were in the air and new styles were being adopted. During this decade there was as much talk, indeed, of the "new" — "new art", "new woman", "new age" – as there was of *fin de siècle*. In retrospect, the year of Nobel's death was an *annus mirabilis* in London, although no one realized it at the time or related one new development to another. This was the year of the first regular cinema shows in Leicester Square, of Marconi's successful wireless demonstrations, of the automobile rally from London to Brighton and of the founding of Alfred Harmsworth's popular newspaper, the *Daily Mail*, price one halfpenny. All these were portents of the century to come. Technical and social history were entering a new phase. It was also the year of the first Olympiad of modern times in Athens – and of two successful flights by S. P. Langley in his new "flying machine".

Inventions of all kinds, including the aeroplane, had always appealed to Nobel, and he invented many things as well as explosives, including artificial silk, artificial leather and artificial rubber. He had great hopes of aerial photography. Yet the ironies as well as the achievements of technical advance preoccupied him also. The nineteenth century was to end and our own century to begin to the sounds of a "Dawn of the Century Victory March" by E. T. Paull. The illustrated cover of the published edition of the "March" showed in the background not only an impressive collection of new nineteenth-century inventions, but suggestions of possible inventions to come. Promise or threat?

With the English fighting a tough war against the Boers

ALFRED NOBEL
1833 — 1896

in South Africa, and with Europeans threatened in violent disturbances in China, the English novelist George Gissing was writing at the end of the century that "a period of struggle for existence between the nations seems to have begun . . . This may very well result in a long period of semi-barbarism, until – perhaps by immense slaughter, perhaps by famine and epidemics – the members of the human race are once more reduced."

Such a note of alarm, backed by a pervasive melancholy, had often been sounded by Nobel in his private papers. Indeed, in a will drawn up in 1893 he had used the same words as Gissing: "If in thirty years they [the kind of people to whom he proposed to give Prizes] have not succeeded in reforming the present system, they will inevitably lapse into barbarism."

Two years after his death, one of Nobel's collaborators, Henry de Mosenthal, wrote an article about him in a periodical that had first appeared in 1877. It was called simply "The Inventor of Dynamite".

Despite the title of his article, Mosenthal dealt as much with Nobel's dreams as with his inventions, stressing that Nobel was always interested in inventions that had no direct military significance, and that he took out as many as 355 patents. "He always considered," Mosenthal added, "that by improving war material and thus increasing the dangers of war, he was contributing his share towards the pacification of the world."

The main point of the article, however, was that everything in Nobel's life culminated in his final will, drawn up without benefit of lawyers in 1895. Nobel wished his fortune not to pass to his family, but to be used to reward both peacemakers – the future of the world lay in their hands –

and scientists of various kinds, a group of people who "as a rule", he felt, had not been in a position to "reap much financial benefit from their labour".

Nobel believed fervently in science, and this was the creed that was to be expressed in the Nobel Science Prizes. "To spread knowledge," he argued, "is to spread well-being," adding that by this he meant general well-being, not individual prosperity. With the arrival of such well-being, the greater part of the evil which was "an inheritance from the dark ages" would disappear. "The advance in scientific research and its ever-widening sphere stirs the hope in us that microbes, those of the soul as well as those of the body, will gradually disappear, and that the only war humanity will wage in future be the one against the microbes."

The reference to microbes pointed to another of Nobel's beliefs that he shared with scientists and non-scientists alike. He was keenly interested in medicine, which had not yet become fully "scientific" by the time of his death, but which had nonetheless been profoundly changed during the nineteenth century both in its concepts and its practices. Nobel himself carried out a number of medical experiments, and, suffering from ill health throughout the whole of his life, put his trust in medical pioneers who found new remedies.

The Nobel Prizes in this field were to be awarded in Physiology or Medicine, a bracketing that the nineteenth century had made possible; significantly, the first winner of a Nobel Physiology or Medicine Prize was to be the German scientist Emil Adolf von Behring, who had been interested in microbes and had worked on "serum therapy especially in application against diphtheria". The 1905 Prize was to go

Left
The yellow building in the background is Alfred Nobel's laboratory, just outside Karlskoga, 155 miles from Stockholm. Today it is a museum.

Right
Nobel's controversial will was filed for probate at a small local court near his manor house. The portrait in the background shows him in his laboratory.

Right
Alfred Nobel lived in Russia, France, and Italy. He was known as ''Europe's richest vagabond''. This is the special fitted case he carried on his travels.

to Robert Koch, who had isolated the bacterium that triggered tuberculosis, the leading cause of death in Europe in the 1890s.

Nobel had always believed in helping living people rather than in supporting old institutions: "I would rather take care of the stomachs of the living than the glory of the departed in the form of monuments", he had once written; he is said to have given away large sums of money, some of it to "dreamers" like himself. His "large fortune", Mosenthal insisted, had not contributed to his happiness while alive, but "on the contrary had made him suspicious" not only of institutions, but of people. He was a lonely man who never married, and he died in unhappy circumstances which he had always feared at his villa in San Remo, inappropriately called at first *Mio Nido* (My Nest), surrounded by French servants, with "no kind hand of a friend or relative to close my eyes and whisper in my ear a gentle and sincere word of comfort". However, although Nobel had often felt despair, he had appreciated also how important was hope, which he once defined as "nature's veil for hiding truth's nakedness".

What the naked truth was in Nobel's case only he could say. His giving has ensured that his name is remembered long after him, and is remembered in more places than he himself ever knew. Yet at least one aspect of the "truth" was that Nobel had been a shrewd businessman, as well as a creative inventor exploring new ideas. Indeed, if an economic historian could tell Nobel's story entirely in terms not of giving but of building what in the twentieth century has come to be called "multinational" enterprise, he would pick out as key chapters the years of exceptional prosperity between 1871 and 1873, when Nobel opened ten manufacturing plants in nine countries, and the 1880s, when he consolidated his companies into two trusts, the English/German Trust and the Latin Trust. The Trust form, developed by J. D. Rockefeller in America, was a new business form on this side of the Atlantic. Nobel himself was instrumental in its growth.

There was to be a sequel, too, to this particular story, for in the late twentieth century giant concerns like ICI and Bofors can be traced back to Nobel through lines of descent, some of them intricate. Only in Russia was a Nobel enterprise to be terminated in the twentieth century – the huge Naftaproduktionsbolaget Bröderma Nobel, with its plant in the Baku oilfields and its headquarters in St Petersburg – and that came to an end not as a result of business failure but of political revolution.

As it was, the ultimate "truth" for Nobel was that he stipulated in his own handwritten will that his assets in the different companies should be withdrawn from business on his death, and that the major part of his estate should be converted into a fund, the income from which should be "distributed annually in the form of Prizes to those who during the preceding year" had "conferred the greatest benefit on mankind". Mosenthal called the will "extraordinary", yet it was not entirely without precedent, or sequel.

The Rumford Medal, awarded by the Royal Society in London since 1810, was presented to "the author of the most important discovery or useful improvement . . . made during the preceding two years on heat or light, the

Biographers have been attracted to Nobel by the complexity of his character, as they have to Rockefeller. When examining this as reflected both in his will and in his earlier pursuits and preoccupations, they have often felt they have been dealing with an enigma. Some of them have used his life – and death – to prove a case rather than to explore apparent and real contradictions. For others Nobel could be disposed of quickly: he was simply "a merchant of death". Not all of them noted that the word "dynamite" derives from the Greek word *dynamis*, which means power.

The sources of Nobel's attitudes and opinions – and he had many "strange ideas" that could shock his contemporaries – doubtless lay in his family and in his upbringing. Deeply attached to his mother, who did not die until 1889, he had had little formal institutional education either at school or at university, and he had had one serious row with his father, Immanuel, who was almost as extraordinary a person as his son was.

Immanuel too had been an inventor, and had laid the foundations of what became the huge cluster of Nobel enterprises by turning to the production of nitroglycerine, and by drawing Alfred and his brothers both into invention and into business. Nobel's father had already experimented with explosives before he left Sweden for Russia in 1842, seeing the business possibilities of the new product, and in 1850 had been awarded the highest Russian honour the tsar could confer on a foreigner, the Imperial Gold Medal.

As restless as his son, he was back in Sweden again in 1858, his contracts abruptly cancelled when Tsar Alexander II dramatically changed his policies. Bankrupt for a second time – the first time had been in the year that Alfred was born – Immanuel lived until 1872. There had been deep tragedy in his life when in 1864 his youngest son, Alfred's brother, was killed, together with four others, in an explosion in the Stockholm workshop that also destroyed his laboratory. Nitroglycerine was dangerous to store and transport, but more dangerous still to experiment with.

It was Alfred, not Immanuel, who invented an invaluable detonator that used gunpowder to ignite nitroglycerine, and two years later, a detonator cap that made possible the initial detonation – indispensable practical improvements. There was more than a touch of rivalry in their relationship, yet father and son shared the Lettersted Prize, a gold medal awarded in 1868 by the Swedish Academy of Sciences, "for outstanding original work in the field of art, literature and science, or for important discoveries of practical utility for mankind".

There may have been intimations here of long-term Nobel vistas, but in the short run, there were conflicts between father and son before Immanuel had a stroke and Alfred took over the explosives business, working without stint as managing director, plant engineer, office clerk and salesman. "Work beautifies everything," he was to write later. Already, however, Alfred had been warned by another brother to "give up inventing as soon as possible. It

preference always being given to such discoveries as . . . tend most to promote the good of mankind"; and seventeen years after Nobel's death, the Rockefeller Foundation was to be created by the other great nineteenth-century trustmaker, J. D. Rockefeller, as remarkable a businessman as Nobel, who did not want his vast fortune to "pass into the unknown with unmeasured and perhaps sinister possibilities". Rockefeller did not endow prizes, but created a Foundation which was to proclaim as its object "the well-being of mankind throughout the world". The two Foundations, Nobel and Rockefeller, were to prove curiously complementary. Thus, of the first sixty-seven people who were to win Nobel Prizes for Physiology or Medicine, thirty-one had previously received help from the Rockefeller Foundation.

only brings disappointment. You have such wide knowledge and such exceptional qualities that you should turn your attention to more serious matters." It was a warning Nobel ignored – with all the extraordinary consequences that followed.

Literature also played an important part in Alfred Nobel's life. Before he reached the age of twenty he had written intensely personal autobiographical poems, in one of which he described his own cradle as looking like a deathbed. In his youth, his favourite poet was Shelley, and later he was to write a tragedy of his own based on Shelley's "The Cenci". "He had every prospect of being a writer of reflective poetry," Professor Henrik Schück, one of his best biographers, has claimed, and in middle life he turned to translation also – from French and from Russian. He made several drafts for novels, too, including *In Lightest Africa* (1861) and *The Sisters* (1862).

During his last years, when he returned to Shelley for consolation, Nobel wrote a play *The Nemesis* (1895), and he also began a satire, "The Patent Bacillus" that made fun of the English legal system, which he believed had cheated him in a famous patents case – the "cordite or smokeless powder case", which went to the Court of Appeal and the House of Lords in 1895. Alfred would never have won a Nobel Literary Prize, but it is obvious why, having left out the idea of such a Prize in the draft of his will of 1893, he finally chose to endow one along with the other Prizes. It is obvious from his life also why one of his memorable aphorisms – and a collection could be made of them – was "Justice is to be found only in imagination."

That Nobel wrote and read six languages was in part the result of his travels. Since he spent much of his life on railway trains and steamships, he never showed signs of settling down. In his own lifetime he came to be called "Europe's richest vagabond"; Victor Hugo is said to have coined the phrase. Born in Sweden, Nobel moved first to Russia with his parents, then back to Sweden again, where he was eventually to return after years abroad. He made his first visit to the United States in 1850, a visit that lasted two years. From 1865 to 1873 his home, his private laboratory and his company's business office were all at Krümmel, near Hamburg, and it was from there that he travelled to Britain, central Europe, and France.

In 1873, soon after Bismarck had defeated Napoleon III, Nobel chose to move to a house in the Avenue Malakoff in Paris, where he cultivated orchids, kept a collection of superb carriage horses and experimented with his new explosives, among them ballistite. In 1891 he moved again, to San Remo on the Italian Riviera, where he was to die. His carriages were as sumptuous as his horses were superb: there was interior electric lighting and the wheels were covered in rubber.

Nobel had another house in Sweden, however, a manor house at Björkborn, where he acquired a factory in 1894, which in the twentieth century was to become the centre of the flourishing Swedish components industry. At Björkborn Nobel reaffirmed his faith in his native country. "If there is one branch of industry which should be entirely independent of supplies from abroad," he claimed, "then it is manifestly the defence branch, and as there are munitions factories in Sweden it is both pitiful and absurd not to keep them going." Perhaps there was irony in this too in that Sweden was to be involved in neither of the two world wars.

Whatever the consequences for Nobel of his last-resort preference for Sweden, it was of great advantage to the future Nobel Prize scheme that its contentious terms of reference were examined by Swedish lawyers and judges and not by lawyers working within the legal systems of Italy, France, Germany, or Britain. Nobel's estate was scattered in eight countries, and, despite his Swedish manor house, his own domicile was regarded as controversial. Whether or not for this reason, the complex and protracted legal processes that took nearly four years to settle were all carried through in a small local court near Björkborn.

After his death, Nobel's flower-decked coffin had been transported from San Remo to Stockholm and a formal funeral service had been held in old Stockholm's cathedral before – at Nobel's express wish – his body had been cremated. Yet even before his body had left San Remo, his young assistant, Ragnar Sohlman, still in his twenties, had been told by telegram that he would be one of the two executors of Nobel's will, along with Rudolf Lilljequist, a Swedish industrialist whom Sohlman had not met. Nobel was exceptionally clever in picking Sohlman as an assistant who he could fully trust. A graduate of the Stockholm Institute of Technology, Sohlman had visited the Nobel plant in Baku while still a student, and when he first joined Nobel in San Remo he arrived there direct from the United States, where he had been employed as an engineer and as an official in the Swedish Section of the Great World Exhibition held in Chicago in 1893.

The publicity Nobel had so disliked was immediate on his death, and it was Sohlman who had to deal with it. As early as 2 January 1897, four days after the formal funeral ceremony, the main text of Nobel's will appeared in a Stockholm newspaper. The publicity was friendly, however, for the newspaper praised Nobel's decision to set aside his money for five prizes in five different fields of human endeavour "as a gift to mankind, intended to further its development and promote its influence, as well as to serve purely idealistic purposes". The gift, the newspaper added, was probably "the most magnificent gift of its kind that a private person has ever had both the desire and the ability to make".

Other early comment on Nobel's will in 1897 and in the first months of 1898, when Mosenthal was writing his article, was far less favourable. It was not only that many members of the Nobel family protested: Sohlman, accustomed to detailed instructions from his master, was worried

– and disappointed – that none existed, while the prestigious institutions that had been invited without prior consultation to administer the various Nobel Prizes were divided about the wisdom of doing so. Some of their officers feared it would divert them from their own purposes.

Some politicians were worried too. Sections of the Stockholm conservative press questioned Nobel's patriotism, while from the Left the Swedish Democratic leader, Hjalmar Branting, headed an article in his own newspaper "Alfred Nobel's Will – Magnificent Intentions – Magnificent Blunder".

More dogmatic than Shaw would have been, Branting added that "a millionaire who makes a donation may personally be worth every respect, but it would be better to be rid of both millionaires and donations". Ironically, Branting was to win the Nobel Peace Prize in 1921. There was irony too in the fact that part of the money given by Shaw for an Anglo-Swedish Literary Foundation was to be used for translating a book on Nobel by Sohlman.

Many detective stories begin with a will. What exactly was stated in Nobel's will, a document of less than 300 words, that cancelled "all previous testamentary provisions", and that was witnessed by four Swedes in the Swedish Club in Paris? It was signed "Alfred Bernhard Nobel, Paris, November 27th, 1895".

In detail, after warning his executors to invest his money in "safe securities", Nobel asked that the "said interest be divided into five equal parts, which shall be apportioned as follows: one part to the person who shall have made the most important discovery or invention within the field of physics; one part to the person who shall have made the most important chemical discovery and improvement; one part to the person who shall have made the most important discovery within the domain of physiology or medicine; one part to the person who shall have produced in the field of literature the most outstanding work of an idealistic tendency; and one part to the person who shall have done the most or best work for fraternity among nations, for the abolition or reduction of standing armies, and for the holding and promotion of peace congresses".

Three points deserve mention. First, in the sciences the emphasis was on discovery, although the Chemistry Prize referred also to "improvement". Second, the words concerning the Peace Prize included a specific reference to Peace Congresses, however sceptical Nobel was about their likely outcome. Third, the words concerning the Literature Prize specifically included a stipulation that was to prove difficult to interpret: "work of an idealistic tendency".

It was even more difficult for Nobel's two executors to follow the closing paragraph, which dealt not with intention but with modes of implementation: "The prizes for physics and chemistry shall be awarded by the Swedish Academy of Sciences; that for physiological or medical works by the Caroline Institute in Stockholm; that for literature by the Academy in Stockholm; and that for champions of peace by a committee of five persons to be elected by the Norwegian Storting." The Caroline (Karolinska) Institute had been mentioned earlier in Nobel's discarded will of 1893, as had the Swedish Academy of Sciences of which Nobel was a proud member, yet there had been no communication with them, or with the Swedish Academy, as to their willingness to participate.

The certificates, with their hand-painted decorations, and the medals for the 1989 Nobel laureates are displayed in the boardroom of the Nobel Founation.

Nor had there been any communication with the Oslo Storting, and there were some Swedes who objected to the fact that Norway's Parliament was to be given charge of these Prizes at a time when Sweden and self-governing Norway were still linked under the same king. Why draw a distinction? It was said, moreover, that the King of Sweden favoured changes in the arrangements that were so sketchily treated in the will.

Most seriously of all, there was opposition to the will from Nobel's relatives, who had arrived at San Remo too late to hear anything from Nobel's own lips. None of them was chosen as an executor. Fortunately, Emanuel, the elder son of Nobel's brother Ludvig, and head of the Russian branch of the Nobel business, proved sympathetic to the will, and co-operative in trying to ensure that its terms were implemented.

The last sentence in the will, which reflected Nobel's cosmopolitan approach to life and to learning, was criticized also: "It is my express wish that in awarding the Prizes no consideration whatever shall be given to the nationality of the candidates, so that the most worthy shall receive the prize, whether he be a Scandinavian or not." The various institutions mentioned in the last paragraph, all of them conservative, were not used to thinking within this framework, while their domestic critics maintained that for this reason alone they would be incapable of effectively discharging international responsibilities outside Scandinavia.

Fortunately, Sohlman was determined to deal firmly with all doubts and challenges, and so also was his fellow executor, Rudolf Lilljequist. Backed by their lawyer, who disposed of many tricky problems, they were indefatigable

Left
The 1990 Nobel laureates gather on stage for the presentation ceremony.

Right
The Prize presentation ceremony begins after the members of Sweden's Royal Family have taken their seats.

– and agile – in seeking to realize Nobel's intentions. For Sohlman the pocket had to be considered as well as the soul, for not only had Nobel's property interests to be transferred into other "safe securities" – and this involved an elaborate process of divestment, particularly difficult in Russia – but the disappointed relatives had to be persuaded not to pursue what would have been protracted and expensive litigation. In consequence, there had to be adjustments and compromises.

Sohlman had to travel almost as much as Nobel had to deal with the complexities. His first visit was to Oslo, where he found the Norwegians more willing to discharge their responsibilities than the Swedes; his second was to Paris, where he met the Swedish Minister to France and the Swedish Consul General. Only next did Sohlman choose to meet the president of the prestigious Swedish Academy,

the historian and politician Hans Forssell. Like many professors in such circumstances, Forssell would have preferred the Academy not to accept the responsibility: he would have liked the money to have gone to the Academy direct and untied. The Permanent Secretary of the Academy, Carl David af Wirsén, took a different view, however, and was to play an especially important, if controversial, role in the early history of the Nobel Prize for Literature.

Wirsén had outside backing also. The Swedish poet and critic Oscar Levertin argued that "permanent contact with the European world of letters", which the Swedish Academy until now had to maintain, would be "wholesome". "For the first time foreign specialists in literature will direct their attention to the distant academy in Stockholm, and everywhere in different countries people with literary

interests will eagerly wait to see which Muse will be the Danaë on whom the Swedish Academy will pour its golden shower."

The Caroline Institute was forthcoming, but the Royal Academy of Sciences, influenced by Forssell, refused to commit itself until the legal position of the relatives was cleared. There was deadlock for a time, before Sohlman and Lilljequist arranged further meetings, first with foreign legal advisers dealing with the estate, and then with representatives of the family. Great progress was now made, and at last in June 1898 the family representatives accepted the will both on their own behalf and on that of their descendants. In return they received the substantial interest on the Nobel assets for 1897.

The Swedish Academy yielded next, and in June 1898 it appointed representatives to organize the Prizes; and so too, in the same month, did the Caroline Institute and the Royal Academy of Sciences. It was agreed that basic statutes should be drawn up in joint consultations, which would include a member of the family of Robert Hjalmar Nobel, and that the statutes should then be submitted for the approval of the Crown. There was no such stipulation in the will, but the decision to proceed in this way further speeded progress.

The Crown duly approved in September 1898, after the Norwegian Storting delegates had approved earlier, although there had been final hurdles to surmount in the dealings between the delegates of the Norwegian Storting and the Swedish Government. Between 1898 and 1905, when the union of the Swedish and Norwegian crowns was brought to an end, there were to be disputes between the Swedish government and the Norwegian Storting, but they did not seriously hold back the Nobel Prize scheme.

The outcome in 1900 was the setting up of a new Nobel Foundation, the body of which still administers the Nobel Prizes, with Trustees and a Board of Directors and a set of statutes which were promulgated officially in June 1900 by the Swedish government. The Foundation was placed in the hands of the Board of Directors, who were to be responsible for the finance and management of the scheme and for the appointment of an Executive Director. The Chairman and his deputy were to be Crown appointments, but the other four members (nowadays five) were to be chosen by sixteen trustees of the Foundation, and these were to be drawn from the four Prize-awarding bodies.

The Statutes not only provided a framework, but filled in points not covered in Nobel's brief will. They also specified precise procedures necessary for the smooth working of the scheme. The Prizes were to be offered at least once in any five-year period, and the phrase "during the preceding year" in the first part of the will was to be taken to mean that "other works" could be considered only in case their significance had not been established until recently. There were to be no posthumous awards.

Prizes, it was agreed, might be given for two works, or to two, or at most three, people. No Nobel laureate was to be given a fraction of a Prize. Prize money that had been impossible to distribute in the absence of a worthy Prizewinner would be returned to the main fund, or placed in separate funds to be used in ways other than Prizes.

To help in the preliminary investigations of works proposed for Prizes, the Swedish institutions named in the will were to appoint a Nobel Committee for each Prize section. These were to consist of three to five members, who were to serve for reasonable terms. They would have the right to summon experts to assist them, and if need be to co-opt temporary members to help them make decisions. They were also to organize scientific institutions and other establishments to be known as Nobel Institutes. Organizing Funds were set aside for each of the Prize Sections, and in addition there was to be a Building Fund.

Each of the Prize-awarding bodies was to be required to draft its own directives and to submit them for approval to the Swedish government; the Norwegian arrangements were to be left to a Committee of the Storting, and were not formally adopted until April 1905.

The first President of the Board of the Foundation was to be a former Swedish Prime Minister who had just left office, implying recognition of the highest political level of the Foundation's importance. Gustav Boström was to become Prime Minister again in July 1902 while still serving as a President of the Board, and although he was to run into difficulties between the two countries that were to lead to the break with Norway, these did not diminish his role in the Nobel Foundation. There was immediate recognition of the Foundation also at the highest academic level, for Forssell joined the Board and Wirsén became a Trustee. The presence of Ragnar Sohlman guaranteed continuity of care, and through him in a sense Alfred Nobel was represented too. The first Executive Director was Henrik Santesson.

Sohlman was later to become Executive Director, giving the post a distinctive authority. Years later, in 1948 – twenty-two years after the Foundation acquired its own office in Stockholm – he summed up the achievements of five decades in the same way as Wallace had summed up the achievements of his "wonderful" nineteenth century. The Nobel scheme had worked well, Sohlman said, and would have pleased Nobel. "In the light of our experience", the task of distributing the Nobel Prizes and managing the Nobel Fund had proved a privilege and "an asset of the highest value to our country". The predictions of great dangers and risks involved in the fulfilment of the duty extended to Sweden and Norway by Alfred Nobel had proved unfounded, Sohlman concluded. "Rather has the discharge of this task contributed to an increased knowledge of and respect for both countries and for northern civilisation in general."

In each case selection procedures followed what became a standard pattern – with letters soliciting nominations being sent each autumn to past and present members of the

Professor Lars Gyllensten, chairman of the board of the Nobel Foundation, delivers the 1988 opening speech.

Professor Maurice Allais of France receives the 1988 Alfred Nobel Memorial Prize in Economic Sciences, certificate and gold medal, from His Majesty King Carl XVI Gustaf.

selecting committees, previous Prize-winners, to academics and academic institutions, and to other people selected by the relevant committees. The constituencies varied over the years, with additions to those institutions and institutions specified as permanent constituents in the first plans. Screening usually began the following February, when detailed reports on names submitted – or produced from inside the committees – were collected. Then there would be discussions before short-lists were drawn up and the final recommendations made and sent for approval to the institutions scheduled in Nobel's will. Thereafter, there was no right of appeal, and the names of the winners were announced in the autumn. One minor complication was that Peace Prize nominations were often sent not to Oslo but to Stockholm (which still occurs). These had to be received by 1 February.

These arrangements, like the constitutional arrangements, have required few changes except for the requirement that the Chairman of the Board should be appointed by the Swedish Government. The requirement remained on paper, but in time the Chairman came to be selected only from among the prize-granting organizations. This in itself was a sign of the independence and increasing prestige of the Foundation, and of its general international recognition. By 1914 the value of the scheme could be taken for granted; it did not need the official support as had been thought necessary at the beginning.

There was to be a later constitutional change in Norway. Parliament decided to exclude from Peace Prize Committee membership all sitting cabinet ministers and members of Parliament. This too was designed to emphasize the independence of the Awards.

What has always required attention – and ultimately substantial change – has been the financial management of the Nobel Fund, or Main Fund. The funds at the disposal of the new Foundation in 1901 had amounted in the first instance to over 31 million *kronor*, 28 million of which constituted the Main Fund. This was not a large sum when compared with the sums of money made available at the outset to giant American Foundations in the twentieth century; and Swedish tax law and the reference in the will to "safe securities" did not help. It was not until 1946 that the Foundation was declared exempt from state income tax, and not until 1953 that, at the request of the Board of the Foundation, the obligation to invest its funds only in government bonds was removed.

Until then, annual income had only slowly increased; each year, one-tenth of the Foundation's previous year's net proceeds were added to current income along with any undistributed monies. This was not enough to cope with changes in costs, and in 1960 the Main Fund still stood at only just under 38 million *kronor*. Even after 1953 other minor state and local government taxes and levies were still being imposed, though the Fund now benefitted greatly from the fact that it could invest abroad, within limits, as well as in Sweden.

There was an even bigger constraint on real growth. Inflation, one of the problems of the twentieth century that Nobel may not have anticipated, had eroded the value of the Fund, which stood at 72 million *kronor* in 1970; and it was to become an even bigger problem during the 1970s when unprecedented inflation was accompanied by unemployment.

Appropriately, on the eve of the great inflation, a sixth Prize had been introduced in Economics in 1968. Based as it was, however, on a donation from the Tercentenary Fund Foundation of the National Bank of Sweden, it imposed no new financial burdens on the Foundation. Nor did it bring in new agencies: the Royal Swedish Academy of Sciences was to choose the Prize-winner.

The fact that by 1988 the paper value of the Nobel Main Fund amounted to 477 million *kronor* certainly did not mean that it was now five times better off than it had been in 1970. What counted was the real value of the Prizes. The first Nobel Prizes distributed in 1901 were worth about 150,000 *kronor* each, seventy times the value of the Rumford Medal; and although their worth had risen to around 225,000 *kronor* by 1960, this increased figure represented only about one-third of their original "real value". In 1989 the real value of the Nobel Fund was 1 billion, 371 million *kronor*, or seventy percent better than the real value of the 1901 capital. The 1901 figure had been deemed equivalent to a university professor's earnings over a period of twenty-five years. The sum now required to cover a science professor's earnings over a period of twenty-five years would be around 4.9 million *kronor*. Meanwhile, of course, science research had become far more sophisticated and costly.

The figure of 150,000 *kronor* was set at a time when there was no substantial institutional support for scientific research at a level that would permit the Prize-winner to continue his research undisturbed. The best-equipped laboratories in the world at that time – already in the United States – were business laboratories, not academic laboratories, and elsewhere even the best-known university laboratories were running on a shoestring.

The biggest change came after the Second World War. The physicists of the 1960s, "poised on the threshold of Big Science", found that a single experiment could now cost millions of dollars. And this was only the beginning. Atom-bashing was to prove almost unbelievably expensive. So, too, was "defence physics" in a "space age". Biologists also were drawn into increasingly costly experimental research as biology took the place of physics on the most exciting frontiers of science. There were new frontiers too in medicine, and new challenges.

Over the years, the Foundation has produced many studies, some biographical, some institutional, relating to its objectives and achievements. The staff of the Foundation also has grown, so that by the 1980s twelve persons were employed. They were involved in organising, supervising,

After a traditional "Ice Cream Parade", a dessert of ice cream with *petits-fours* is served each year. Following the banquet, an evening of dancing takes place in the splendid Golden Hall in Stockholm.

or reporting on a far more varied range of activities than their predecessors had been. The Foundation today is a very different kind of Foundation from that of 1901, and it is operating in a very different kind of world.

By 1945 its Institutes had already become sizeable institutions, taking initiatives as well as providing services. Thus the Nobel Institute of the Royal Academy of Sciences had established a Department of Physics as early as 1905, and a Department of Chemistry in 1944; while the Nobel Institute attached to the Royal Caroline Medico-Chirurgical Institute, as it came to be called, had established a Department of Biochemistry in 1937 and Departments of Neurochemistry and Cell Research and Genetics in 1945. Meanwhile, the Institute associated with the Swedish Academy had built up an impressive library of modern literature in all languages, and the Norwegian Nobel Institute had acquired an equally impressive library of books on peace and international relations.

Some of the activities of the Foundation drew on new sources of finance. Thus, during the 1970s, the Foundation inherited two Italian vineyards, which it subsequently sold to provide income for international scientific co-operation; and it also became the sole legatee of Georg von Békésy's valuable collection of Asian art and antiques which it subsequently distributed among various Museums in Stockholm. Békèsy, an American citizen, had won the Nobel Prize for Physiology or Medicine in 1961 for work on the human ear.

In one respect, the Foundation has refused to extend its activities beyond those envisaged in Nobel's will. It has refused to endow new Prizes in such key subjects as mathematics, engineering, and the humanities. The absence of mathematics has been a regular source of complaint, particularly since the sciences (including economics) increasingly depend upon them, and because in an age of computers' possibilities of research, and of action following it, have been greatly advanced.

The ubiquity of the computer in the late twentieth century owes most to engineers – and engineers in particular still lack the kind of international prize that would do justice to their contribution to human development, both in "large projects", the glamour projects of engineering, and in "small projects", the kind of projects that directly – if quietly – influence everyday life. Their skills and their imagination have transformed the environment, raising huge new problems in the process.

The environmental sciences figure only in part in the Nobel scheme, and other sciences, like astronomy or geology, would have got left out if the Nobel Prize Committees had not interpreted their terms of reference broadly, as they did in 1974, for instance, when two British astronomers, M. Ryle and A. Hewish, shared the Physics Prize, or in 1973, when the Physiology or Medicine Prizes went to three

"animal watchers", Karl von Frisch, Konrad Lorenz and Niko Tinbergen.

Historians have won the Literature Prize, although none since Winston Churchill, far more than a historian, in 1953. Literary critics have had a harder time. Georg Brandes, often proposed, never won a Literature Prize for this reason. Nor for this – and doubtless for other reasons – did the Hungarian Georg Lukacs. Sociologists, social physiologists and psychologists have been left out too. There was to be no Nobel Prize for Freud, although Romain Rolland suggested his name in 1936.

The history of the Nobel Prizes, which have come to be considered symbols of excellence, has gone through several different phases since 1900, and ceremonies were not held during two world wars. The Physics Prize and the Chemistry Prize were not awarded on six occasions while the two wars lasted, and the Physiology or Medicine Prize was not awarded on seven. The technical term applied to such years, when no Prizes of any kind were awarded at all, was "reserved", and they included 1916, 1941, 1942 and 1943, as well as some peace-time years. There were several war-time Prizes, however. Thus, in 1915 the Physics Prize was awarded jointly to two Englishmen Sir William Henry Bragg, born in 1862, and his son William (later Sir William) Lawrence Bragg, born in 1890, who still holds the record of being the youngest Nobel Prize-winner. They were honoured for "their services in the analysis of crystal structure by means of X-rays".

Not surprisingly, there were no Nobel Peace Prizes in either War – and in several years of so-called peace – or, more accurately, "cold war". Nonetheless, the winner of the 1915 Literature Prize was a well-known pacifist, Romain Rolland, a popular French writer who was awarded his Prize "as a tribute to the lofty idealism of his literary presentation and to the sympathy and love of truth with which he has described different types of human beings". The word "idealism" relates back to the terms of the will. There are several writers on the list of Nobel Literature Prize-winners, including some before Romain Rolland, who would have hated to have the word applied to them.

Nobel citations are often similar in style to citations for honorary degrees, but some are calculated to appeal to a wide public, which is increasingly interested in who wins the Awards – and why – as the century has gone by. An interesting anthology could be made of them. They are not the only citations which count, however. American historians of the sciences have made much of the number of citations in other scientists' work before and after they became Prize-winners. The record is impressive.

Each Nobel Prize has its own distinctive story, some more exciting than others, some with a human angle that has always attracted the Press and now attracts television. Of the very first Prizes, few were in this category, although the first Physics Nobel Prize-winner, W. C. Röntgen, discoverer of X-rays, had hit the headlines even of the popular Press in 1896 when details were given of his "photographing through opaque matter". His photographs of skeletons were among the best publicized photographs of the nineteenth century.

Some stories are linked over the years, particularly that of the Curie family. In 1903 the Physics Prize went to Marie Curie, Pierre Curie, and to their teacher Antoine Henri Becquerel, who had first been proposed in 1901. Marie, who was to become one of the best-known scientists of the twentieth century, was to go on to win the Nobel Chemistry Prize in 1911. By then she had been very much in the news, and her name was as well-known in school classrooms as it was in scientific libraries. She was to remain regularly in the news until her tragic death from leukaemia, the result of exposure to radiation, in 1934. Yet that was not the end of the Curie story, for Marie's daughter Irène followed in her mother's footsteps, as did Irène's husband, Frédéric Joliot. Together they were to win the Nobel Prize for Chemistry in 1935 "in recognition of their synthesis of new radio-active

elements". And Joliot was to play an important part in history at the beginning of the Second World War when he was responsible for bringing to Britain precious supplies of "heavy water" from Norway. These were essential for future nuclear research.

One other of the two double Nobel Prize-winners, the American Professor Linus Pauling, who won the Nobel Chemistry Prize in 1954, stands out in that the other Prize he won was the Peace Prize in 1962, when nuclear warfare seemed to be the apocalyptic horror. Pauling received the Peace Prize for mobilizing world scientists to demand a political nuclear test ban. Not all his fellow scientists approved, but the idea of mobilizing Nobel laureates, particularly scientists, to support peace causes was here to stay. They were the kind of élite constituency in which Nobel put his trust.

Not surprisingly, there are many stirring as well as controversial episodes in the history of the Peace Prize, which on a number of occasions has been won by institutions rather than individuals. There were links with the Nobel past when the Baroness Bertha von Suttner won in 1905, and with the nineteenth-century past as a whole when the first Peace Prize-winners were associated with great nineteenth-century achievements. The first joint holders in 1901 were Henri Dunant – the Swiss founder of the Red Cross in

1863 and a still well-known figure in the history books – and Frédéric Passy, a French exponent of free trade and a founder of the *Ligue Internationale de la Paix*. Passy's name, like the names of at least a quarter of the Nobel Peace Prize-winners, is little-known in our century.

Institutions, not individuals, were to win the Nobel Peace Prize on several occasions, but the League of Nations was not one of them. The first, in 1904, was the Institute of International Law at Ghent; the last was the United Nations Peacekeeping Forces, a body in which Nobel might have put his trust, in 1988. In 1981 the Prize had been won by the United Nations High Commissioner for Refugees in Geneva, and in 1985 by the International Physicians for the Prevention of Nuclear War.

The most bold and courageous decision taken in the choice of a Nobel Peace Prize before the Second World War was made in 1936 when the 1935 Prize went, a year late, to Carl von Ossietzky, German journalist and pacifist. The delay is explained by the fact that there were many hurdles to cross. When Von Ossietzky's name was first brought forward, he was being detained in one of Hitler's concentration camps; and the Gestapo, which under international pressure freed Von Ossietzky from camp, did its best to stop the Prize award, which was bitterly attacked in private and in public by Hitler. Support for the Prize was backed at the time by a vigorous and well-managed international campaign, which succeeded in mobilizing influential opinion in many countries. One of its leaders, Willy Brandt, then exiled in Norway, was to win a Nobel Peace Prize in 1971 as Chancellor of the Federal Republic of Germany.

Von Ossietzky's backers among previous Nobel Prize-winners included the American social worker Jane Addams, who had won the Peace Prize in 1931; the German novelist Thomas Mann, also in exile, who had won the Literature Prize in 1929; the physicist Albert Einstein, also in exile, who had won the Physics Prize in 1921; and the French writer, Romain Rolland, who, as noted, had won the Literature Prize in 1915. The fact that another Nobel Prize-winner, the Norwegian novelist Knut Hamsun, who had won the Literature Prize in 1920, wrote articles sharply criticizing Von Ossietzky, did not count against him, for Hamsun was known at that time as a strong supporter of Nazi Germany. In Norway itself, nonetheless, there was other conservative opposition to the award, and this accounted for the delay.

After it had been announced that Von Ossietzky had won the Prize, he could not attend the ceremony, and he died soon after in 1938, an isolated figure, not now in a concentration camp, but in a sanatorium. It was Thomas Mann who found the right obituary words. "The figure of this brave and pure-minded journalist," he said, "could grow in time to a fighter for humanity and a martyr of legendary proportions." When the Berlin Wall came down in 1989, Von Ossietzky was honoured on each side.

Meanwhile Hitler issued a decree forbidding any German to accept a Nobel Prize in the future. The Committee in fact made awards to Germans anyway, although they were not allowed to collect them until Hitler was no longer in power. The decree handicapped Germany, which had dominated the early years of the Nobel Science Prizes. Indeed, it lost many future Nobel Prize-winners to Britain and to the United States. Before 1936 Germany had won a quarter of the Nobel Prizes awarded; after 1936 both Britain and the United States forged ahead. Two Germans awarded Nobel Physics Prizes in 1938 and 1939 had to decline the award, but later, in completely changed circumstances, were to receive the Medal and Diploma.

It was after the 1960s that stories of heroic Peace Prize-winners captured the headlines again, including those who had suffered personal persecution. Nonetheless, the two contrasting winners in 1952 and 1953 had often been in the news: Albert Schweitzer and General George Marshall. Schweitzer's name had first been proposed in 1932; Marshall's name at that time would have been little known. On making an address in Oslo after receiving his Award, Schweitzer stated that "only when an ideal of peace is born in the minds of the peoples will the institutions set up to maintain this peace effectively fulfil the functions expected of them". Marshall, initiator of the bold American plan to restore prosperity to Europe, put his trust in effective practice. In retrospect he stands out in the first phase of the cold war as an even bigger person than he did at the time.

The 1961 Nobel Peace Prize went to the secretary general of the United Nations, Dag Hammarskjöld, which was made posthumously. This was possible because Hammarskjöld's name was already before the Committee when he was killed in an aeroplane crash. In 1974 the rules were changed so that only if a Prize-winner died *after* the October announcement could he or she still receive an award.

Africa was to figure directly in many awards after 1961. Indeed, it had already figured in 1960 when the Zulu leader Albert John Lutuli, a pioneer of the African National Congress, was given the Prize and the South African government allowed him to spend only one week in Oslo to collect it. Four years later, the best-known supporter of human rights in this century, Martin Luther King, won the Award, four years before his murder in Memphis, Tennessee. At the age of thirty-five, he was also the youngest person to win the Nobel Peace Prize. His belief in universal civil rights had obvious relevance for all parts of the late-twentieth-century world.

When the Russian physicist Andrei Sakharov won the Peace Prize in 1975, he was attacked in *Pravda* by a group of thirty-five Soviet academics, who described his work as "radically alien to Soviet scientists", and eighty-nine Nobel laureates wrote to Podgorny supporting Sakharov. His day, too, was to come, quicker than Von Ossietzky's. He was to be rehabilitated by President Mikhail Gorbachev, who himself was to win the Peace Prize in 1990. And in this same year Lech Walesa, who won the Prize in 1983 as a fighter for

Solidarity, was elected President of Poland. On receiving his Nobel Prize, Walesa had described peace and justice as being like bread and salt for mankind.

Politicians on the Nobel Peace Prize list have always been greeted more sceptically than victims of persecution, like the Dalai Lama, who won the Prize in 1989, or saints like Mother Teresa, who won the Prize in 1979, or relatively unknown people like the Belgian Georges Pire, who won the 1958 Prize for his work with refugees. When the Prize was given to President Theodore Roosevelt in 1906, there were cries of disapproval, although his successor Woodrow Wilson, who took the United States into the First World War and did much to promote democratic nationalism as a key war aim was more generally accepted in 1919.

Menachem Begin, Prime Minister of Israel, who won the Peace Prize jointly with President Sadat of Egypt in 1978, was subject not so much to scepticism as to attack. So also was Henry Kissinger, Nixon's secretary of state, who won the Peace Prize jointly in 1973 with the Vietnamese Le Duc Tho, who was one of the rare Prize-winners to decline. Others were Jean-Paul Sartre, who refused the Nobel Literature Prize in 1964, and Boris Pasternak, who was forced to decline it in 1959.

In the latter case there was a happy ending. The year 1990 is the centenary year of Pasternak's birth, and in 1989 his son Evgeny, who had recently published a book about his father, travelled to Stockholm to receive the gold medal that his father had not been able to receive thirty years earlier. The following evening, the Russian cellist Mstivlav Rostropovich, a close friend of the Pasternaks, played in Pasternak's honour. If there had been a Nobel Music Prize, Rostropovich would certainly have received it.

The very first Nobel Prizes to attract public attention had been those for Literature, and it was a wise decision on the part of the Literature Committee to insist from the start that the term "literature" covered not only *belles lettres*, as they were then called, but any other works which by reason of their content or their style, or both, were deemed to have literary value. This provision was to make it possible to elect to the Prize in 1903 a great but aged German historian of the ancient world, Theodor Mommsen.

When the first Literature Prize had been awarded there had been immediate difficulties. The French novelist Émile Zola was the first name considered, but he cannot have been considered for long since few of his readers, or non-readers – least of all the members of the Swedish Academy – would have considered Zola an idealist, and since it was known also that Nobel himself had disliked him. Another great name, Tolstoy, was ruled out, too; although forty-two Swedish authors and artists signed a tribute to him, he had not been officially nominated. He had achieved one other distinction, however, in 1901: he was excommunicated from the Russian Orthodox Church.

The writer chosen in 1901, the Frenchman Sully Prud-homme, attracted little interest, far less than the joint first winners of the Peace Prize. Indeed, the first Nobel Literature Prize-winner who stands out in retrospect is Rudyard Kipling (1907), whose citation speaks of his "power of observation, originality of imagination, vitality of ideas and remarkable talent for narration". Two years later, Wirsén, who hitherto seems to have been the key figure on the Committee, objected bitterly to the choice of Selma Lagerlöf, a Swedish writer little known outside Sweden. The only really well-known Swedish writer, Strindberg, also opposed by Wirsén, was considered only once – and turned down.

The Belgian Maurice Maeterlinck, praised for his "poetic fantasy", won the Prize with little dissent in 1911, although when the Indian Rabindranath Tagore won his Prize in 1913, he faced competition from the French literary historian Émile Faguet. One very aged Western novelist, Anatole France, was to win the Literature Prize in 1921. Henri Bergson was very old too when he won the Prize in 1928. The great Irish poet W. B. Yeats had won the Prize in 1923; it was said to be a tribute to the new Irish Free State. Thomas Mann was given the Prize in 1929 "principally for his great novel *Buddenbrooks*," which has won steadily accepted recognition as one of the classic works of contemporary literature". The use of the word "principally" was strange, as was the fact that *Buddenbrooks* had been published as long ago as 1901, the year of the first Nobel Prizes.

The first two Americans to win the Prize – Sinclair Lewis in 1930 and Eugene O'Neill in 1936 – had little in common at the time they were elected, although O'Neill in his speech accepting the Prize remarked that it was not only his own work which was being honoured "but the work of all my colleagues in America". William Faulkner had to wait until 1949. He was preceded by a remarkable trio: the German/Swiss novelist Hermann Hesse in 1946, the French writer André Gide in 1947, and the English poet T. S. Eliot in 1948. Faulkner was followed in 1950 by Bertrand Russell, honoured three years before Churchill, with whom he had nothing in common. Ernest Hemingway got his Literature Prize in 1954. His recent novel *The Old Man and The Sea* (1952) was one of his novels picked out: it included the line "A human being can be annihilated but not vanquished."

Many great twentieth-century writers have *not* won the Nobel Prize for Literature. Indeed, the list of the non-winners, who include Henry James, Chekhov, Joseph Conrad, Mark Twain, Marcel Proust, Thomas Hardy and James Joyce, is as impressive as the list of those who did. In recent years moreover, the tendency has been to choose Nobel Literature Prize-winners who have been relatively little read, even in translation, in Western Europe. Ivo Andrić, a Bosnian from Yugoslavia, was chosen in 1961, and Shmuel Agnon from Israel in 1966, Miguel Asturias from Guatemala in 1967, Yasunari Kawabata from Japan in 1968, and Pablo Neruda from Chile in 1971. Yet in this same decade of change Prizes also went to Jean-Paul Sartre (declined) in 1964, the Russians Mikhail Sholokhov and Alexander

Wole Soyinka, the 1986 Literature laureate sits at the centre of his fellow award-winners: Gerd Binnig (Physics), Stanley Cohen (Medecine), Yuan T. Lee (Chemistry), James Buchanan (Economics), Heinrich Rohrer (Physics), Ernest Ruska (Physics), John C. Polanyi (Chemistry), Rita Levi-Montalcini (Medecine), and Dudley R. Herschbach (Chemistry).

Solzhenitsyn in 1965 and 1970, and the Irish playwright Samuel Beckett in 1969.

The award of Nobel Prizes may have broadened the reading public for foreign writers, some of whom, like the Columbian Gabriel García Márquez, who acknowledged his debt to Faulkner, have built up a world audience. Yet, unlike their scientific colleagues, not all of them have been successful in establishing their international reputation. Poetry, so dear to Nobel himself, has been difficult to translate, and the poems of two recent Prize-winners – the Spaniard, Vicente Aleixandre (1977) and the Greek, Odysseus Elytis (1979) – are still little-known in most countries. The difficulty the judges have faced in deciding whether to choose poets, novelists, or playwrights for Prizes had been apparent from the start. Wirsén described the choice as "like deciding on the relative merits of the elm, the linden, the oak, the rose, the lily or the violet".

When the first Prize was awarded, a prominent Austrian had suggested that the statutes should be altered so that only Europeans could be considered, and that the value of the Literature Prize should be reduced. There was not even any discussion as to whether either of these two suggestions should be considered. It was a landmark date, however, in 1986 when the Nobel Literature Prize went for the first time to a black African, Wole Soyinka, from Nigeria, although, like the Australian Patrick White, who won the Prize in 1973, he already had his enthusiastic readers in Europe and other parts of the world. Later, in 1989, Arabic was spoken for the first time at the Nobel Prize ceremonies in Stockholm when a friend of Naguib Mahfouz read the Prize-winner's speech in Arabic and then in English.

While each Nobel Prize has its own distinctive story, it is possible to make a number of generalizations about the Nobel Science Prizes within the context of the intellectual and academic history of each of the scientific disciplines which constitute the Nobel "fields", a much-used twentieth-century word. It is also possible to assess the impact of these Prizes both on research and on public opinion.

During the early years, the biggest problem was not to find names of eligible scientists, but to determine the order in which Science Prizes would be given to "great men". Indeed, the Foundation honoured itself in conferring honours upon many of those chosen. The first of the Physics Prize winners, W. C. Röntgen, had received no fewer than seventeen out of twenty-nine nominations for the Prize. Other pre-1914 scientists whose names stand out in the history of science include in Physics, which was undergoing a profound revolution, Sir J. J. Thomson (1906) and Albert Michelson (1907).

Paradoxically, however, the New Zealander, Ernest (later Lord) Rutherford received his Nobel Prize in 1908 not for Physics, but for Chemistry, an award which surprised and disturbed him. He had worked with Thomson and "trained no fewer than eleven Nobel Laureates". Two other of the early Nobel Prize-winners in Chemistry – the Dutch professor, Jacobus Henricus Van't Hoff, the first Prize-winner in 1901, and the Swedish Svante August Arrhenius (1903), were studying the nature of atoms and molecules. Arrhenius, little known today in Britain or the United States, is said to have swayed the choice of more Nobel Science Prize-winners than any other person.

The range of contribution of Nobel Prize-winners to Chemistry, the key science of the nineteenth century, was to prove extraordinarily wide in the twentieth. Indeed, one of the Prize-winners, the American Willard Libby (1960), specialist on carbon dating, made as substantial a contribution to archaeology and to history as to chemistry. Others made as invaluable contributions to health care as the Prize-winners in Physiology or Chemistry. Thus, two German chemists, Heinrich Wieland (1927) and Adolf Windaus (1928), studied cholesterol and produced drugs to cope with heart disease; while Frederick Sanger (1958), working on the insulin molecule, pointed to new ways of treating diabetes. In 1945 Sir Alexander Fleming, knighted a year earlier, Ernst Boris Chain, and Howard (later Sir Howard) Florey had won the Physiology or Medicine Prize for their "discovery of penicillin and its therapeutic effect for the cure of different infectious maladies". Penicillin, which would have fascinated Nobel, was the most powerful killer of microbes yet discovered.

If the boundaries between physics and chemistry were imprecise before 1914, at a time when a new age of physics was emerging, the boundaries between chemistry, biology, and medicine were equally imprecise after the 1950s when a new age of biology was emerging. Physics too played its part. Of the remarkable team of three that won the Physiology or Medicine Nobel Prize in 1962 for their discovery of the double helix structure of DNA, Francis Crick and Maurice Wilkins had taken their first degrees in physics. The discovery had profound consequences; and, as Watson and Crick pointed out, their objective of understanding the replication of genes was an objective that seemed out of reach to an older generation of geneticists.

In a very different period in the history of science Sir Ronald Ross won a Physiology or Medicine Prize in 1902 "for his work on malaria", and the German Paul Ehrlich a Prize in 1908 for his work on "immunity". The best-known early Prize-winner, however, was the Russian Ivan Petrovic Pavlov, who won it in recognition of his famous work not on "the reflex activity of the cerebral hemispheres" – which brought the word "reflex" into the common language – but on "the physiology of digestion, through which knowledge on vital aspects of the subject has been transformed and enlarged".

Pavlov was not the only scientist to be cited for work that is not well-known to the general public. Theodor Svedberg, for example, a Swedish chemist who received the Nobel Chemistry Prize in 1926, received it for studies of Brownian motion, not for his invention of ultracentrifuge, which was to influence the whole development of microbiology. Most significant of all, Enrico Fermi received his Physics Prize in 1948 before having fully explored the process of nuclear fission, the subject for which he will always be remembered.

Some great scientists still at work at the beginning of the century had not figured at all in the Nobel lists. Thus, the Russian chemist Dmitri Mendeléyev, one of the best-known scientists of the century, who died in 1907, and who through his work on the atomic table remains well-known, did not receive an award. Nor did Lord Kelvin, among the best-known British scientists, who also died in 1907 and was buried in Westminster Abbey. His name had been proposed by Röntgen but the Committee believed that his best work belonged too far back in the past. Mendeléyev, got near: he lost to the much less well-known H. Moissan from France by a vote of five to four, one year before his death. Such details of votes have rarely been revealed, for Committee decisions are meant to remain secret for fifty years. How the judges reach their decision, therefore, is usually a matter of gossip rather than of intelligence. There are exceptions, nonetheless, for it has proved difficult in this century to jettison memory. One reason is that we can record it, another is that public curiosity has been enhanced. For each of these outcomes pioneers in communications have been responsible, and it was fitting that in 1909 Guglielmo Marconi shared the Nobel Physics Prize with a great scientist K. F. Braun. It was not so much for his own scientific knowledge that Marconi won his Prize but for his achievement in turning "wireless" into a reality. No pioneer of television was to win a Prize, however. Nor did Thomas Edison.

There were some obvious candidates for later Nobel Prizes with rare scientific qualifications who had to wait long for their awards. Thus, the British neurophysiologist, Sir Charles Sherrington, who did much to popularize science, had to wait thirty years before he finally got the Prize for Physiology or Medicine in 1932. Thus, Peyton Rous, who discovered in 1911 that a malignant tumour was produced by a virus, did not get the Prize for Physiology or Medicine until 1966 when he was eighty-five years old. His theories had never been accepted in influential circles, and according to one knowledgeable Professor at the Caroline Institute, if Rous had been offered a Prize as late as 1959, "the world would have said we were crazy". A later Physiology or Medicine Prize-winner, the American Barbara McClintock (1983), observed that her genetics work on home-grown maize that led to her discovery in 1944 that genes were able to "jump" around on chromosomes was ignored because it defied "biological dogma".

Much has been written recently about the history of the Science Prizes for, as Wilhelm Odelberg, a member of the Royal Swedish Academy of Sciences, has noted, academic interest in the history of science – and, he might have added, scientists – has increased enormously since 1945 on both sides of the Atlantic, and numerous chairs in the subject have been established. There has also been an increasing interest in the sociology of science, particularly in the United States, where the sociologist Robert Merton was a pioneer, and in the economics of science, particularly in Britain, where in recent years there have been serious cuts in research expenditure. The relationship between adequate or more than adequate national funding and the number of Nobel awards has been raised more than once. In fact, as Harriet Zuckerman has shown in a thorough analysis of Nobel Science Prize-winners, *Nobel Laureates in the United States* (1977), there has most often been a "complex interaction of merit and privilege".

As a result of the growing interest in the history of science, it has also become possible to chart the way in which particular scientists have come to be awarded Nobel Prizes, at what stages in their lives, and with what results. It has become possible, too, to trace how Nobel Prize-winners have viewed their own achievements, including the award of the Prize, and how one Nobel Prize-winner's work has influenced the work of others, including other Nobel Prize-winners, some of whom they "begat" intellectually. Finally, it has become possible to reveal that while some scientific themes have emerged from time to time within the Nobel Prize lists at widely separated dates – for example, the conquest of cancer – other themes have been regarded as novel from the start. Of course, what at first seemed novel could in retrospect look pioneering, like a 1977 paper by Sidney Altman, winner of the Nobel Chemistry Prize in 1989. Only very rarely do the Nobel judges seem to have made errors, when in the light of all available evidence, including hindsight, the wrong scientist got a Nobel Prize.

Science has to be studied, of course, in longer perspective than one century, not least because our own century has produced more scientists than all previous centuries put together. It is necessary to go back at least to the eighteenth century and to ponder on the achievements and limitations of the nineteenth century, Nobel's century, when the word "scientist" was invented. Significantly, when the Royal Swedish Academy of Sciences celebrated its 250th Anniversary in 1989, it held a symposium on the history of science, "Solomon's House Revisited", the title of which led back to one of the greatest figures of the past – Francis Bacon, a forecaster of the future.

As was noted by Lars Gyllensten, the Chairman of the Board of the Nobel Foundation, one of Bacon's main propositions, "knowledge is power", was being re-examined in the late twentieth century, not least in the light of environmental damage and dislocation. The ethics of science, too, were receiving almost as much attention as science policy since the revolution in the life sciences had begun. From this angle, the spread of scientific knowledge is as important as its creation, and the Nobel Prizes have done much to direct attention to scientific achievement – and so too have the Prize ceremonies which can attract almost as much public attention as the choice of Prize-winners.

There is in fact a Nobel Week as well as a Nobel Year, which focuses on 10 December, the anniversary of Nobel's death when the Prizes are presented in Stockholm by the Swedish King, and in Oslo by the chairman of the Norwegian Committee in the presence of the Norwegian King. "There's something spooky about the Nobel", the winner of the Nobel Physics Prize, Leon M. Lederman, stated in 1989. "It has its own special aura." The reason he gave – "because of its earlier winners" – is substantially but not entirely accurate. The aura is now institutional. Few Nobel Prize-winners are entirely surprised when they learn that they have been awarded Prizes. Most have been surprised when they return from Stockholm after receiving them.

The Nobel Week includes other events besides the handing out of the Prizes. First, there is the arrival at the Grand Hotel, usually on 6 December on what for some Prize-winners is their first visit to Sweden. Next there are receptions held in the main meeting room of the Swedish Academy on 7 December, following press conferences for the Prize-winners in Physics, Chemistry, and Economics. On 8 or 9 December each of the Prize-winners offers formal lectures, and on 9 December a reception is given at the Swedish Academy by the Nobel Foundation.

On the great day, 10 December, the King presents the Prizes in the afternoon at the Stockholm Concert Hall. In the evening, there is a Nobel banquet held in the Blue Hall of Stockholm's City Hall, a monument to the Sweden of the 1920s. Over 1,000 guests now attend, with university students lining the steps of the hall and carrying their banners. The banquet is followed by a ball in the Golden Hall. Meanwhile, there are festivities in Oslo where the Nobel Peace Prize is presented to its winner. After receiving the Oslo Prize, the new laureate delivers a lecture which usually receives special publicity. When Secretary-General Pérez de Cuellar accepted the Prize on behalf of the United Nations Peace keeping forces in 1988, he began his speech with what is still the fundamental contrast: "Peace – the word evokes the simplest and most cherished dream of humanity. Peace is, and always has been, the ultimate human aspiration. And yet our history overwhelmingly shows that while we speak incessantly of peace, our actions tell a very different story."

There are other contrasts, too, which can affect Nobel Prize officials as well as Prize-winners, a few of whom, like the American physicist R. P. Feynman (1965), have regretted receiving it. The Chairman of the Committee of the Swedish Academy resigned in 1989 – with two other members of the Swedish Academy – when his colleagues failed to make a public statement attacking the death threat to Salman Rushdie.

Even the ball is not quite the end of the Nobel Week – at least in Sweden. On the following morning hotel guests are wakened up to the sound of singers ushering in the Feast of St Lucia, Sweden's Festival of Light.

The Nobel lectures vary in range, and a few of them reflect uneasiness about the gap between the Nobel élite and the masses of the population, and, even more relevantly, about the dependence of the Prize-winners on large numbers of scientific helpers who do not receive the Prize. In 1988 Gyllensten had drawn attention to another gap – between the culture of scientific researchers on the one hand and humanists on the other, although he suggested that steadily increasing demand for responsibility on the part of both the researchers and the humanists is now bridging the gap between the two cultures.

It is undoubtedly true that awareness of the need to bridge gaps has grown since the 1960s when C. P. (later Lord) Snow drew attention to this issue. Yet much scientific language remains inaccessible to most people even in societies which pride themselves on a high level of educa-

tional development, and there are cultural gaps also within the sciences themselves.

The tendency towards increasing academic specialization – and with it separate scientific languages, which developed in the nineteenth century, has continued through from the nineteenth century into the twentieth, although recently team work, often interdisciplinary in range, has reversed the tendency in some fields. As Gyllensten stressed rightly in relation to one major area of concern, "the matter of protecting our environment and our resources so that we can all live a decent and dignified life in the future, this is not a task for specialists". "It is the concern of everyone, and it is a global problem."

Gyllensten left out the social sciences, as Snow had done, and so too, as we have seen, does the Nobel Foundation – with the exception of the Economics Prize which was not added until 1968; and these sciences, along with history, which is sometimes treated as one of them, are necessary to its understanding. It is only within this framework that we can investigate why there are deep and growing popular suspicions not only of scientists, but of science as a whole, even when the prestige of Nobel Prize-winners remains high.

As our own century enters its last decade, a decade of greater uncertainties than there were 100 years ago, it is possible at last for historians to discern something of its shape so that we too will doubtless begin to draw up our own accounts.

As long ago as 1967, in a decade which was turning to "futurology", the twentieth century was described by the then Vice-President of the European Economic Community, Dr S. L. Mansholt, as "our accelerating century". With the Second World War already half a generation behind him, he picked out six features of twentieth-century experience that would have to be taken into account in looking ahead towards the century's end: the continuation of the industrial revolution; the two World Wars that had "devastated Europe without solving a single problem": a substantial improvement in the well-being of the industrial countries, which had left a vast gap between the less developed countries and "the industrial west"; an ideological conflict between the East and West over the nature and future of the socioeconomic system; "extremely inadequate international organisation, because we have not created a single body which can cope with the major problems of the future"; and "rapid progress in science and technology", progress that, nonetheless, would lead in the very near future to "an explosive development in productivity and living standards and habits, together with an equally explosive increase in population".

The result, Mansholt's presentation concluded, was a world living in anxiety concerning the future, "caught between fear of war and hope of peace". It was a very different world from that of the *belle époque* between 1900 and 1914, a world of sunshine and shadows, where there were also threats of war, and when beneath a glittering surface there were dark undercurrents. It was a world of changed perceptions, too, as a result of great geo-political changes and above all of the communications revolution.

There was to be exceptional tension in 1968, the year after Mansholt had given his lecture. Tension turned in places into conflict, and soon the war in Vietnam entered into a violent new phase. Most ominously for Mansholt, however, the tension derived not only from the international situation but from changes in domestic relations, and, above all, in the organization of work. The upthrust of technology had changed ways of thinking and feeling as well as ways of working and relaxing, and for him the great question was, would it be possible for mankind "to cope with the great spiritual tensions which accompany life in a society dominated by technology?"

It was during the decade of the 1960s that "futurology" came into fashion and that people began to look towards 2000. In 1990, a generation later, it is now possible to measure the angle of deviation between what they predicted or prophesied and what has actually happened. Mansholt spoke of the continuation of the industrial revolution: Daniel Bell, prominent among the futurologists, coined the adjective post-industrial to suggest that the late-twentieth century world was genuinely new. Peter Drucker in 1969 wrote a book called *The Age of Discontinuity*, while Alan Bullock wrote in 1971 of a "Promethean Age". Other writers have referred subsequently to an "age of transparency".

There are as many, or more, question marks in the early 1990s than there were in 1900. Mansholt in 1967 predicted the absence of a world war between his time of writing and the end of the century, yet we cannot be too sure even about that, for while since he wrote the cold war has ceased, the gap between north and south has greatly widened. Moreover, the ideological conflict between East and West took a dramatic new turn in 1989 when Communism collapsed in eastern and central Europe, and when the Soviet Union, under the leadership of Gorbachev, changed many of its established policies.

The future constitutional position within the Soviet Union is still in doubt, however, as is the compatibility of political and economic reforms, while international organization remains "inadequate" and is being tested in the Middle East, an area which has remained torn by conflict since the end of the Second World War. Progress in science and technology has continued with particular momentum in the life sciences and medicine, which has a direct bearing on life and death and hence on the future of world population, still increasing alarmingly. With computing has come robotry, and in both these developments Japan, which has so far produced seven Nobel Prize-winners, has been a pioneer.

Mansholt's speech would have been worthy of a Nobel Prize-winner. As it is, Nobel Prize-winners in their speeches themselves often gaze into the unknown future. British scientist Sir Nevill Mott, winner of the Physics Prize in 1977, predicted large-scale generation of electricity from sunlight: it would involve covering large areas, perhaps of the deserts, with solar cells. Ten years later, Donald Cram, American winner of the Chemistry Prize, predicted that before the end of the century AIDS – not yet there in 1967 – would be curable, that the immune system would be well understood and that faulty genes would be repairable.

Each Prize-winner has his or her own vantage point in time and place, and the range of vision of each, like that of Mansholt, is determined by a combination of age, temperament, academic field, and practical experience. Writers in this century have traversed the frontiers of knowledge as experimentally as scientists and with as strong a sense of curiosity. And both the visual and the performing arts have joined in the enterprise.

Mansholt had little to say either about media and the continuing communications revolution – and its effects on perceptions, expectations, and aspirations – or about the continuing challenge of education, which within a late-twentieth-century context requires to be thought of as lifelong education. He mentioned environmental issues, however, at a time when, in his own words, it was "only with the help of a private fund in the United States that a modest beginning can be made in studying these environmental problems jointly". From the early 1970s awards they were to figure increasingly on international agenda, like Dr Gyllensten's, and in the curricula of universities, raising metaphysical as well as scientific and technical questions, questions dealing, as in their own way did questions raised by the media, "with the way we see the world".

How we see it has been fundamentally transformed both by the communications revolution and by the move out into space. It was not until 1969, of course, two years after Mansholt's speech, that the first human being walked on the moon. Yet already before 1967, Sputnik, the first satellite, had shaken the United States in 1957 and the Soviet Union had put the first man into space in 1961. In a brilliant lecture delivered at Edinburgh University in that year, the year of the Berlin Wall and of the Cuba Missiles Crisis, Ritchie Calder had already described "humanity's family estate" in terms of "a biosphere, the living-space, for the evolutionary process which, we like to think, had its consummation in Man".

The idea of evolution emerged from Nobel's century. The idea of the planet as one belongs very much to our own. The twenty-first century will test the capacity of human beings to deal effectively and imaginatively both with their own affairs and with those of the planet. They will have to go beyond techniques of problem solving, difficult though these have proved to be, to acquire and develop a sense of long-term trusteeship. If Nobel Prizes direct attention to such obligations, they will make an even greater contribution to the new century which we shall soon enter than they have made to our own.

Asa Briggs,
Oxford

Each Nobel medal is struck in 23-carat gold and measures about 2½ inches in diameter. The medal's thickness varies, depending on the value of gold. Each is currently valued at about 20,000 Swedish *kronor*.

1 PEACE

Just outside the meditation room of the United Nations' General Assembly Hall in New York is this window by Marc Chagall. The room was planned by Dag Hammarskjöld when he was UN secretary general during the 1950s. Also near the entrance is a display case with his Nobel certificate and medal, awarded posthumously in 1961.

Introduced by Irwin Abrams

When Alfred Nobel was considering a provision in his will for a Peace Prize, he wrote to his friend, the peace leader Baroness Bertha von Suttner, that he thought it should be awarded no longer than thirty years. If peace in Europe had not been established by then, he believed, the continent would be headed straight back to barbarism.

Thirty years after the first Prize was awarded in 1901, the world was struggling to recover from the cataclysm of the First World War and was about to plunge into an even greater conflict, one which would produce the ultimate deadly weapon – the atomic bomb.

The twentieth century has been witness to much barbarism, not only great wars and civil violence, but an unprecedented descent into the Holocaust. It is against this dark backdrop of inhumanity that the Nobel century should be reviewed, as a period of triumphs of the human spirit in the fields of endeavour that Alfred Nobel chose to honour.

Of the five original awards, the Prize for Peace has been in many ways the most important – as well as the most controversial. Achievements in the sciences, medicine and literature demonstrate human potential in works of the intellect and creativity. Achievements in peace have to do with human survival. The atomic age was born in this century, and in 1982, Dr Tore Browalldh, deputy chairman of the Nobel Foundation, declared, "The unthinkable has been made possible: to transform Spaceship Earth into a nova, an exploding star, by means of a new world war. Today the Nobel Peace Prize stands as the symbol of the struggle to prevent the extinction of man as a species."

Yet after the awarding of ninety Peace Prizes, the world is still rife with violent conflicts. Some cynics have suggested that the Norwegian Nobel Committee should shut up shop and give its funds to some needy cause. But peace is not just a goal. Peace is a process, a continuing effort, and the Nobel Committee makes grants for partial achievements and for efforts that may not succeed. Above all, the Committee makes its most significant awards to individuals whose untiring labours for peace can raise the level of our expecta-tions about the human potential for dedicated service to humanity.

There are detractors who like to say that Nobel's Peace Prize was set up to assuage the guilt of a munitions maker, but the fortune Nobel left to establish the Prize was the result of his development and production of dynamite for such peaceful uses as the building of canals and railroads and the digging of tunnels and mines.

There can be no question about Nobel's sincere interest in peace. His correspondence with Baroness von Suttner shows this. It was she who convinced him that the young peace organization, just holding its first world congresses in the 1890s, was a serious and hopeful endeavour, worthy of Nobel's financial support. In his last letter to her, written only a few weeks before he died on 10 December, 1896, Nobel said that he was delighted to see the progress that the peace movement was making, and he paid tribute to her efforts.

In writing the Peace Prize clauses for his will, Nobel had the movement very much in mind. The award was to go "to the person who shall have done the most or the best work for fraternity between nations, for the abolition of standing armies and for the holding and promotion of peace con-gresses". Working for disarmament and the organizing of congresses were activities of the peace societies about which the Baroness had been sending him regular reports.

When the earliest Peace Prize recipients were selected, the Norwegian Committee gave recognition to pioneer peace activists like the Baroness and to international law-yers, the groups whose activities laid down the intellectual and moral foundation for the international organizations that were to come. But in the very first Prize in 1901, the Committee made clear that it would interpret freely Nobel's directive to award the "best work for fraternity between nations". The Committee divided the Prize between the leading veteran of the peace movement and Henri Dunant,

"The Signing of the Peace in the Hall of Mirrors, Versailles, 28th June, 1919" is one of the paintings produced by Sir William Orpen in his role as an official War Artist.

the humanitarian founder of the Red Cross. How better to demonstrate fraternity than to give succour to victims on both sides of a fratricidal conflict? And in 1906, the Committee for the first time gave its prize to a statesman, President Theodore Roosevelt, who had helped bring the Russo-Japanese War to an end.

Later Committees broadened their mandate so that the Nobel roll of honour includes not only peace activists, international lawyers, humanitarians and statesmen, but religious figures, labour leaders and scientists. Along with individuals, both private and official organizations have also been singled out for the honour. In recent times Committees have awarded the Prize to champions of human rights. A chairman of the Committee said to me in reference to these awards, "Nobel's will does not state this, but it was written in another time. Today we realize that peace cannot be established without a full respect for freedom."

In bestowing Prizes on human rights activists, the Committee has acted to assist their efforts – not just with the prize money – but with the international prestige that goes with the award. For example, Bishop Desmond Tutu was strengthened in his fight against apartheid in South Africa. The Nobel Prize made it more difficult for the Soviet government to persecute Andrei Sakharov, and it gave world recognition to the struggle of the Dalai Lama of Tibet against the Chinese suppression of his people.

The Committee has engaged in peacemaking in other ways as well. Its award to Willy Brandt in 1971 helped him with his policy of reconciliation with Germany's wartime enemies. President Arias of Costa Rica was clearly aided by the award in his efforts to bring peace to Central America. President Gorbachev thought that the Prize was given to him in 1990 in support of his policy of *perestroika*. He said, "I perceive this action of the most authoritative organization of the global community . . . as a recognition of the significance of the immense cause of *perestroika* for the destiny of the entire world." The Committee explained, however, that the Prize had gone to the Soviet leader because of his role in ending the cold war and liberating Eastern Europe.

Prizes to statesmen have been the most open to criticism. Theodore Roosevelt's skilful diplomacy did help end a war that the belligerents wanted to conclude, and he did promote international arbitration. But Roosevelt is better known for his imperialist policies, and he himself once declared that his most important contribution to peace was sending the US Navy around the world.

Perhaps the most unpopular Prizes, in world public opinion, were those that went to Henry Kissinger in 1973 and to Menachem Begin in 1978. Kissinger stayed away from the award ceremony to avoid a demonstration against his Vietnam policy. Begin's government started a war in Lebanon not long after he received his award.

Critics have pointed out that statesmen are paid to keep the peace. That is their job. What they achieve because of their office cannot be compared to the achievement of a

Soviet President Mikhail S. Gorbachev, recipient of the 1990 Peace Prize, said in his Oslo lecture, "If *perestroika* fails, the prospect of entering a new peaceful period in history will vanish, at least for the foreseeable future."

person who had committed his life to the cause of peace and humanity. There are too few statesmen like Brandt, Arias, and American Secretary of State Elihu Root, who continued significant work for peace after leaving office.

Those laureates who are outstanding have shown their devotion to peace in many ways. Fridtjof Nansen, a famous explorer as a young man, devoted the last part of his life to care for world refugees. Lord Cecil worked for a lifetime to make a success of the League of Nations. Ralph Bunche and Dag Hammarskjöld devoted all their considerable talents to making the United Nations effective. Jane Addams made Hull House in Chicago a haven for the disinherited, then led a movement of women to stop the First World War and founded the Women's International League of Peace and Freedom. Carl von Ossietzky fought German militarism as a journalist and was sent by the Nazis to a concentration camp where mistreatment led to his early death.

Albert Schweitzer gave up careers as theologian, teacher, and musician to train as a doctor so he could tend the sick in the African jungle. Mother Teresa was a teaching missionary when she answered an inner call to minister to the sick and dying in Calcutta's slums and went on to found the worldwide Missionaries of Charity. Linus Pauling, winner of the Nobel Prize in Chemistry in 1954, mobilized the scientists of the world to demand a partial nuclear test ban and received the Peace Prize in 1962. The complete list is a distinguished roster.

Who are the judges whose decisions make headlines all over the world each October? What is the procedure they follow? In his will, Nobel gave the responsibility for the Peace Award to a committee of five to be appointed by the Norwegian parliament. Why Norway, when all the other Prizes are presented by the king of Sweden in Stockholm? (So many peace nominations are sent to Stockholm by mistake that every month a bundle of them has to be forwarded to Oslo. Not long ago, proposals for President Reagan's nomination were sent in error to Stockholm.)

Nobel never explained why he gave this job to Norway, but back then the country was joined with Sweden in a monarchic union. Norwegian parliamentary deputies were actively involved in peace causes, and that might have influenced Nobel.

Some people believe that the Norwegian government is responsible for the Committee's decisions. This is not true. Nazi Germany tried to put pressure on the Oslo government to prevent the award from going to Von Ossietzky, and more recently, governments have complained to Norway about Prizes that have gone to dissidents in their countries. But the Norwegian Nobel Committee answers for its choices neither to its government nor to the parliament which appoints its members. To make this independence clear cut, the parliament decided some years ago to exclude from Committee membership any sitting cabinet ministers and parliamentary deputies. The Committee which chose Gorbachev for the 1990 award is typical. It was chaired by a prominent woman writer, and the others were a former premier, a church official, an historian, and a labour executive.

Since there is no single group anywhere in the world that can claim to be authoritative about peace, those eligible to submit nominations represent a greater variety than those who suggest laureates for the Stockholm Prizes. Those who can send nominations to Oslo include members of governments and national assemblies; past and present members of the Oslo Committee; holders of the Peace Prize, members of the Institute of International Law, of international courts, and of the council of the International Peace Bureau; and university professors of political science, law, history, and philosophy.

Nominations each year must be received in Oslo before 1 February. The Committee receives almost a hundred names annually. The secretary submits these nominations with relevant data to the Committee which then makes up a short list and assigns reports to be written by advisors on each candidate. By the end of the summer these carefully researched reports are ready for Committee deliberations. Members are pledged to absolute silence about how they arrive at their decision. (The Norwegian Committee, smaller than the Stockholm bodies, has a far better record over the years of keeping matters confidential.)

In his will, Nobel wrote that his prizes were to be awarded to persons who "shall have conferred the greatest benefit on mankind". To this objective, the Norwegian Nobel Committees have sought to remain faithful throughout this century. That they have for the most part succeeded is shown by the considerable prestige which their Prize enjoys the world over, far surpassing any other award for service to peace and humanity.

Through their best selections, the Committees have set before us an array of great spirits, men and women who in the midst of this age of violence and barbarism give us reason to have faith in humankind and inspire us to follow them in working for a more peaceful world.

I.A.

Bertha von Suttner

A Plot for an Operetta

The story of Bertha von Chinio und Tettau's life has all the ingredients of a nineteenth-century Viennese operetta: a poor, fatherless governess falls in love with a younger man; his parents oppose the match; she is sent away – but true love wins out.

Bertha's father, a field marshal, died before she was born. Brought up by her mother and a guardian who was a member of the Austrian court, Bertha studied music and considered a career in opera. Her mother, however, gambled away their money, and at the age of thirty Bertha took a job as teacher-companion to the four daughters of the Suttner household. Baron Arthur Gundaccar von Suttner, the youngest son, and Bertha, fell in love. Arthur's parents had expected him to marry an heiress and restore the Suttner wealth.

Arthur's mother persuaded Bertha to apply for a job with a gentleman in Paris who had advertised for someone to manage his household and his social affairs. The man was one of the world's wealthiest: Alfred Nobel. Bertha went for an interview; Nobel admired her intelligence, seriousness, and knowledge of languages. After less than a week on the job, however, Bertha received a telegram from Arthur saying he could not live without her. Bertha rushed back to Vienna, and the couple eloped.

The first act ends with their love duet. Act II:

Because of the Von Suttners's disapproval, the young couple went to live in the Caucasus, where Bertha had friends. For the next nine years the two made their living as writers.

By 1885 the Von Suttner family had become reconciled to the marriage, and Bertha and Arthur returned to Austria and the literary life. It was then that Bertha wrote *The Machine Age* (1889), which was highly critical of the armament build-up going on in Europe at the time. The book was widely reviewed and discussed. Both Bertha and Arthur became increasingly interested in writing about and working for peaceful solutions to Europe's problems. Bertha next wrote *Lay Down Your Arms*, a novel in which the heroine experiences all the horrors of war. The book's impact has been compared to that of *Uncle Tom's Cabin*; it created an immediate controversy, and turned its author into a leader in the cause of peace.

Had Alfred Nobel fallen in love with Bertha during the week she worked for him? He never married, and the two kept in touch for the next twenty years. Nobel admired Bertha's books, and was much interested in her peace work. In 1892, at a peace convention in Switzerland, Nobel said to Bertha and her husband, "If you keep me in touch with developments, and if I hear that the Peace Movement is moving along the road of practical activity, then I will help it on with money."

When Nobel died, Bertha heard about his will. She was thrilled, and believed that he had carried out his promise, hoping she might be a recipient, as her need for money was pressing. She was, however, passed over by the Committee. In 1905, one of the witnesses to Nobel's will told the Committee that Nobel himself had wanted the Baroness to have the Prize; she was the first woman to win the award.

Despite her life's work, however, Bertha saw that the world was preparing not for peace but for war. As the black-gowned widow in her sixties told the crowd at the Oslo ceremony:

"Let us look round us in the world of today and see whether we are really justified in claiming for pacifism progressive development and positive results. A terrible war, unprecedented in the world's history, recently raged in the Far East. This war was followed by a revolution, even more terrible, which shook the great Russian Empire, a revolution whose final outcome we cannot yet foresee. We hear continually of fire, robbery, bombings, executions, overflowing prisons, beatings, and massacres; in short, an orgy of the Demon Violence. Meanwhile, in Central and Western Europe which narrowly escaped war, we have distrust, threats, sabre rattling, press baiting, feverish naval build-up, re-arming everywhere."

In 1914 – the year the Baroness Bertha Felicita Sophia von Suttner died – the Great War began.

Peace is not something to lecture about, but something to put into practice.
FATHER GEORGES PIRE, 1958

The advocates of pacifism are well aware how meagre are their resources of personal influence and power. They know that they are still few in number and weak in authority, but when they realistically consider themselves and the ideal they serve, they see themselves as the servants of the greatest of all causes.

BERTHA VON SUTTNER, 1905

By 1901 Bertha von Suttner was the leader of the peace movement in Europe, and one of the most famous women of her time. She edited a peace journal, wrote articles and books, and made speeches. In 1904 she lectured in the United States, and President Theodore Roosevelt, who would be awarded the Peace Prize the following year, received her at the White House.

Woodrow Wilson

Thomas Woodrow Wilson did not learn to read until he was twelve years old. His parents thought he was lazy; more likely, he was dyslexic.

Wilson's father was a Presbyterian minister. His mother, who suffered from depression and was withdrawn, adored her charming son. At seventeen, ill-prepared academically, Woodrow was sent to a small college. He was homesick, dropped out, and went on to Princeton University, where he flourished. Woodrow loved to sing Gilbert and Sullivan songs and took the role of Mark Antony in a play called *The Sanguinary Tragedy of Julius Sneezer*. He became an orator. He was a great admirer of British statesmen, and highly critical of what he saw as the deficiencies in the American form of government; he especially deplored the poor quality of its elected officials.

After graduating, Wilson studied law at the University of Virginia, but when his law practice failed, he decided to try an academic career. After teaching at Bryn Mawr and Wesleyan, and publishing a successful book, Woodrow was hired by Princeton as a teacher. He was named president of the University in 1902. Because he wanted to make drastic changes that meant breaks with long-held traditions, Woodrow encountered problems with the University board. He was about to be dismissed from his post when the chance to run for governor of New Jersey was offered to him. Wilson won the election, with one of the largest majorities in the state's history.

Elected to the US presidency in 1913, Wilson believed his role had been pre-destined by God, and that he was meant to preserve neutrality during the First World War in order to bring peace to the world. He negotiated between the British and Germans, but when the Germans sunk four American ships, Wilson led his country into war. He created a fourteen-point peace plan, and went to Europe to convince its leaders to accept it. Wilson failed to persuade the US Senate to allow the country to join the League of Nations, an organization that was born of his own plan.

The Nobel Peace Prize was awarded to Wilson in 1920 as founder of the League of Nations, but poor health prevented him from going to Norway, to accept the award.

In 1924, as Wilson lay dying, his doctor brought a team of specialists into his room. As they entered, Wilson's last words were "too many cooks spoil the broth".

Wilson admired all things Scottish and played golf every day he could. He was a popular teacher at Princeton University because of his passionate and spontaneous lectures. As president of the University, Wilson made a reputation as an educational reformer.

> *As the world community develops in peace, it will open up great untapped reservoirs in human nature. Like a spring released from pressure would be the response of a generation of young men and women growing up in an atmosphere of friendliness and security, in a world demanding their service, offering them comradeship, calling to all adventurous and forward-reaching natures.*
>
> EMILY GREENE BALCH, 1946

At the Versailles peace conference, these were the "Big Four": Baron Sonnino of Italy, Lloyd George of England (who wanted to squeeze the defeated Germans like an orange "until the pips squeaked"), Georges Clemençeau of France, and Woodrow Wilson.

It is to be observed that every case of war averted is a gain in general, for it helps to form a habit of peace, and community habits long continued become standards of conduct.

ELIHU ROOT, 1912

If the peoples of the world get together and with one united voice demand world unity and peace, they will get it.

LORD BOYD ORR, 1949

Wilson was re-elected president in 1916 with the slogan "He kept us out of war," – and a year later led the United States to join the Allies fighting in Germany. Although nominations to award him the Nobel Peace Prize came from all over the world, Wilson was a highly controversial choice because in order to join the League of Nations, he had to agree to the Treaty of Versailles.

Fridtjof Nansen

Following the First World War, Fridtjof Nansen of Norway used the fame he had won as an explorer to help millions of refugees. His relief work earned him the 1922 Peace Prize.

As a youth, Nansen excelled in winter sports. He was strong enough to ski fifty miles in a day, which was good training for his first expedition: the interior of Greenland had never been explored, and Nansen crossed it. On another adventure, Nansen and a companion travelled more than 140 miles over rough ice to get nearer to the North Pole than any previous explorers.

Nansen wrote books about his experiences, taught at university, and served as Norway's first minister to Great Britain.

In 1914, with the war in Europe under way, Nansen became interested in international political affairs. Later, when working for the League of Nations, he found ways to repatriate half a million prisoners from Russia. He invented the "Nansen Passport" for stateless refugees, an identification card recognized by fifty-two governments. Nansen arranged the exchange of more than one million Greeks living in Turkey with one-half million Turks living in Greece.

In 1921, millions of Russians were dying in a famine. Despite most nations' mistrust of the new Soviet government, Nansen gathered and distributed enough supplies to save the lives of an estimated ten million people.

It is hard to believe that anyone could find fault with Nansen's energetic, selfless endeavours, but he had critics, and in his Nobel Prize lecture, he denounced them:

"They call us romantics, weak, stupid, sentimental idealists, perhaps because we have some faith in the good which exists even in our opponents and because we believe that kindness achieves more than cruelty. It may be that we are simple-minded, but I do not think we are dangerous. Those, however, who stagnate behind their political programs, offering nothing else to suffering mankind, to starving, dying millions – they are the scourge of Europe."

Eight years later, Nansen died on a skiing trip at the age of sixty-eight.

Above
His skill as a skier was appropriately documented in front of a painted studio backdrop. At eighteen he won the Norwegian national cross-country skiing race, and continued to come in first for the next eleven years. Before he was seventeen he won the national distance ice-skating championship of Norway, and he was a skilled horseman, hunter, and fisherman as well.

Left
After the First World War Nansen became a familiar figure in a broad-rimmed hat at the League of Nations, where a journalist called him "one of the sights of Geneva – the proudest after Mont Blanc".

These children were among the victims of the famine that devastated the Soviet Union in 1921. Nansen sent out an appeal for aid: the League of Nations turned down his request, but the United States contributed twenty million dollars. With donations coming from other countries as well, Nansen's relief effort is credited with saving ten million Russian lives.

Nansen's specially designed ship, the *Fram* (*Forward*), could drift with ice-floes, and took him on an expedition to the Arctic in June of 1893. On his return home in 1896, Nansen became research professor at the University of Christiana, where he worked on the mass of scientific data he had collected during his travels.

Jane Addams

In 1914, Archduke Francis Ferdinand, heir to the Austrian-Hungarian throne, was on an official visit to Sarajevo. A bomb was tossed on to his car, and bounced out into the street just before it exploded. Later that same day, a young Serbian fired seven shots into the car, killing the Archduke and his wife. The sparks for the Great War were ignited; all Europe was arming.

Jane Addams, a social worker and the most admired woman in America, turned her considerable skills to peace activism. She wrote, "Women, who have brought men into the world and nurtured them until they reach the age for fighting, must experience a particular revulsion when they see them destroyed."

Addams was born in Illinois in 1860, the eighth child of a prosperous miller who served eight terms in the state senate, and who was a friend of Abraham Lincoln. Jane wanted to become a doctor, but poor health and her father's death while she was in her early twenties ended the dream.

During a tour of Europe, she visited a settlement house in London's East End, which inspired her to open Hull House in Chicago. Her work on behalf of the poor made her a heroine. Then the Germans invaded Belgium and France.

In 1915 Addams helped to form a Women's Peace Party. She became the Party's chairman, and in Amsterdam presided over an international congress of 1,500 women at which resolutions on peace were passed. After the congress, delegates of women visited statesmen in London, Berlin, Vienna, Rome and Paris, urging them to try mediation as a means of reconciliation rather than war.

Her fame established by the highly-publicized success of the first settlement house in Chicago, Jane Addams (right) became an activist in the pursuit of women's rights. Addams believed that "just as it is quicker to punish an unruly child than to bring him to a reasonable state of mind; . . . so it is quicker to fight armies of men than to convince them one by one . . . ."

Although Addams urged President Woodrow Wilson to mediate, in April 1917, after the Germans had sunk five American ships, he asked Congress to declare war.

Addams continued to speak out, and frequently was reviled by patriots, who thought her pacifism was treasonous. On one occasion she created an unpleasant controversy when she said she had talked to young soldiers during her tour of Europe, and had been told that just before battle the English were given rum, the Germans took ether, and the French used absinthe "not because the young men flinched at the risk of death but because they had to be inflamed to do the brutal work of the bayonet, such as disemboweling, and were obliged to overcome all the inhibitions of civilization". One newspaper reported that Addams had said that soldiers could not go into a bayonet charge until they were half drunk. In a letter to *The New York Times*, adventure-writer Richard Harding Davis accused Addams of being "a most choice specimen of a woman's sentimental nonsense".

When the War ended, the Hague delegates met again in Zürich and formed a permanent organization – the Women's International League for Peace and Freedom. Addams became its president, and for the rest of her life presided over meetings, raised money, and donated her own money to the US chapter, as well as her share of the Peace Prize, which was awarded to her in 1931.

Right
In September 1889, Jane Addams moved into a decaying mansion, Hull House, in the Chicago slums, and began an experiment in social work among the impoverished immigrants who teemed in areas such as Chicago's Maxwell Street.

Below
Jane Addams's Hull House offered immigrants from nearby Chicago tenements a variety of educational and recreational programmes. She was the head resident, administrator, counsellor, public relations director, and fund-raiser. When Addams died in 1935, the Chicago City Council declared she was "the greatest woman who ever lived".

Norman Angell

The Age of "Angellism"

Norman Angell of Great Britain was awarded the Peace Prize in 1933. As he wrote in his autobiography, *After All*, published in 1951, he thought he should have received it twenty years earlier: "It would have been more logical to have awarded it at the earlier date, since the kind of work I had been doing in the intervening years was being done – often far better – by others; while what I was doing in 1912 did break new ground, in a new way for peace; in a way that had secured for the peace problem a world-wide attention." In 1912 Angell had expanded a pamphlet he had written into a book entitled *The Grand Illusion*. It appeared in more than twenty languages, sold four million copies, and triggered a peace movement called "Norman Angellism".

Angell's father was well-to-do, and as a boy Norman went to private schools in England, France, and Switzerland. At seventeen, with fifty pounds from his father, he sailed to the United States where he worked as a cow-hand, rancher, ditch-digger, prospector, mail-carrier, and newspaper reporter.

At twenty-six Angell returned to Europe and became editor of an English-language newspaper in Paris. He felt his experiences gave him special insights into the British, Americans, and French, and he began to promote peace. He was interested in education because he believed that an educated citizenry would be a rational citizenry, and always choose peace. At one point Angell devised a card-game to promote an understanding of currency; he thought it would be a useful tool for economic education – and hoped as well that it would replace bridge.

Surely those who have seen at first hand the destitution pervading our misgoverned Europe and actually experienced some of the endless suffering must realize that the world can no longer rely on panaceas, paper and words. These must be replaced by action, by persevering and laborious effort, which must begin at the bottom in order to build up the world again.

FRIDTJOF NANSEN, 1922

In 1898, he married a New Orleans woman who proved to be highly unstable. They were separated by 1914, but she was an emotional and financial burden until 1955, when she died. He remained secretive about her all his life.

Angell held a seat in the House of Commons for one term, advised political leaders, and was active in the creation of the League of Nations.

Despite two world wars, he continued his promotion of peace by lecturing and by writing more than forty books until just a few years before his death in 1967 at the age of ninety-four.

We must recognize the fact that adequate food is only the first requisite for life. For a decent and humane life we must also provide an opportunity for good education, remunerative employment, comfortable housing, good clothing, and effective and compassionate medical care. Unless we can do this, man may degenerate sooner from environmental diseases than from hunger.

NORMAN E. BORLAUG, 1970

Right
As the Second World War approached, Angell became an outspoken critic of Prime Minister Neville Chamberlain's policy of appeasement towards Nazi Germany. Angell urged his country to open its borders to Jewish refugees, and he himself took a family of refugees into his home.

Left
In 1966 Norman Angell visited the United States to make a formal presentation of his papers, which had been purchased by Ball State University in Muncie, Indiana. This last visit gave him a chance to get back into the saddle. In 1983, sixteen years after his death, newspapers carried a notice that his Nobel medal was being auctioned at Sotheby's in London.

Carl von Ossietzky

When the 1935 Peace Prize was awarded to the German journalist Carl von Ossietzky, a cartoon in the New York *World Telegram* showed a furious Führer saying, "It is a political demonstration against the Third Reich!"

Von Ossietzky, who had been imprisoned by the Nazis, was given the award for his record of anti-militarism. This clearly was a departure for the Oslo Committee. Two previous Peace laureates had recommended Von Ossietzky, and, because of the treatment he received from the Nazis, and because of friends working on his behalf, he attracted worldwide attention.

Until the campaign for the Peace Prize began, Von Ossietzky was unknown outside Germany. In 1931, as editor of a weekly that promoted peace, he was convicted of treason for publishing information about Germany's secret re-arming. He served a six-month sentence, then returned to his desk to attack the Nazis once again. In February 1933 Hitler proclaimed his dictatorship; his enemies – including Von Ossietzky – were arrested.

Von Ossietzky was moved through a series of concentration camps. He had tuberculosis and a heart condition, and his health was deteriorating. A Red Cross representative who visited Von Ossietzky described him as being "a trembling deadly pale something, a creature that appeared to be without feeling . . . a human being that had reached the uttermost limits of what could be borne".

In 1934 a friend decided to call attention to Von Ossietzky's plight by nominating him for the Peace Prize. German emigrés in Paris enlisted some of the most prominent men and women of the day to work on the journalist's behalf.

Willy Brandt in Oslo used his contacts there. Albert Einstein, not eligible to nominate because his prize was in Physics and not Peace, persuaded Jane Addams to propose Von Ossietzky. Ludwig Quidde, German Nobel laureate in 1926 and an exile in Geneva, sent in his nomination as well.

While support for Von Ossietzky grew, the German foreign office warned Oslo that a Prize given to Von Ossietzky would have grave consequences.

The Committee's telegram notifying Von Ossietzky that he had been awarded the Peace Prize reached him in hospital, where he had been moved from prison. His reply was, "Thankful for undeserved honour." The Norwegians were informed that the Germans regarded the award as an insulting provocation; Hitler decreed that no German ever again would be allowed to accept a Nobel Prize, in any field.

The award to Von Ossietzky was the

In 1934 Von Ossietzky was questioned by an officer at the Papenburg-Esterwegen concentration camp. His imprisonment caused outrage around the world, and sympathy for his plight was expressed by fellow journalists. A Nobel Committee spokesman called him a champion of peace.

first to be made to someone who was being persecuted by his or her government for their convictions of peace. It foreshadowed later awards to such controversial figures as Chief Albert John Lutuli of South Africa, Andrei Sakharov of the Soviet Union, Lech Walesa of Poland, and Desmond Tutu of South Africa.

Von Ossietzky spent the last two years of his life in a private sanatorium. Most of his Prize money was embezzled by a lawyer. When he died in 1938, the Nazis buried his ashes in secret, but after the Second World War, a Berlin street was named after him.

Peace can be reached only through fighting against the ancient Adam in ourselves and in others.

NATHAN SODERBLOM, 1930

In 1938, Von Ossietzky (centre) was escorted to prison by two friends. Petitions to the Nobel Committee were signed by Thomas Mann, Norman Angell, Jane Addams, Albert Einstein, and Bertrand Russell. Although he could have fled the country, Von Ossietzky believed that fighting "the rottenness in a nation" must be done from inside.

Albert Schweitzer

During his first tour of duty as a doctor in Africa, Albert Schweitzer took a small steamer 160 miles upstream from his hospital to aid the wife of a missionary who was ill. On the journey, Schweitzer sat on deck working on a book, trying to sort out his thoughts. On the third day, at sunset, the words "reverence for life" suddenly came to him. In his autobiography, *Out of My Life and Thought*, he recalls, "The iron door had yielded: the path in the thicket had become visible. Now I had found my way to the idea in which affirmation of the world and ethics are contained side by side!"

In 1932 the Nobel Committee in Oslo was urged to break with its tradition of giving the Peace Prize to a statesman or to a leader of a peace society. Instead of starting an organization to spread his beliefs, the Committee was told, Albert Schweitzer had lived his creed by raising money, building a hospital in Africa (at Lambaréné in the Gabon), and devoting himself to providing medical care for the natives. The Committee moved with deliberate speed; it took twenty years before it was convinced.

Albert Schweitzer was born in 1875 in Alsace. His father was a Protestant minister, and at nine Albert began playing the organ at church. At school he was a disciplined, successful student, but troubled by the poverty of his classmates. While studying at university, Schweitzer decided he would live for science and art until he was thirty, and then he would devote himself "to the direct service of humanity". He proceeded to write books about Christianity, J. S. Bach, and the organ. He played the organ in churches and gave concerts. He preached, taught, and lectured. Then, at thirty, Schweitzer

For me it is essential to have the inward peace and serenity of prayer in order to listen to the silence of God, which speaks to us, in our personal lives and in the history of our times, about the power of love.
ADOLFO PEREZ ESQUIVEL, 1980

began seven years of medical training.

He says in his autobiography, "I wanted to be a doctor that I might be able to work without having to talk. For years I had been giving myself out in words, and it was with joy that I had followed the calling of theological teacher and of preacher." As a doctor, Schweitzer planned to practise what he had been preaching.

During the First World War, the French considered Schweitzer and his wife to be Germans, and consequently interned them with others from Alsace at St Remy de Provence in a former monastery. The large day-room, bare and ugly, seemed familiar to Schweitzer; he was certain he had seen the iron stove before. He then realized he knew the room from a Van Gogh drawing, one the artist had made years earlier when the building was used as a hospital. "Like us," Schweitzer remarked, "he had suffered from the cold stone floor when the mistral blew! Like us, he had walked around and around between the high garden walls!"

Schweitzer was back in Africa at his

On the path to the leper facilities, the doctor's white helmet and shirt glowed against the deep jungle greens. It was Schweitzer's custom to make nightly rounds to all of his patients. The hospital grounds also became a refuge for pets of all kinds: dogs and cats, as well as a trio of noisy pelicans, baby antelope, and wild pigs.

greatly expanded hospital when his nephew, Dr Guy Schweitzer, brought word that the Peace Prize was his. The prize money was used to build and equip a hospital for lepers.

Schweitzer died at the age of ninety, and was buried near his Lambaréné hospital.

Above

The Ogowe River near Schweitzer's hospital at Lambaréné in the Gabon provided access by water, and patients were brought from as far away as 200 miles. They came in dug-out canoes, and family members stayed with the ill, often for months. Common illnesses included malaria – almost all the patients had it – sleeping sickness, sores, ulcers, dysentery, strangulated hernia, elephantiasis and leprosy.

Left

With the Prize money he received, Schweitzer built a special ward for leper patients set apart from the main hospital. Its buildings were constructed of corrigated metal, which lasted much longer and provided better shelter and ventilation than huts of bamboo and grass; the floors were of poured concrete rather than foot-packed earth. More than 300 patients could be treated in the new facilities. Sixty victims of leprosy, their disease arrested by the use of sulphone drugs, were able to help in the construction of the new building.

George C. Marshall

1953

A Man with a Plan

Ironically, the man who was to receive the Nobel Peace Prize also supervised the development of the atomic bomb, and in 1945 recommended that the United States use it on Hiroshima and Nagasaki. Marshall said, "The bomb stopped the war. Therefore it was justifiable."

On the same day in 1901 that young George C. Marshall was notified that his commission in the US Army had been approved, the first Nobel Peace Prize was awarded to Henri Dunant, founder of the Red Cross. Fifty years later, a member of the 1953 Oslo Committee pointed out that Marshall was president of the American Red Cross, the first high military officer ever to be honoured with the Peace Prize.

At twenty-one, probably the youngest and most inexperienced second lieutenant in the US Army, George Marshall was sent to command troops in a remote part of the Philippines. One day, on a training march, the men were led across a stream. Seeing crocodiles, some of the soldiers panicked, knocked Marshall down, and stampeded over him. When he crawled out of the water and on to the bank, instead of yelling at the men, Marshall ordered them to fall in behind him and to cross the stream again. They did as told, and Marshall led them back across the crocodile-infested water. He then inspected and dismissed them. Marshall's reputation as an imaginative leader was born.

Although he felt handicapped because he was not a West Point graduate, Marshall's career moved briskly. In the early 1930s, with the Depression at its worst, the Army and Marshall were involved in the Civilian Conservation Corps. He considered the programme "the greatest social experiment outside of Russia". During the First World War, Marshall became an aide to the legendary General Pershing, and in the Second World War, Roosevelt named Marshall chief-of-staff.

Germany surrendered in May of 1945; three months later the Japanese did too.

In his retirement speech that year, Marshall cited his concern about postwar Europe, a concern that would become the Marshall Plan and earn him the Nobel Peace Prize. He said, "Along with the great problem of maintaining the peace, we must solve the problems of the pittance of food, of clothing and coal and homes." Two years later, as secretary of state, he was asked to set the European recovery programme in motion.

One of his assistants, Dean Acheson, said that when Marshall appeared, everyone in the room was immediately aware of him. "It was a striking and communicated force," Acheson recalled. "His figure conveyed intensity, which his voice – low, staccato, and incisive – reinforced. It compelled respect. It spread a sense of authority and calm."

The mistakes that had followed the First World War and led to the Second were not repeated. In citing the General's accomplishments, the Oslo Committee chairman said, "The years that have gone by since he submitted his program have demonstrated its constructive character. And the organs which have grown from the Marshall Aid have, more than anything else in these difficult years, contributed to what Nobel termed 'the idea of a general peace in Europe.'".

If there is to be peace, there must be compromise, tolerance, agreement.
LESTER PEARSON, 1957

Right
The conquering hero is rewarded with a bouquet and smiles. United States Secretary of Defense Henry Stimson called Marshall "the finest soldier I have ever known". Truman referred to Marshall as "the greatest living American".

Below
Julius B. Stafford-Baker's drawing of "Berlin. The Headquarters of the S.S., the Gestapo and the Security Police" shows the devastation caused by Allied bombing. The United States spent more than twelve billion dollars on the Marshall Plan, which is credited with making Germany's economic miracle of the 1950s possible.

Dag Hammarskjöld

Just off the vast lobby of the United Nations' General Assembly Hall, on New York City's East River, is a meditation room. It was planned by Dag Hammarskjöld when he was secretary general during the 1950s. At the entrance is a large stained glass window by Marc Chagall, and a display case with the Nobel Peace Prize certificate and medal, awarded posthumously in 1961. The inscription that is cut into a black marble plaque at the entrance was written by Hammarskjöld: "This is a room devoted to peace and those who are giving their lives for peace. It is a room of quiet where only thoughts should speak." Hammarskjöld also wrote the text of a pamphlet for visitors to the room. It begins, "We all have within us a centre of stillness surrounded by silence . . . "

Dag Hammarskjöld was born in 1905, the son of a Swedish prime minister. While at Uppsala University he studied humanities, literature, history, English, French, and German, and was an outstanding student of his day. He was interested in poetry, painting, music, mountain-climbing, and skiing. He took advanced degrees in law and economics. After teaching in Stockholm for a year, Hammarskjöld entered public service, rising to head the Bank of Sweden.

He then became a deputy foreign minister and delegate to the UN. In 1953 he was elected secretary general and reelected to a second five-year term in 1957. Low-key and meticulous, the UN chief worked tirelessly in trying to resolve conflicts all over the world. In a memorable moment in UN history, Soviet Premier Nikita Khrushchev pounded on the podium with his shoe and demanded that Hammarskjöld resign. The secretary

Discouraged people are in sore need of the inspiration of great principles. Such leadership can be the rallying point against intolerance, against distrust, against that fatal insecurity that leads to war. It is to be hoped that the democratic nations can provide the necessary leadership.

GEORGE C. MARSHALL, 1953

At a United Nations press conference, secretary general Dag Hammarskjöld answered questions in a half-dozen languages. His father had been a prime minister of Sweden, and Hammarskjöld wrote that he had "inherited a belief that no life was more satisfactory than one of selfless service to your country – or humanity".

general faced him down and received an ovation. It was his finest moment. While on a 1961 peace-seeking mission in the Congo, Hammarskjöld was killed in a plane crash.

The soft-spoken diplomat left behind a notebook, which he called a "sort of white book concerning my negotiations with myself and with God". It is made up of highly personal – often cryptic – commentary, aphorisms, poems, *haiku*-like observations of nature, and Psalms. These fragments were translated into English and then adapted by the poet W. H. Auden. Curiously, the best-selling book, *Markings*, reveals almost nothing about Hammarskjöld except that he was obsessed by love – or by the lack of it in his life – and loneliness and death, words that appear in his notebook over and over again.

The stained glass window at the entrance to the UN chapel is only one of the memorials to Hammarskjöld. After his death, friends in Sweden set up a foundation in his name. It organizes seminars and conferences on problems in Third World countries, and publishes books and monographs on that subject.

During his years as secretary general of the United Nations, Hammarskjöld was often on the road, travelling to trouble-spots all over the world. His greatest success was his handling of the Suez Crisis. He once said that the United Nations Charter should have an article stating that the secretary general "should have an iron constitution and not be married". Hammarskjöld's health was fine, and he never married.

Martin Luther King Jr

The story of Martin Luther King Jr's life is also an account of the US Civil Rights movement. From the 1955 bus boycott in Montgomery, until his death from a sniper's bullet on the balcony of a Memphis motel in 1968, King was in the forefront. He was propelled by African Americans who were fearful; he was pushed by Black activists who wanted to move faster; white supremacists focused their hatred on him. J. Edgar Hoover singled King out for special FBI surveillance; and the media chased after him, helping to fuel his charismatic image. Although his birthday in January has become a US national holiday, more than two decades after his death King continues to be a highly controversial figure. It has been alleged, for example, that he plagiarized parts of his doctorial thesis.

Early in his career, while in a Harlem department store autographing copies of his first book, *Stride Toward Freedom*, King was stabbed in the chest by a mentally disturbed woman. During recovery in hospital, he decided to go to India on a trip sponsored by the Quakers to see what Gandhi had accomplished by using nonviolent tactics. Changes in the treatment of what had been known as the "untouchable" caste confirmed King's belief that Gandhi's approach to the struggle for equal rights could work in the US.

Today, what is most memorable about the man is his voice, a rich baritone that gave his often grandiose phrases and familiar sentiments great emotional power. In 1964, when he delivered his Nobel lecture in Oslo, he told the overflowing crowd: "The oceans of history are made turbulent by the ever-rising tides of hate." At thirty-five, King was the youngest person to receive the Peace Prize.

After his assassination in 1968, King's funeral service at Atlanta's Ebenezer Baptist Church was packed with family, friends, followers, elected officials, and candidates running for national office, many of whom might have been reluctant to be associated with him while he was alive. King's body was then taken three-and-a-half miles by mule cart for a second lengthy ceremony on the Morehouse College campus. He was buried in Southview Cemetery, where a marble monument is engraved with one of his famous, flowing sentences: "Free at last, free at last, thank God Almighty, I'm free at last."

Old systems of exploitation and oppression are passing away, and out of the womb of a frail world new systems of justice and equality are being born. Doors of opportunity are gradually being opened to those at the bottom of society. The shirtless and barefoot people of the land are developing a new sense of "somebodiness" and carving a tunnel of hope through the dark mountain of despair.

MARTIN LUTHER KING JR, 1964

On 23 August 1963, the Civil Rights movement's largest crowd – a quarter of a million people – gathered in front of the Lincoln Memorial in Washington DC. King's powerfully moving sermon brought him international attention. ''I have a dream,'' King told the crowd, ''that one day right there in Alabama, little Black boys and Black girls will be able to join hands with little White boys and White girls as sisters and brothers.''

Peace can only last where human rights are respected, where the people are fed and where individuals and natures are free.

DALAI LAMA, 1989

A picture of a man he greatly admired, Gandhi, hangs in the King dining room. In 1960 King spent a month in India studying the great pacifist's techniques. Then, during 1963, King led mass protests in Birmingham, Alabama, and the protestors were met by water cannons, police dogs and clubs.

On 4 April 1968, Martin Luther King Jr lies dying on a Memphis motel balcony. King's aides point in the direction the bullet had come from. In a prophetic sermon preached the night before, King had said, "I've seen the promised land. I may not get there with you . . . I'm not worried about anything. I'm not fearing any man. Mine eyes have seen the glory of the coming of the Lord."

At the height of the Montgomery, Alabama bus boycott, King was arrested and found guilty of "loitering on the courthouse steps". He had come to attend the trial of a close associate. King was sentenced, but when he decided to serve the fourteen days in jail, his fine was paid by a city commissioner, to prevent King from using the imprisonment "for his own selfish purposes".

Andrei Sakharov

1975

Victorious Dissident

Andrei Sakharov and Yelena Bonner, a physician, met at a dissident rally. His first wife had died in the late 1960s, and Sakharov and Bonner were married in 1971. Over the years she provided constant support, but in some quarters she was blamed for inciting him to commit acts of dissidence.

What kind of education does it take to make a Nobel Peace laureate and world-class scientist?

By the time he was four years old, Andrei Sakharov had begun to learn to read. His grandmother, when she was fifty, taught herself English and then read English novels and plays aloud to her grandchildren.

In his *Memoirs*, published after his death in 1989, Sakharov says that by the time he was an adolescent he had read Dumas's *The Three Musketeers*, Hugo's *Les Miserables*, Dickens's *David Copperfield*, *Dombey and Son* and *Oliver Twist*,

We, you and I, are privileged to be alive during this extraordinary age, this unique epoch in the history of the world, the epoch of demarcation between the past millennia of war and suffering, and the future, the great future of peace, justice, morality, and human well-being.

LINUS PAULING, 1962

Harriet Beecher Stowe's *Uncle Tom's Cabin*, Swift's *Gulliver's Travels*, Mark Twain, Jules Verne, Jack London, Ernest Thompson Seton, H. G. Wells, Goethe's *Faust* and Shakespeare's *Hamlet* and *Othello* – and many more.

This list of books conjures up a picture of a little boy squinting constantly at pages of print through the "Mongol eyes" he says he inherited from his mother's side. He also read Pushkin and Gogol, and says that he and his grandmother discussed almost every page of Tolstoy's *War and Peace*.

During the Second World War, Sakharov worked in a munitions factory and then spent the next twenty years in a "secret city", developing thermo-nuclear weapons. The Soviets called him the "Father of the Hydrogen Bomb". He was named a Hero of Socialist Labour three times, and was honoured with the Stalin Prize and the Order of Lenin. However, Sakharov began to be haunted by the weapons he had helped to create. His dissent started in 1957, when he complained about the radioactive hazards posed by nuclear test explosions in the atmosphere. At first Kremlin leaders listened to his concerns with respect. Then, in a public letter, he outlined a campaign that would bring openness and restructuring to the Soviet society. At the time he was turned out of his laboratory, but twenty years later his letter read like a blueprint

for *glasnost* and *perestroika*.

When the Nobel Peace Prize was given to Sakharov in 1972, he was branded "a laboratory rat of the West" by the Kremlin. He was not allowed to go to Norway, but his wife, who was in Italy for eye treatment, went to Oslo and read his speech. In 1979 Sakharov criticized the invasion of Afghanistan, and was sent with his wife to Gorky, a city off limits to Westerners. His hounding there by the Soviet authorities provoked an international outcry. Seven years after his exile began, the Soviet leader Mikhail Gorbachev telephoned Sakharov and told him he could return to Moscow and take his place in the changing society.

In the final year of his life Sakharov was elected to the new Soviet Congress and found himself honoured, as his earlier pleas, criticisms, and recommendations for his country began to find their way into official doctrine.

Growing crowds of dissidents became more and more visible in Moscow throughout the 1980s. When Sakharov and his wife returned from Gorky in 1986, he took an active role in pushing for rapid change.

Mother Teresa

In December 1979 an elderly nun in a white summer sari stepped off a plane into the bitter cold at Oslo airport. Mother Teresa had arrived to accept her Nobel Peace Prize. When she discovered there was to be a lavish banquet held in her honour, Mother Teresa asked that it be cancelled and the money be used to feed Calcutta's hungry. A reception was held for her instead, and the banquet money was contributed to Calcutta's poor.

Such purposeful directness has always been Agnes Gonxha Bojaxhui's most potent weapon. Born in Skopje, now in Yugoslavia, in 1910, she decided at twelve that she wanted to help the poor. At eighteen Agnes left home to join the Sisters of Loretto, an order of Irish nuns with a mission in Calcutta. She taught in their convent school, and in 1946 received permission from Rome to devote herself to living and working among the poor. In 1950 she founded her own order, the Missionaries of Charity, to tend to the slum dwellers for whom no one else cared.

The squalour she found in Calcutta's crowded slums inspired Mother Teresa to establish a Home for the Dying in 1954. Her order demands devotions at four in the morning, a single change of clothing, the same food that is given to the poor, and sixteen-hour days spent tending to the dying, diseased and orphaned.

Without television, Mother Teresa might never have become an international celebrity. She was made for the medium: her message – "We serve Jesus in the poor" – and her image – the instantly recognizable white sari – are simple yet memorable. She was

launched into the public consciousness in 1967 by the British commentator Malcolm Muggeridge. He was meant to be interviewing Mother Teresa but managed only a couple of questions before she took over the programme. Since then there have been many interviews, documentary films, and countless newspaper and magazine articles about her.

In her Prize lecture, Mother Teresa departed from her written text to tell stories. One was about a man "we picked up from the drain, half-eaten with worms, and we brought him to the home. He said 'I have lived like an animal in the street, but I am going to die like an angel, loved and cared for.' And it was wonderful to see the greatness of that man who could speak like

Until early 1990, Mother Teresa travelled widely, always attracting the media. In a cover story in 1975, *Time* magazine called her a living saint. She gets up at four every morning to hear Mass before going to work. "It is not how much we do," she says, "but how much love we put into it. The moment we have given it to God, it becomes infinite."

Let us always meet each other with a smile, for the smile is the beginning of love, and once we begin to love each other, naturally we want to do something.
MOTHER TERESA, 1979

Above

Members of her order, which includes more than 1,600 sisters, come from all over the world. Among their projects are hostels for the dying, homes for orphans, schools, mobile clinics, leprosy centres, and food kitchens. The order also stands ready to help out in times of natural catastrophe – floods and earthquakes, epidemics, and refugee relief.

When will we learn that human beings are of infinite value because they have been created in the image of God, and that it is blasphemy to treat them as if they were less than this? To do so ultimately recoils on the offender.

DESMOND TUTU, 1984

Left

Among Mother Teresa's many facilities in Calcutta is a hospice for the dying. In 1985, she helped open a church-sponsored hospice for patients with AIDS in New York City.

Along with vows of poverty, chastity, and obedience, the order's members are expected to give "whole-hearted free service to the poorest of the poor – to Christ in his distressing disguise." Mother Teresa explained, "We are really contemplatives in the heart of the world. For we are touching the body of Christ twenty-four hours . . . Christ in our hearts, Christ in the poor that we meet, Christ in the smile that we give and the smile that we receive."

that, who could die like that without blaming anybody, without cursing anybody. Like an angel – this is the greatness of our people."

As her order expanded, Mother Teresa had to spend much of her time as a fund-raiser and trouble-shooter: picking up honourary degrees all over the world; flying to Bangladesh to ask President Zia to stop his customs officials from bothering her nuns; then to Kathmandu to settle on the site of a new house.

Tireless, Mother Teresa always insisted on tending the most desperately ill herself, but she claimed that what she wanted most was the contemplative life. In 1990 she got her wish. Because of failing health, she began to relax the firm control she had maintained for four decades. Her order now includes 230 houses in more than sixty countries.

Retirement, however, has not diminished her extraordinary charisma. With the simplicity of true faith, Mother Teresa speaks to us all:

"People today are hungry for love, for understanding love which is much greater and which is the only answer to loneliness and great poverty. That is why we are able to go to countries like England and America and Australia where there is no hunger for bread. But there, people are suffering from terrible loneliness, terrible despair, terrible hatred, feeling unwanted, feeling helpless, feeling hopeless. They have forgotten how to smile, they have forgotten the beauty of the human touch. They are forgetting what is human love."

The abject poverty she found among the homeless in Calcutta's slums appalled Mother Teresa. During the 1950s, she led a small group of volunteers to rescue the dying, abandoned infants and lepers. Word of her work brought contributions from all over the world.

During a visit to Rome, Mother Teresa shared a ride in the Pope's bulletproof car. As her mission grew and expanded to countries outside India, the Vatican placed her order directly under its own jurisdiction.

Lech Walesa

1983   *The Carpenter's Son*

Long before Danuta Walesa got on the plane for Oslo, she was nervous – so nervous that she prayed government officials would not give her a passport. She was to stand in at the Nobel ceremonies for her famous husband; the hero of Solidarity.

The auditorium at the university was banked with flowers. The hall was filled with diplomats and Norway's leading political and cultural figures. At one o'clock sharp on the afternoon of 10 December 1983, the King of Norway entered and everyone stood. The orchestra played a polonaise.

The Nobel Committee chairman, Emil Aarvik, said, "The electrician from Gdansk, the carpenter's son from the Vistula valley, has managed to lift the banner of freedom and humanity so high that the world can once again see it." Then he presented the Peace Prize diploma and gold medal with Alfred Nobel's profile in low relief to Danuta, the former flower-shop girl and mother of seven.

As Mrs Walesa read her husband's acceptance, her poise charmed everyone. Walesa, in Gdansk listening on the radio, told reporters that he had fallen "in love with her all over again". Friends suggested slyly that he may also have been a little jealous of all the attention she got. He had not gone to accept the prize in person because he was afraid the authorities might not let him return to Poland.

At the press conference in Oslo, hundreds of correspondents were on hand to question Danuta Walesa. She impressed them with her grasp of Poland's history. That evening, Danuta and the Walesas' thirteen-year-old son

Bogdan stood in the frigid cold on the balcony of their hotel as a torchlight parade of union workers marched in tribute below.

When Danuta and Bogdan arrived home with the medal and certificate, Walesa drove them from the airport to the shrine of Our Lady of Czestochowa. Walesa placed the awards on an altar where kings had left their crowns and generals their medals. On the road back to Gdansk, the car was stopped thirteen times by the police, and its occupants were body-searched.

Above
Many of the demonstrations in Poland during the 1980s were inspired in large part by Walesa. In December of 1990, the forty-seven-year-old former electrician – who has only a vocational school education – won a landslide runoff victory in Poland's first direct presidential election ever.

Right
Walesa exchanges a hug with two of his children in their six-room Gdansk apartment. He is noted for his earthy sense of humour, and his speeches have great appeal.

74

During the late 1970s, when the Polish government had increased food prices, Walesa and others had encouraged rebellion. Dozens of demonstrators were killed. An activist priest was murdered by the police. Because of his protests, Walesa was sacked. He took odd jobs and joined the dissidents, editing an underground newspaper and signing a charter of workers' rights that demanded the right to strike. Wildcat strikes, boycotts and violence were commonplace. Then, in 1980, the workers in the Gdansk shipyard went on strike. Walesa climbed over a twelve-foot fence to cheer on the strikers and challenge the Communist authorities. The government was forced to negotiate with Walesa, and workers won the right to organize a free trade union and to strike: Solidarity was born.

The dramatic events brought world fame to Walesa, but the next year, as the economic situation in Poland continued to deteriorate, Solidarity took a more radical turn and martial law was declared. Walesa was detained.

In 1982, when the Nobel Committee in Oslo met to decide on the laureate, Walesa was being held. Although there was much support in Norway for him and his cause, the Prize went to others. The following year, Walesa had given up: "If they didn't give it to me last year at a time when it could have really helped," he told a journalist, "I cannot see why they should give it to me now." Then in October, while Walesa was out picking wild mushrooms, reporters found him and told him that he was to receive the Nobel Peace Prize.

The Polish authorities were not pleased. Norwegian and American music was banned from state radio, and the Norwegian ambassador was reprimanded because his prime minister congratulated Walesa. Walesa thought he should not leave Poland. "How can I go to get this nice prize and sip champagne when my colleagues are in jail and hungry?"

Six years later the Berlin Wall was knocked down, and it became clear that the Soviets were no longer going to prop up Communist rulers in the satellite countries. Walesa, the popular chairman of Solidarity, found himself in a delicate position, trying to support a new, struggling, democratic government while his union members wanted jobs and pay increases.

As the leader of the battle that toppled the Communists, Walesa has overwhelming recognition in Poland. He announced in 1990 that he had decided to go into politics and run for the presidency "to speed the nation's transition from Communism to democracy". In December 1990, the forty-seven-year-old former electrician won a landslide victory in Poland's first direct presidential election.

We should go on talking, we must not close any doors or do anything that would block the road to an understanding. And we must remember that only peace built on the foundations of justice and moral order can be a lasting one.
LECH WALESA, 1983

Desmond Tutu

1984

The Dancing Priest

As a little boy, Desmond Tutu collected comic books. His favourite heroes were Batman and Superman. He learned his English from the comics. Perhaps that is why to this day his speech always seems to be punctuated with exclamation points.

A little man with eyes that sparkle, Desmond Tutu has been described as laughing, quick, impish, feisty, uninhibited, confident, vivid, bright, pulsating with life, enthusiastic, spontaneous and joyful.

As a teenager, he was isolated for twenty months with tuberculosis and read books brought to him by Trevor Huddleston, an Anglican priest who became his mentor. Instead of falling behind in school, Desmond moved ahead of his classmates. He had begun to follow in his father's footsteps as a teacher when it was decided that South African Blacks had no need of a European-style education – they all were to be labourers.

Tutu turned to the Anglican Church, and that institution found that it had an extremely able student.

During his first days in London to study for the priesthood, Tutu was in line at a bank when a White man pushed ahead of him. The teller told the man politely that Tutu was next. Tutu was astounded. When he thanked the clerk, she said she would have done the same for anyone, and he was even more surprised. He was experiencing life in a non-apartheid country for the first time.

During the 1970s, angry Blacks in South Africa turned to violence, which was put down by the police. Hundreds were killed. Tutu had warned the government, and as a result, he began

This is Africa's age – the dawn of her fulfilment, yes, the moment when she must grapple with destiny to reach the summits of sublimity, saying: Ours was a fight for noble values and worthy ends, and not for lands and the enslavement of man.

CHIEF ALBERT JOHN LUTULI, 1961

Above
Tutu has told Black audiences, "Be nice to Whites. They need you to rediscover their humanity." Black militants were angered by his insistence on moderation. There are more than 233 million Blacks in a country where 4.5 million Whites had all the power. Tutu warned that "oppressed people will become desperate". He refused to carry the pass that all Blacks in South Africa were required to have at all times.

Right
"I was not moved by very high ideals," Tutu said of his decision to become an Anglican priest. "It just seemed to me that if the church would accept me, this might be a likely means of service." As general secretary of the South African Council of Churches, Tutu led their opposition to racial segregation. When his Nobel award was announced, the newspapers in South Africa expressed outrage that such a man should receive a Peace Prize.

to be viewed with suspicion and mistrust. His open criticism of official policies caused his passport to be confiscated twice – an action considered to be a serious warning of governmental displeasure.

In 1984 when Tutu went to Oslo to accept the Nobel Prize, he took along his wife, their four children and friends, including a trio of singers. There was a bomb threat and the auditorium was emptied while a search was made. When the audience was allowed back in the hall, Tutu had his trio sing gospel songs and then accepted his scroll and medal. Tutu used his Nobel money to set up scholarships for Blacks to study in the United States. He continued his attacks on apartheid while, at the same time, advocating conciliation.

With the release of Nelson Mandela from prison, Tutu lost his role as chief spokesman for South African Blacks. He has been elevated to Archbishop of Cape Town and head of the Anglican Church of South Africa. A dignified religious leader in gold and scarlet robes? Never. The irrepressible Tutu has been seen more than once dancing up and down the aisles.

The obstacles to peace are not obstacles in matter, in inanimate nature, in mountains which we pierce, in the seas across which we fly. The obstacles to peace are in the minds and hearts of men.
NORMAN ANGELL, 1933

The Organizations

1904–1988   *Despite Nobel's Wishes*

Alfred Nobel never intended that his Peace Prize should go to an organization or institution, but the Oslo Committee provided for such an eventuality from the beginning. At the time, their decision was criticized, especially by peace activists. Bertha von Suttner, who received the award in 1905, knew what her friend Nobel had in mind, and protested that "the soul of a society always resides in an individual".

Three years after the awards were initiated, in 1904, the Prize went to the Institute of International Law, a group organized in Ghent in 1883 when ten representatives from nine countries met and another twenty-four sent in agreements that they would join. The Institute has helped the world move gradually toward the rule of law; it has been quiet, inconspicuous – and effective.

Six years later, the Permanent International Peace Bureau in Bern received the Prize. In its early days, the Bureau encouraged the use of arbitration in disputes, but after the Second World War it was declared defunct, and its assets were taken over by the Swiss government. Today's International Peace Bureau revived the old name, and organizes seminars on peace issues.

The first Peace Prize was shared by Henri Dunant, a Swiss humanitarian who founded the International Committee of the Red Cross. In 1917 his organization was awarded the Nobel Peace Prize for its work with prisoners-of-war during the First World War. In 1944, again because of its work in war time, the Red Cross was given its second Peace Prize, and in 1963 it received a third.

The International Labour Organization, which was established in 1919 by the Treaty of Versailles, became an agency of the United Nations in 1946, and was given the Peace Prize in 1969. Initially, the group had tried to set international labour standards, but it then shifted its emphasis to the promotion of economic development in the Third World.

In 1977 the award went to Amnesty International. Based in London, the organization seeks by letter-writing campaigns to put pressure on governments to free those who have been imprisoned or tortured because their opinions or religion are unacceptable to their governments.

In 1985 the Peace Prize went to the International Physicians for the Prevention of Nuclear War, Inc. The organization was started by Bernard Lown, a Harvard cardiology professor, and Yevgeny Chazov, director of Moscow's Cardiology Research Centre, who met in 1960 when they collaborated on research into the mechanism of sudden death syndrome. By 1985 the physicians had more than 135,000 members in forty-one countries. At the presentation of the award in Oslo, the chairman said, "This year's prize is more concerned with the problem of disarmament, but is also at a deeper level concerned with human rights – perhaps even the most fundamental right of them all – the right to live."

Over the years, the problems of refugees have been of continuing concern to the Oslo Committee. More than a half-dozen awards have gone to organizations that help the world's displaced. In 1990 there were an estimated fifteen

The world has passed through a long night of tribulation and suffering, millions of our fellow creatures have been sacrificed to the demon of war; their blood has saturated every plain and dyed every ocean.

But courage, friends, courage! The darkness is ending, a new day is dawning, and the future is ours. Hurrah! Hurrah!

WILLIAM RANDAL CREMER, 1903

million people living outside their homelands, often in great poverty. Applications to Europe, the United States and Canada rose from 25,000 in 1973 to 600,000 in 1990. There are 55,000 Vietnamese confined in camps in Hong Kong, 3.2 million Afghans in Pakistan, and 2.3 million more in Iran. Civil strife in Africa has produced 4.4 million refugees in a complex exchange that has 658,000 Ethiopians in the Sudan; 384,000 Sudanese and 324,000 Somalians in Ethiopia; and 600,000 Ethiopians in Somalia. The recent war in the Persian Gulf has produced more than a million refugees.

The problem today is not only war, but poverty. According to Thorvald Stoltenberg, the United Nations High Commissioner for Refugees, "the majority of the world live in deep poverty. First, there was the information revolution. People now, even if they are very poor, know how people live in other parts of the world. Second, it is much easier than before to be

transported over long distances. We cannot hide away anymore''.

In 1921, when Nobel laureate Fridtjof Nansen was named High Commissioner for Refugees of the League of Nations, he estimated that the problem would be solved in ten years. He died in 1930, and there were still refugees in the world. The League set up an office named for him, with the mandate to complete its work in eight years. The Nansen International Office for Refugees in Geneva was awarded a Nobel Peace Prize in 1938, but the refugee problem grew worse as the Nazis began their persecution of Jews in Germany and Austria.

The Friends Service Council in London, and the American Friends Service Committee (1947) were cited for war relief and reconstruction, as was the Office of the UN High Commissioner for Refugees (1954 and 1981). The Children's Fund (UNICEF) received the Prize in 1965, and in 1988 it went to the United Nations Peace keeping forces.

These soldiers from Nepal, the United States, Australia, France, Canada, Ireland, Norway, and Sweden were serving in Lebanon in 1978 to restore peace and security. The first United Nations Peace keeping operation was an observer mission established in 1948 in the Middle East. Peace keeping operations around the world cost the UN about $230 million annually; the Nobel Prize paid the costs of only one day's peace keeping in southern Lebanon.

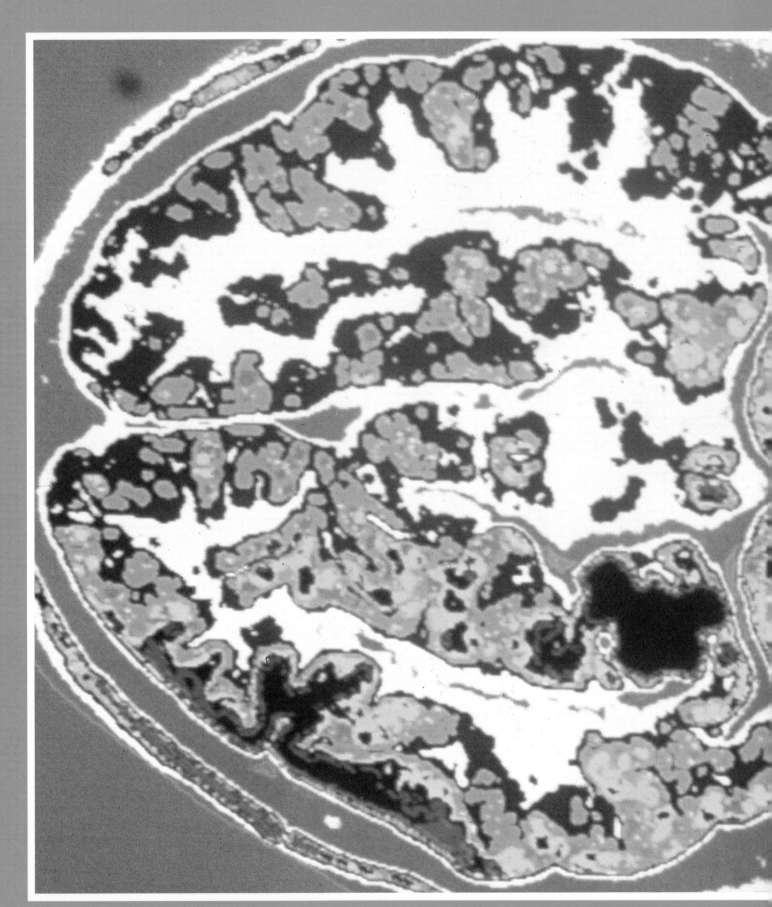

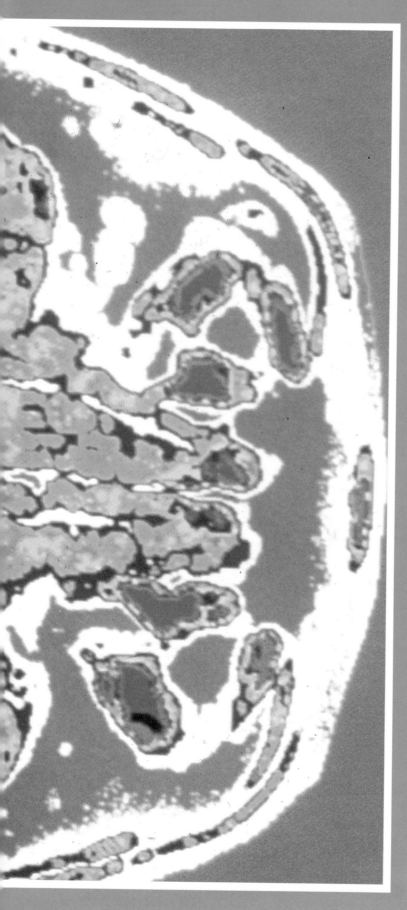

2 PHYSICS

X-ray images, enhanced by a computer, produced this CAT-scan colour-enhanced picture of the human brain.

Introduced by Frank Kendig

The twentieth century is the age of physics. The origins of today's most visible artifacts – radios, telephones, television sets, lasers, computers, space ships, and the atomic bomb – lie in the discoveries of the twentieth-century physicists. And these are only the *visible* side-effects.

At times during this century, the pace at which nature's secrets were being revealed seemed so great that physics appeared ready to swallow the other sciences whole: first chemistry, then biology. But physics does not exploit nature; that is left to engineering and politics. Physics does not even try to explain, but only to describe.

The universe that physicists have painstakingly assembled during this century is their greatest triumph. It is a universe in which galaxies exist – an unknown fact until well into the century – where stars are born and die, and where black holes gobble up their remains. It is a universe of curved space, antimatter, and supergravity, in which everything is comprised of mysterious stuff called quarks, found in three families of two quarks each.

The universe can be seen either as a swarm of particles, or as an ocean of waves with equal clarity. It is a universe born in an unfathomable primal explosion that may someday cease to exist. It is a universe that, in J. B. S. Haldane's words is not only a queerer place than we imagined, but perhaps a queerer place than we *can* imagine.

The first Nobel Prize in Physics went to the German physicist Wilhelm Röntgen in 1901. The selection and timing were right. At the end of the nineteenth century, virtually every scientist believed that the universe according to Isaac Newton and James Clerk Maxwell – what is now called classical physics – was a complete, accurate, and unassailable description of the fundamental laws of nature. Alexander Pope's famous couplet:

> *Nature and Nature's laws lay hid in the night:*
> *God said, Let Newton be! and all was light.*

had achieved the status of scientific dogma.

Yet cracks were already beginning to show in the grand edifice of Newtonian physics, and what is now called the second scientific revolution was ready to be launched. "It seems probable," said the American physicist Albert Michelson, "that most of the grand underlying principles have been firmly established . . . the future truths of physics are to be looked for in the sixth place of decimals." Michelson's premature announcement of the end of physics was made to a conference of scientists in 1894.

The following year Röntgen discovered X-rays. The year after that, the year of Alfred Nobel's death, the French physicist Antoine Henri Becquerel discovered spontaneous radiation; in 1897, the British physicist Joseph John Thomson deduced the existence of electrons, which he called "corpuscles"; in 1898, Marie Curie, the discoverer of radium and polonium, coined the term "radioactivity". By the turn of the century the atomic age had begun, and from it came what textbooks now refer to as twentieth-century, or "modern", physics. In 1903 Becquerel shared the Nobel Prize with Marie Curie and her husband Pierre; Thomson became a laureate in 1906.

As for Michelson, he lived to regret his statement, and received a Nobel Prize in 1907 for his experiments in optics. Today, he is best remembered for an experiment he conducted with chemist Edward Morley in 1887, perhaps the most important failure in the history of science. Michelson set out to prove the existence of the so-called ether which at the time was thought (wrongly) to pervade space. His failure to prove its existence was to become the cornerstone of Albert Einstein's theory of relativity.

Einstein received his Prize in 1921, but not for relativity. That theory generally is acknowledged to be his most important work, along with quantum theory, one of the two great triumphs of modern physics. Instead, Einstein's Prize was for his work on the photoelectric effect, one of the foundations of quantum theory, and an idea that Einstein himself never could accept.

The roster of Physics laureates since and including Röntgen is a remarkably representative list of the giants of twentieth–century physics. "The Nobel has had a very good record," said American physicist Leon Lederman not long after he won the Physics Prize in 1988. Lederman is the

Guglielmo Marconi believed that science kept him young. "It encourages one to go on dreaming," he said. "Science demands a flexible mind."

former director of Fermilab, the high-energy physics centre in Illinois that was named after the 1938 Physics laureate Enrico Fermi. Lederman's ambition is to reduce physics to a single equation. ". . . the biggest mistake was Fermi," Lederman said. "They gave him the prize for discovering transuranic elements when he really had discovered fission. But that's the kind of mistake you like to make. There have been very few mistakes, some curious choices, like the man who got the prize for inventing some kind of reflector for lighthouses." (Lederman was referring to Swedish physicist Nils Dalen, who received his prize in 1912 "for his invention of automatic regulators in conjunction with gas accumulators for illuminating lighthouses and buoys.")

There have been unaccountable delays and strange omissions, of course: Einstein waited seventeen years after the publication of his work to receive his award, and Lederman himself waited almost three decades. He used to tell his children the delay was because the Nobel Committee "couldn't make up its mind which of my accomplishments to recognize". And every physicist can name favourite theorists or experimenters who should have won the Prize but did not.

The most celebrated also-ran undoubtedly is the great New Zealand-born physicist Ernest Rutherford, the first to uncover the structure of atoms. Rutherford, who at age twenty-four went to England to work with J. J. Thomson in 1895, was the consummate experimentalist: a gruff, purposeful man one colleague described as graced with an unparalleled gift for getting experiments to work by cursing at them. Over his long career, Rutherford trained no fewer than eleven Nobel laureates, and strongly believed he deserved a Physics Prize of his own. In 1908 he did receive a Prize, but it was in Chemistry. It distressed and bewildered him for the rest of his life. He was, after all, the man who once declared "all science is either physics or stamp-collecting".

Looking back over the careers of the more than 100 men and women who have won Nobel Prizes in Physics, the mix of experimentalists and theorists is somewhat weighted toward the theorists; getting nature to yield her secrets to experiment has become increasingly difficult and expensive. Nevertheless, as 1923 Physics laureate Robert Millikan put it, "science walks forward on two feet, namely theory and experiment. Sometimes it is one foot which is put forward, sometimes the other, but continuous progress is made only by the use of both." Röntgen, on the other hand, made the case for the experimentalists. When asked what he thought about while he was discovering X-rays, Röntgen responded, "I didn't think. I experimented." Einstein, who became the personification of theoretical physics, much preferred "thought experiments" to those conducted in a laboratory, but he realized the importance of both.

As the outstanding theoretical physicist Steven Weinberg stated in his acceptance speech for the 1979 Prize he shared with Sheldon Glashow and Abdus Salam: "Our job in

Man's great leap into space during this century was made possible by scientists who wanted to know the answers to everything. Here, astronaut Dale A. Gardner prepares to dock with a spinning *Westar VI* satellite.

physics is to see things simply, to understand a great many complicated phenomena in a unified way, in terms of a few simple principles. At times, our efforts are illuminated by a brilliant experiment . . . but even in the dark times between experimental breakthroughs, there always continues a steady evolution of theoretical ideas, leading almost imperceptibly to changes in previous beliefs.''

What is most surprising about the roster of Physics laureates is how few of these men and women – among them some of the most brilliant minds of this century – achieved wide public recognition outside the realm of science. Even before he received his Nobel Prize, Einstein was a worldwide celebrity, but, with the possible exception of the Curies and Marconi, it is difficult to think of a Physics laureate who is as well known as even a minor rock star.

The relative obscurity of the majority of Nobel Prize-winning physicists is due both to the language of physics – mathematics, a language that translates poorly – and the mind-boggling universe it describes. The great British astronomer Arthur Stanley Eddington clarified the problem when he was interviewed shortly after the publication of the theory of relativity, an idea that physicists say is a stroll in the woods compared to the thorny jungle of quantum theory. When asked if it was true that only three people in the world understood Einstein's theory, Eddington quipped, ''Who is the third?''

In the world of science, however, the roster of Nobel Physics laureates could double as an honour roll of the most famous names of the century. A brief list of eponyms makes the case: Planck's constant (after Max Planck, who received the Prize in 1919); the Compton effect (Arthur Compton, 1927); De Broglie waves (Prince Louis-Victor de Broglie, 1929); the Heisenberg uncertainty principle (Werner Heisenberg, 1933); Cerenkov radiation (Pavel Cerenkov, 1958); Josephson junctions (Brian Josephson, 1973); and Feynman diagrams (Richard Feynman, 1965) – to name only a few. A number of Physics laureates have been awarded the singular honour of having their names given to units of measurement – the röntgen, the curie, and the fermi come to mind. Einstein had an element of nature named after him: einsteinium, the ninty-ninth element, discovered shortly after his death; the 102nd element, first isolated in Sweden in 1958, was named nobelium after Alfred Nobel.

Outside the world of science, there is a popular if distorted picture of the physicist as a down-to-earth scientist whose discoveries immediately and irrevocably change the way we live. In some ways, Röntgen fits that description: barely a month after the discovery of X-rays, Eddie McCarthy of Cartmouth, New Hampshire became one of the first to have his broken arm set by a physician using X-ray images.

Marconi's wireless had a similar impact on everyday life,

as did the discovery of colour photography by French physicist Gabriel Lippman (1908 laureate); the development of laser theory by American physicist Charles H. Townes (1964); and the invention of the transistor by American physicists William Shockley, Walter Brattain, and John Bardeen (1956 laureates). To date, Bardeen is the only laureate to win two Physics Prizes. He was honoured again in 1972 along with Leon Cooper and Robert Schrieffer for work in developing a theory of superconductivity, which may change the way we live in the not-too-distant future.

Of course, the most visible and ominous invention of twentieth–century physics was the atomic bomb, the result of work by a long list of Nobel laureates, Einstein among them. The bomb itself was the by-product of an effort to solve the most intriguing problem of modern science, namely, what is the structure of the atom and how do its parts behave? "The constitution of the atom is, of course, the great problem that lies at the base of all physics and chemistry," said Lord Rutherford early in the century, "and if we knew the construction of atoms we ought to be able to predict everything that is happening in the universe." Today's physicists no longer accept Rutherford's promise of prediction – not since 1933 laureate Werner Heisenberg abolished the notion of absolute certainty in science – but the central question remains the same.

Over the course of the century, the majority of Physics laureates have devoted their lives to understanding the workings of the atom and its parts. Because of the nature and complexity of this effort, the results and breakthroughs more often than not are beyond the grasp of the general public. Nobel's Physics Prize, in a sense, makes up for this lack of general recognition, and there is no doubt that it is cherished as much for its prestige in the community of physicists as for its monetary reward.

Consider the case of Nils Bohr, the Danish physicist who won the Prize in 1922 for "his services in the investigation of the structure of atoms and of the radiation emanating from them". The torch-bearer of the quantum revolution, Bohr donated his Nobel medal to Finnish war relief at the beginning of the Second World War. Soon after the War began he was entrusted with the medals of the German physicists Max von Laue (1914 laureate) and James Franck (1926). Before he escaped from occupied Denmark in 1943, Bohr, a meticulous man who was known to write drafts of postcards, dissolved the medals in acid in order to get them safely out of the country. After the War, he precipitated the gold from the acid, and had the medals re-cast.

As this century comes to a close, the picture of the universe provided by modern physics appears fairly complete. It describes a universe that operates according to the laws of quantum mechanics and relativity, and is governed by four basic forces – gravity, electromagnetism, weak nuclear, and strong nuclear. The forces themselves are mysteries; nobody can explain them. Physicists call them explanatory principles which themselves cannot be explained, but they nevertheless govern the behaviour of everything from electrons to elephants.

As the new century approaches, the dream of physicists is to combine these four mysteries into one, to successfully marry quantum mechanics and relativity and produce a single set of simple, elegant equations that perfectly describe the first moment of time and everything since then: a theory of everything.

Some physicists, among them the British physicist Stephen Hawking, predict that such a theory is close to hand. Others point to Michelson's announcement of the death of physics in 1894, and Max Born's prediction in the late 1920s that "Physics as we know it will be over in six months." The answer to the question of physics' ultimate demise will probably not be settled until the next century. But then in physics, answers have never been as important or interesting as the questions.

It is the questions, not the answers, that are the triumphs of twentieth-century physics. How did the universe begin? How will it end? Will time someday reverse itself? What goes on inside the atom? If space is primarily empty, why does the ground hold us up? Why is the sky dark at night? In posing these questions in a unique, precise way, physics in this century has extended the sphere of human knowledge, illuminating regions previously explored only by philosophers – and children.

F.K.

Wilhelm Conrad Röntgen

1901

Those Naughty Rays

Should a lady permit herself to be X-rayed? Röntgen's discovery, announced in 1896, was an immediate source of jokes and ribaldry. While doctors lost no time using it to diagnose broken bones, the popular press printed a cartoon showing a maid with an X-ray machine peeking through a bedroom door.

A poem entitled *X-actly So!* began and ended with the following:

The Röntgen Rays, the Röntgen Rays,
What is this craze ? . . .
I hear they'll gaze
Thro' cloak and gown – and even stays,
These naughty, naughty Röntgen Rays.

Wilhelm Röntgen, professor of physics at the University of Würzburg, tried to ignore the sudden attention, but he finally was persuaded to give an interview to an American magazine. The reporter was an Englishman, H. J. W. Dam, and his article appeared in *McClure's* in April 1896. It is a memorable portrait of a genius: "Professor Röntgen entered hurriedly, something like an amiable gust of wind. He is a tall, slender and loose-limbed man, whose appearance bespeaks enthusiasm and energy. He wore a dark blue sack suit, and his long, dark hair stood straight up from his forehead, as if he were permanently electrified by his own enthusiasm. His voice is full and deep, he speaks rapidly, and, altogether, he seems clearly a man who, once upon the track of a mystery which appeals to him, would pursue it with unremitting vigor . . ."

The following dialogue from their encounter was also recorded:

"Now, then," said he, "you have come to see the invisible rays?"

A shy, reticent man, Röntgen was annoyed by his fame. He enjoyed the outdoors, hunting with friends, and climbing in the Bavarian Alps.

"Is the invisible visible?"

"Not to the eye; but its results are. Come here . . ."

The reporter was then seated inside a large, dark box and given a thoroughly convincing demonstration.

Röntgen increasingly detested the business of being famous. When he was asked to sit for a sculptor who was creating a monument for Berlin's Potsdamer Bridge, he refused. Then he was told that the Kaiser had suggested this tribute, and if he failed to pose, the statue might not resemble him. Röntgen sat, but after he saw the finished bronze he was furious, and claimed he looked ridiculous. He would, he said, appear for posterity with an insect spray-gun – it was supposed to be an X-ray tube – in his hand.

But not even this bit of infamy was to last. During the Second World War, the bronze of Wilhelm Röntgen was melted down and used by the German military.

My scientific career in physics has been mostly concerned with two topics: magnetic resonance and lasers. In neither case did I anticipate the large number of applications that would evolve from the scientific principles which my colleagues and I originally studied.

NICOLAAS BLÖEMBERGEN, 1981

Left
Within a short time after Röntgen's discovery, X-rays were being used by doctors to inspect broken bones like the one in the arm of this child. Röntgen never sought a patent or any financial return. He felt his reward was in knowing that his discovery had great value to medicine.

Below
This is a famous, and one of the earliest, X-ray photographs made by Röntgen. The metal ring on his wife's finger is denser than the bones and therefore darker. Röntgen's discovery, "that all bodies are transparent to the agent, though in very different degrees," was immediately confirmed by other scientists.

THE NEW ROENTGEN PHOTOGRAPHY.
"LOOK PLEASANT, PLEASE."

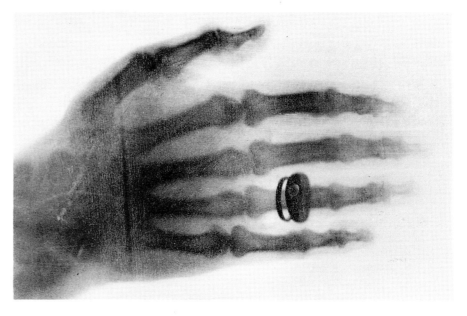

Above
A cartoon from the old humour magazine *Life* appeared in February 1896. The caption read, "Look pleasant, please." Röntgen's discovery contributed to the physics revolution at the turn of the century. He gave his Nobel Prize money to the University of Würzburg to be used in the interest of science.

The Curies and Henri Becquerel

In 1896, Paris physicist Henri Becquerel accidentally discovered that uranium constantly emits radiation. His student, Marie Curie, chose this phenomenon for her doctoral research, and began checking other substances to see if anything other than uranium emitted so-called "Becquerel rays".

The following year, Curie began studying what she called "radioactivity". Her husband Pierre had been investigating crystals and magnets, but he dropped his projects to join his wife in her research.

The couple used acids and hydrogen sulphide to separate pitchblende, an ore comprised mainly of uranium oxide, into its chemical parts. Curie calculated that uranium alone could not account for its high degree of radiation. She surmised that the ore must contain some as yet undetected element or elements that were more radioactive than uranium. She then isolated polonium, which is hundreds of times more radioactive than uranium, and then radium, which is even more radioactive than polonium. She named both elements.

In 1902, after four years of processing pitchblende, the Curies isolated half a gram of radium – the equivalent of all the radium to be found in the entire world. It took eight tons of pitchblende to produce one full gram of radium. The radium salt the Curies produced glowed a faint blue and gave off heat. Their discovery of this fantastic element, which was found almost immediately to have medical applications, caught the world's fancy. The Curies became famous, and shared the 1903 Nobel Prize with Professor Becquerel

"in recognition of their joint researches on the radiation phenomena discovered by Professor Henri Becquerel".

In his Nobel lecture, Pierre Curie acknowledged the potential dangers of radioactive substances in the wrong hands, but said that he was "one of those who believed with Nobel that Mankind will derive more good than harm from the new discoveries". The Curies also believed that scientific knowledge should be shared freely, and refused to patent their extraction process.

Greer Garson and Walter Pidgeon starred in an uplifting Hollywood biofilm entitled *Madame Curie*. In this scene, the actors dramatized the labour involved in processing radium from tons of ore. Pierre Curie was the first to identify the radiation that eminated from radium as atomic energy, and the first to measure its power. He subjected his arm to a burn and published two papers on the physiological action of radium rays.

(Turn to page 128 for the story of the Curies and chemistry.)

The Curies lived in near poverty, giving up most recreation, except for an occasional bicycle outing, to devote themselves to their scientific research. They were married in a civil ceremony, and their honeymoon was a three-week bicycle tour. Marie Curie was the first woman to teach at the Sorbonne.

Gabriel Lippmann

1908

The first colour photographs were made in 1848 by a French physicist who used a silver plate covered with silver chloride. He could not explain how the process worked, and the image quickly faded.

Gabriel Lippmann, professor of experimental physics and director of the research laboratory at the Sorbonne, produced the first permanent colour photograph in 1891. His photographic plate imitated the construction of an insect's eye, and produced a negative without using a lens. His plates were made of clear glass that was coated on one side with gelatine, silver nitrate, and potassium bromide. During the long exposure – one minute in bright sunlight – colour-linked patterns from the subject were combined with reflected light from the plate-holder, which was backed with mercury to create a mirror. Lippmann described this process as a type of mould of the luminous rays held within the thickness of the plate. He was awarded the 1908 Nobel Prize "for his method of reproducing colours photographically based on the phenomenon of interference".

Above
Although Gabriel Lippmann was awarded the Nobel Prize because of his method of permanent colour photography, his lasting contribution to science was his construction of a capillary electrometre, which is still in use today.

Above right
Technical improvements have enabled everyone to explore the possibilities of colour photography, as this shot of a fishing boat in the Greek Islands, taken with conventional colour film on a 35mm camera, shows.

Below right
This original Lippmann plate of the garden at Versailles appears to be in colour because of selective reflection – the plate gives out to the eye only those colours that were impressed on it.

Lippmann spent five years perfecting his colour process, but pointed out that one of its major problems was the length of exposure required, which was so long that he was unable to make pictures of human beings. "It was fifteen minutes when I first began my work," he said. "Perhaps progress may continue. Life is short and progress is slow."

Colour photography as we know it today evolved in an entirely different way. In the 1850s the Scottish physicist James Clerk Maxwell suggested the three-colour use of absorbent dyes, a more practical approach, and today's films require exposures of only fractions of a second.

Guglielmo Marconi

1909

The Father of Radio

In 1895, twenty-year-old Guglielmo Marconi strung up a wire on the roof of the family home in the Italian countryside. He then assembled a primitive oscillator, a resonator, curved zinc reflectors, and a battery in the attic. He sent his brother out into the field with a receiver and a white handkerchief tied to a stick. Guglielmo tapped out waves of Morse code. When his brother received the signal, he raised the flag. One day, Guglielmo sent his brother out of sight over a hill into a vineyard. The brother took along a rifle. When three dots – a Morse "S" – were received, the brother fired the gun into the air. At that point Marconi knew for certain his invention had great potential.

Guglielmo Marconi was an astute businessman as well as an inventor. In 1900 he applied for his patent, Number 7777, and set up a company to build signal towers to send and receive messages. In the hope that investors and workmen would think he was older, he grew a moustache. Later, when his hair began to turn white, he dyed it to appear younger.

In 1901 he established wireless communication across the Atlantic Ocean, and in 1904 he provided daily news for ocean liners. When the *Titanic* sank in 1912, the ship's cry for help over the wireless brought a rescue ship in time to save a few passengers. The event made Marconi a hero, and the Italian government gave him the rank of *marchese*.

For many decades, Marconi travelled the world, setting up transmitting stations, constantly refining his invention, and expanding his prosperous

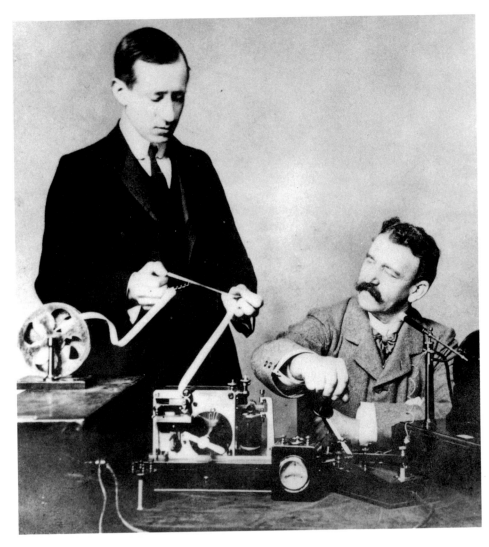

business. The inventor was knighted by Britain's King George, a rare honour for a foreigner.

Marconi and his assistant G. S. Kent operated a sending station in 1899. After radio amateurs found that short waves from low-power transmitters were effective, Marconi developed a reliable worldwide network of communication.

Above
Today, radio is used to scan the heavens. Shock waves and trails of galaxies produced the rings and other features in this photograph. The image was made during observations at the Very Large Array Radio Telescope in New Mexico.

Left
From 1921 Marconi used his steam yacht *Electra* as his home, his laboratory, and as a mobile receiving station. While in port at Genoa, he used his equipment to turn on thousands of electric light bulbs in Sydney, Australia – about 11,000 miles away.

Albert Einstein

The best-known scientist of the twentieth century, Albert Einstein did not speak until he was three years old. Shy, gentle and eccentric, Einstein brought an astounding creativity and imagination to physics. He once explained that all his life his ideas came to him in concepts and diagrams: "I rarely think in words at all," he said. "A thought comes, and I may try to express it in words afterward."

Legend has it that as a sixteen-year-old Swiss student, Einstein became obsessed by a problem he himself had thought up: What would a beam of light look like if a man moved along beside it at the speed of light? After ten years of mulling this over, Einstein created a new, consistent system, now known as his Special Theory of Relativity. He deduced that the light would not look as if it were standing still, as classical physicists thought, but that the beam would move away at the speed of light, just as if the observer were standing still.

At age twenty-six Einstein published five papers, three of which are among the most important in the history of physics. One gave the quantum explanation of the photoelectric effect, for which he was awarded the Nobel Prize in 1921. The second dealt with the Brownian motion, the apparently erratic movement of particles suspended in

Einstein, photographed on board ship in 1921, said of his fame: "It strikes me as unfair, and even in bad taste to select a few individuals for boundless admiration, attributing super-human powers of mind and character to them. This has been my fate, and the contrast between the popular estimate of my powers and achievements and the reality is simply grotesque."

a liquid. It was conclusive proof of the existence of atoms and molecules. The third paper was Einstein's famous Theory of Relativity.

Within months after the appearance of the three papers, physicists were saying their author was a genius. From then until his death in 1955, Einstein was famous in a way no other scientist has ever been – he became the veritable symbol of science. The novelist and scientist C. P. Snow said that people did not understand what they were revering, but they believed Einstein was someone "of supreme, if mysterious, excellence".

Einstein once told Louis Victor de Broglie, who was awarded the Physics Prize in 1929 for his wave theory, that all physical theories should be simple enough "that even a child could understand them".

One of Einstein's good friends was Marie Curie. Shortly after she had received her second Nobel Prize in 1911, Marie and her two daughters went on an outing in Switzerland with Einstein and his son. Eve, the younger Curie daughter, recalled the day. Einstein, lost in thought, climbed up the rocks and strolled along sheer cliffs without noticing anything. Suddenly he stopped, grabbed Madame Curie's arm, and said, "You understand, what I need to know is exactly what happens to passengers in an elevator when it falls into emptiness." The children, Eve wrote, howled with laughter; but Einstein's "thought experiment" led to his general theory of relativity, published in 1915.

Einstein spent the last twenty-two years of his life in Princeton, New Jersey. In 1952 he was offered the job of president of Israel, but turned it down. In despair over weapons and wars, the father of the atomic age once told J. Robert Oppenheimer, who headed the team that developed the atom bomb, that if he had to live his life over again he would be a plumber.

Einstein began playing the violin when he was six. A keen bicyclist and sailor, he claimed to be interested in everything: "I want to know how God created this world," he once said, "I am not interested in this or that phenomenon, in the spectrum of this or that element. I want to know His thoughts. The rest are details."

Louis-Victor de Broglie

Life is a Wave

Louis-Victor, Prince de Broglie, descendant of an aristocratic French family, grew up with an interest in history. His shift to science while in college was influenced by Henri Bergson, the philosopher who inspired a revolution in French thinking.

Bergson, winner of the 1927 Nobel Prize in Literature, attached much importance to the image of the wave, as he wrote in *Creative Evolution*: "Life appears in its entirety as an immense wave which, starting from a centre, spreads outwards . . ." Bergson often used music as a metaphor in his writing, and De Broglie, a connoisseur of chamber music, resorted to music too. For example, De Broglie perceived the atom as a musical instrument that would sound a basic tone and then a series of overtones.

De Broglie theorized that electrons, protons, or neutrons possessed the property of waves. He was inspired by the work of Arthur Compton, who was awarded a Physics Nobel Prize in 1927. In 1923 Compton had discovered that light rays were made up of particles called photons. De Broglie suggested that if particles could be waves, then waves could be particles. Both men were correct: waves and particles are simply two different ways of looking at the same thing. De Broglie's explanation of a fundamental aspect of the universe was rewarded with the 1929 Nobel Prize.

Albert Einstein greatly admired De Broglie's wave theory and called it "a stroke of genius". De Broglie "had lifted a corner of the great veil".

De Broglie never married. In addition to attending musical concerts, he enjoyed walking, reading and chess. In 1987 he died in a Paris hospital at the age of 94.

Left
Louis de Broglie's ancestors served French kings in diplomacy and war for hundreds of years. In 1740, one was made a *duc* by Louis XIV. The son of that first duke helped the Austrians in the Seven Years' War, and was given the title *prinz*. With the death of his older brother in 1960, De Broglie became both a French *duc* and a German *prinz*.

Above
Waves are created by the vibration of water molecules – particles – disturbed, for example, by passing swans. De Broglie waves, however, are not the result of vibrating particles; the particles themselves are waves. Modern science pictures matter as having a dual existence as both waves, as De Broglie theorized, and as particles.

Enrico Fermi

Enrico Fermi supervised the building of the first atomic pile, in which graphite blocks were stacked high on top of each other to moderate the chain reaction. Uranium was placed between the blocks, and on 2 December 1942, cadium control rods were slowly withdrawn to start the world's first self-sustaining chain reaction. "Fermi," an associate later wrote, "had unlocked the door to the atomic age."

In November 1938, Enrico Fermi, professor of theoretical physics at the University of Rome, learned that he had been awarded the Nobel Prize "for his demonstrations of the existence of new radioactive elements produced by neutron irradiation, and for his related discovery of nuclear reactions brought about by slow neutrons". The Prize came at a crucial time in Fermi's life: Benito Mussolini had aligned himself with Adolf Hitler, and had begun enacting anti-Semitic civil service laws. Fermi was half-Jewish, his wife was Jewish, and they had two young children. It was imperative they leave Italy immediately.

That year there were only two Nobel Prize recipients: Fermi, and the American writer Pearl Buck. On the day of the ceremony, seated on the centre of the stage, the two were to receive their medals from Sweden's King Gustavus V, who was sitting in the front row of the audience. When Fermi's turn came, he crossed the stage, descended the four steps to the floor, and shook the King's hand rather than giving a Fascist salute, an act of defiance for which he was excoriated in the Italian Press. Fermi followed this with a very different kind of bravado: acting on the belief that one never turns one's back on royalty, he retraced his steps backwards, and without even a glance over his shoulder, made a perfect landing into his leather-backed chair.

As soon as the presentation ceremony was over, the Fermi family sailed from Stockholm to New York. On entering the United States, the world-renowned physicist was required to undergo the standard mental agility test for would-be immigrants: add 15 and 27 and divide 29 by 2. He passed and was given the official designation "enemy alien". In 1944 he and his family became naturalized American citizens.

A few days after arriving in New York, where he was to teach physics at Columbia University, Fermi received a visit from the Danish nuclear physicist Niels Bohr with the news that the Germans had just succeeded in splitting the uranium atom. Fermi had accomplished the same feat in 1934, but at the time had not realized that he had achieved nuclear fission.

With funding from the United States government, Fermi immediately began experimenting to see if a chain reaction resulting in an enormous explosive force were possible. He and Emilio Segrè, a fellow Italian physicist and former student, believed an atomic bomb might be fuelled by plutonium 239, an element that did not then exist. To produce it they would need to build a uranium reactor.

Fermi was instrumental in persuading Albert Einstein to write his famous letter to President Roosevelt, urging the United States to develop a nuclear weapon before the Axis powers did. In 1942, the Manhattan Project was set up to build an atomic bomb, and Fermi and his research team were moved to the University of Chicago.

On 2 December 1942, in a squash court beneath the stands of the University's football stadium, Fermi achieved the first controlled, self-sustaining nuclear reaction. A Harvard professor later recalled hearing the incredible news over the telephone; his caller said

Few centuries have begun less auspiciously than our own: the disaster of the First World War followed a generation later by the Second – and by charming innovations such as the battlefield use of poison gas and nuclear weapons.

Now, astonishingly, the cold war appears to have ended, raising the hope that the conflict atmosphere of the last forty years may have changed fundamentally. As this grimmest of centuries draws to an end, we may thus, suddenly and unexpectedly, have the possibility that we can focus our energies on real problems – disease, poverty, and environmental destruction.

LEON COOPER, 1972

This dramatic photograph of the interior of an AGR nuclear reactor shows the fuel rods in position.

simply, "The Italian navigator has reached the New World."

In August 1944, Fermi went to Los Alamos, New Mexico to work with J. Robert Oppenheimer, Bohr, and Segrè on developing the A-bomb. Although he defended the dropping of the fission bomb on Hiroshima and Nagasaki in 1945, Fermi later, along with Oppenheimer, opposed the building of the far deadlier H-bomb.

After the War Fermi returned to the University of Chicago to join the newly formed Institute for Nuclear Studies. He died in Chicago at the age of fifty-three. The following year the 100th chemical element was discovered; it is named fermium.

Edward Appleton

In 1924, the British physicist Edward Appleton provided the first experimental proof of the existence of the electrically charged layer of the earth's atmosphere, which today bears his name. Appleton's discoveries cleared the way for worldwide radio broadcasts by showing that radio waves bounce off the ionosphere, which is why radio transmission is not limited to line-of-sight.

Appleton's researches opened a new branch of physical science – radio physics – with applications extending far beyond radio telegraphy. His work played an important part in the later development of radar, and the methods he used for investigating the ionosphere have proved of immense importance in astronomy, geophysics, and meteorology.

Radar was credited with turning the tide in the air battle over Britain in the Second World War. More recently, the spacecraft *Magellan*, in orbit around the planet Venus, produced radar images of a thin plastic crust unlike anything ever seen before. The radar pictures showed deep craters, volcanic cones, flowing lava, and a pattern of intersecting fracture lines.

In 1948 Appleton interviewed himself for a magazine and wrote: "Chubby in build and cheery in face, Sir Edward likes human beings . . . " Another scientist described him as a short man of abundant energy, who was known for his warmth and great kindnesses.

Appleton was awarded the Nobel Prize in 1947 "for his investigations of the physics of the upper atmosphere especially for the discovery of the so-called Appleton layer".

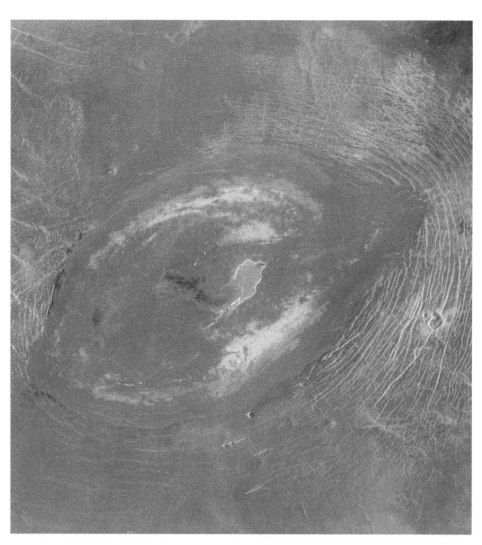

Above
Radar has become a vital tool in space exploration. In 1990 the American spacecraft *Magellan* sent back radar images of the surface of Venus that were ten to 100 times more detailed than previous surveys. Colour has been added to this image to simulate the appearance of the Venus surface.

Right
Although early in the Second World War the Nazis had a superior air force, a team of researchers assembled by Appleton applied its knowledge to the radio-location of aircraft, and developed the technology that made it possible for the Royal Air Force to gain the upper hand. Radar became Britain's greatest secret weapon.

Above
When the First World War began in 1914, Appleton became a signal officer in the Royal Engineers, where he worked with radio communications, investigating the problem of fading radio signals. He devised a method of using a transmitter that sent out short bursts of radio energy, and then measured the time it took for the reflected signal to return.

William Shockley, John Bardeen, and Walter H. Brattain

The announcement of a major twentieth-century invention appeared as a brief item in the radio column of the 1 July 1948 *New York Times*:

"A device called a transistor, which has several applications in radio where a vacuum tube ordinarily is employed, was demonstrated yesterday at Bell Telephone Laboratories, 463 West Street, where it was invented.

The device was demonstrated in a radio receiver, which contained none of the conventional tubes. It also was shown in a telephone system and in a television unit controlled by a receiver on a lower floor. In each case the transistor was employed as an amplifier, although it is claimed that it can also be used as an oscillator in that it will create and send radio waves.

In the shape of a small metal cylinder about a half-inch long, the transistor contains no vacuum, grid, plate or glass envelope to keep the air away. Its action is instantaneous, there being no warm-up delay since no heat is developed as in a vacuum tube . . .

The transistor was developed with the collaboration of physicists, chemists, metallurgists, and engineers over many years. Credit for the 1948 breakthrough – and the 1956 Nobel Prize – went to three men at Bell Laboratories: William Shockley, John Bardeen, and Walter H.

Right

John Bardeen, William Shockley, and Walter Brattain. The invention of the transistor is a superb example of the research teamwork that increasingly has marked advances in physics. Since 1951, multiple awards of the Nobel Prize have been far more frequent than single awards.

Right
The word "transistor" is a combination of "transfer" and "resistor". It is a semiconductor that processes electric signals. The first transistor, seen here, had contacts supported by a wedge-shaped piece of insulating material, separated by only a few thousandths of an inch. The contacts are made of gold, and the semiconductor is germanium.

Right
The word "transistor" is a combination of "transfer" and "resistor". It is a semiconductor that processes electric signals. The first transistor, seen here, had contacts supported by a wedge-shaped piece of insulating material, separated by only a few thousandths of an inch. The contacts are made of gold, and the semiconductor is germanium.

Below right
With subsequent advances in technology, as many as a million transistors can now be incorporated in a single silicon chip, and the number is rising. These chips have permitted the rapid development of computers and communications equipment.

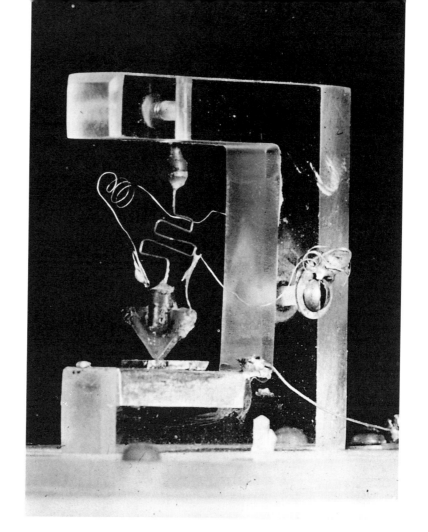

Brattain. (In 1972 Bardeen shared another Nobel Prize with Leon Cooper and J. Robert Schrieffer for a theory of superconductivity.)

Much effort went into finding a material that would work as a transistor. Sand, for silicon, which had the right qualities, covers one-third of the earth, but refining it was a problem. Germanium, the other element used in early experiments, has to be extracted during the refining of zinc or coal carbon, and is by weight worth more than gold.

Transistors make possible things that were never possible before: today we can watch events in Moscow or Hong Kong as they happen; a computer, not a clerk, keeps our account at the bank; airline seats are reserved worldwide in an instant; and jets have automation systems with transistors to guide them. Transistors have made possible communications satellites, powerful computers, and space exploration. Without transistors there would be no electronic calculators or digital watches, no transistor radios, portable tape-recorders, or bugging devices. To diagnose many illnesses doctors now depend on equipment made possible by the transistor, which also allowed the development of the hearing-aid and the heart pacemaker.

The transistor has proved to be the forerunner of a new kind of electronics that has had the revolutionary capacity to change our culture.

Donald A. Glaser

1960   *Bubble-maker*

The story goes that the American physicist Donald Glaser got his inspiration for the bubble chamber – which led to his 1960 Nobel Prize – by watching the bubbles in a glass of beer. Glaser wanted to see if the foam could be affected by radioactivity. Eventually he found that under certain conditions radiation caused superheated liquids to boil.

Glaser's tests and calculations led to the development of a bubble chamber, a laboratory device that replaced C. T. R. Wilson's cloud chamber. Wilson, who had received a Nobel Prize in 1927, had built a sealed chamber to produce a track of liquid droplets in a gas, like minute versions of the condensation trails left by jets across the sky. With his chamber, Wilson proved the existence of atoms, molecules, and ions.

A bubble chamber is like a pressure-cooker, in which water can be heated well above the boiling point, but it will not boil. In a bubble chamber, the liquid is superheated liquid hydrogen. When a charged particle passes through the liquid, its friction leaves a visible track of the particle's path.

Glaser's bubble chamber, which was as big as a Volkswagen bus and cost $2 million, produced a track of gaseous bubbles in liquid that could be photographed. Very high energy particles from the biggest accelerators could be examined in the new device.

By 1956 Glaser was using liquefied xenon gas in his bubble chamber. This allowed physicists to take pictures of the tracks of neutral as well as charged particles, and permitted the observation of many more reactions.

Above
During 1959 and 1960 Donald Glaser collected nearly half a million photographs of the paths of particles using the bubble chamber. Such instruments yielded thousands of times more information than C. T. R. Wilson's earlier cloud chamber.

Right
This photograph, taken in a bubble chamber, has been artificially coloured. After he received his Nobel Prize, Glaser became interested in applying physics to molecular biology, and adapted equipment used to analyse photographs in the bubble chamber to scan bacterial species.

Charles H. Townes

Charles H. Townes shared the 1964 Nobel Prize with the Russians Nikolai Basov and Alexsandr Prokhorov "for fundamental work in the field of quantum electronics, which has led to the construction of oscillators and amplifiers based on the maser-laser principle".

He wrote the following piece about his past work, and what he foresees in the future.

"I like to explore. And for me, exploration occurs in those places which are not very crowded with others.

"After my experience with radar in World War II, I recognized that a brand new field of spectroscopy was possible, with precision and resolution far beyond what had previously been available – microwave spectroscopy using the tools which radar had made available. It involved work on molecules, not a very popular field with physicists at that time, but one which opened up many new measurements not only of molecular structure, but also of nuclear properties and quantum mechanical effects. To extend it further, I wanted to go beyond the microwave region (involving waves of centimetre or in extreme cases millimetre wavelengths) and find ways of producing oscillators in the infrared which would be as potent as electronic oscillators then available in the microwave region.

"Many efforts which failed eventually led to the recognition that to obtain shorter waves one must use the natural resonances of molecules and atoms. How to do it came to me while musing on a park bench, and first produced the maser-microwave amplification by stimulated emission of radiation. The first such new device was made by my student Jim Gordon as a thesis project, with help from a new PhD, Herb Zeiger. This was followed by three years of exciting work with masers, providing extremely accurate frequency standards and a large increase in the available sensitivity of amplifiers. Many types were invented. But these initial efforts were at wavelengths which could be produced electronically, even though masers allowed new precision and sensitivity.

"Late in 1957, I decided I must push on into the infrared. Microwave masers had become too popular to be new territory for much exploration, and most of those in the field seemed little interested in pushing into the shorter wavelengths. I simply sat down at my desk to figure out the best ways for providing radiation of much shorter wavelength, which may seem an unglamorous way to do it. However, I then found not only an appropriate way, but that it would be just as easy to push on into very short waves – even visible light. Discussions with my friend and colleague Arthur Schawlow led him to suggest important additional ideas for light generation, and we wrote the first paper on light amplifiers and oscillators using atomic amplifications – optical masers or lasers (for Light Amplification by Stimulated Emission of Radiation).

"Our paper on light oscillators created great interest and started many projects to build them. Hence when in 1959 I went to Washington to do a public service job and left a graduate student working to produce a laser as a thesis at Columbia University, I felt sure lasers would be produced somewhere soon. The first was made by Ted Maiman at Hughes, the second by a group at IBM, and the third at Bell Telephone Laboratories. Industry had taken hold and from then on did much of the laser invention and construction.

"When I again took up a normal academic position and returned to full-time scientific work, the laser field or quantum electronics were very popular and rather densely populated. My taste for exploration took me to other fields I felt were still rather neglected – the search for molecules in interstellar regions, and infrared astronomy. Both were fields in which I had been interested for some time but was too busy to explore. I was also puzzled why they had not yet been more fully appreciated. This work led to the discovery of stable and polyatomic molecules in space, a field now so popular that my taste has persuaded me to move on again.

"In addition to astrophysical spectroscopy in the far infrared, I am now busy with trying to open up the field of high resolution spatial interferometry of astronomical objects in the infrared. My belief is that this can make a new chapter in astronomy as we become able to see many more details of astronomical objects and use infrared radiation to penetrate the dust of interstellar space which obscures much we would like to see. So far, this is a still-unpopulated field, and one which fits my own instincts for exploration."

Charles H. Townes stands in front of a galaxy centre. Using laser oscillators, he has introduced advanced methods of infrared detection for astronomical exploration. His mobile, infrared telescopes yield a hundred times more detail than conventional radio telescopes.

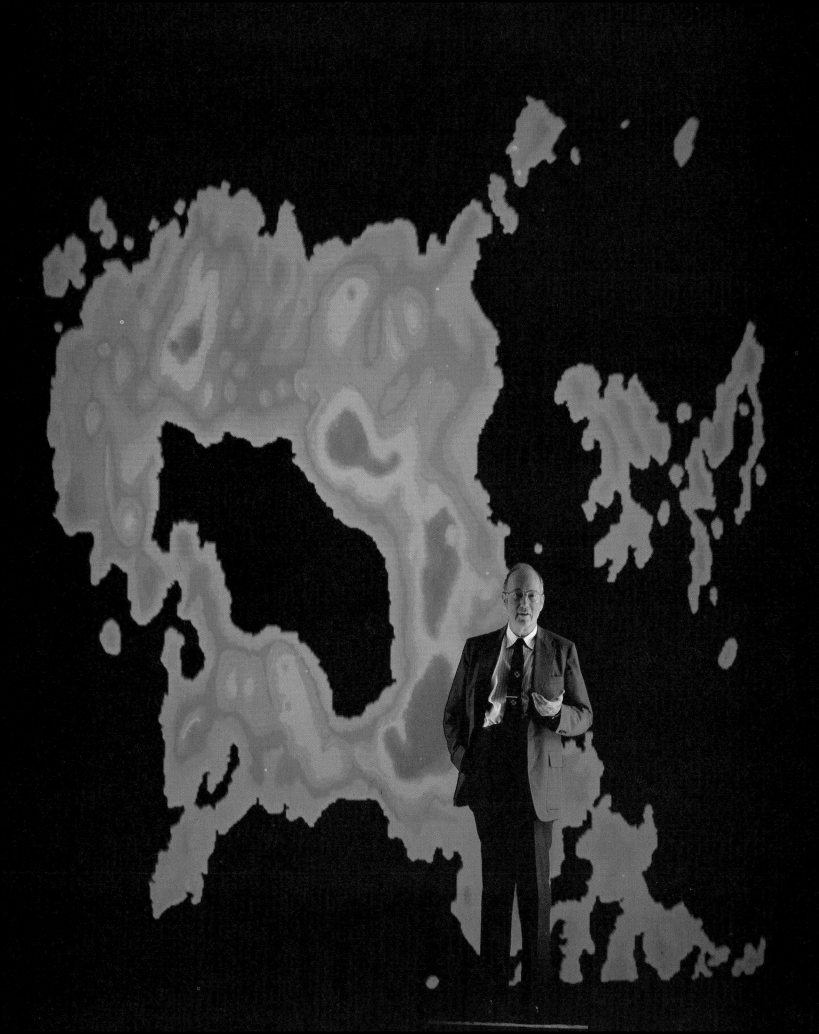

Murray Gell-Mann

1969   *"Three quarks for Muster Mark!"* (James Joyce, *Finnegans Wake*)

The American physicist Murray Gell-Mann suggested in 1964 that there are three quarks in every proton or neutron. Quarks come in several varieties: up, down, strange, charmed, and bottom. A sixth, called top, has not yet been detected in experiments. "I didn't want some pompous name," Gell-Mann explained, but he did choose a word from one of the most esoteric works in the English language.

Gell-Mann presently is working on a book called *The Quark and the Jaguar, Adventures in the Simple and the Complex.* He explained that "through the sciences of simplicity and complexity we will reach an understanding of the way the universe works, from the structure of galaxies to the generation of creative thought in the human mind, from prebiotic evolution to the rise and fall of pre-historic societies".

Gell-Mann's quarks, proposed as the fundamental units of matter, are described in dictionaries as theoretical. For years some physicists disputed their existence, claiming they were nothing more than mathematical devices for making calculations. In the late 1960s, however, Jerome Friedman, Henry W. Kendall, and Richard E. Taylor confirmed the existence of quarks while shattering atoms in a linear accelerator.

Left
Murray Gell-Mann, professor of physics at the California Institute of Technology; Gell-Mann entered Yale at age fifteen.

Right
"Chaos" fractal graphics illustrate Gell-Mann's statement that the complexity of the universe lies mostly in "completely unpredictable accidents".

Dennis Gabor

Early in this century, Dennis Gabor's father took him to visit Budapest's Museum of Technology. The wonders the little boy saw there triggered a lifelong interest in science.

In 1920, while studying engineering at Budapest Technical University, Gabor, opposing the monarchy that had been restored in Hungary, fled to Berlin. During his years as a student there, he often visited the University of Berlin and heard lectures by Max Planck, Walter Nernst, Max von Laue, and Albert Einstein – all eventual Nobel laureates. Shortly after Hitler came to power in 1933, Gabor decided to emigrate to England.

In the late 1940s, Gabor developed his theory of the hologram. To produce a hologram of a vase of flowers, for example, a coherent beam of light is directed at the vase but is split into two before reaching it. One beam, the reference beam, is recorded directly on to a photographic plate or film. The other beam is reflected from the vase and is then recorded. When they come together on the plate or film the two beams create an "interference pattern". When light of the same frequency is then shone through the film, a three-dimensional image of the vase of flowers is produced. Interestingly, even a tiny portion of the film will produce the same image. If the film is cut in half, each half will produce the entire image of the vase.

Gabor's theory has found widespread application. Holography is used for such things as the photographic storage of hundreds of pictures in one emulsion, for medical diagnosis, mapmaking, diagnosing problems in high-speed equipment, testing tyres and laminated structural materials for faulty bonding, and for computing and information storage.

In 1977 a museum of holography opened in New York City, and Dennis Gabor was its first member. Perhaps a father will take his small son to visit, and that boy too will be inspired to invent wonders in the twenty-first century.

The quality of a hologram such as the one above can only be suggested in pictures reproduced in a book. The potential of Gabor's invention was not realized until 1960, when the laser was invented. In a new technique, many holograms – vast amounts of information – may be stored on a single polymer film, at densities 100,000 times as great as conventional hard computer disks.

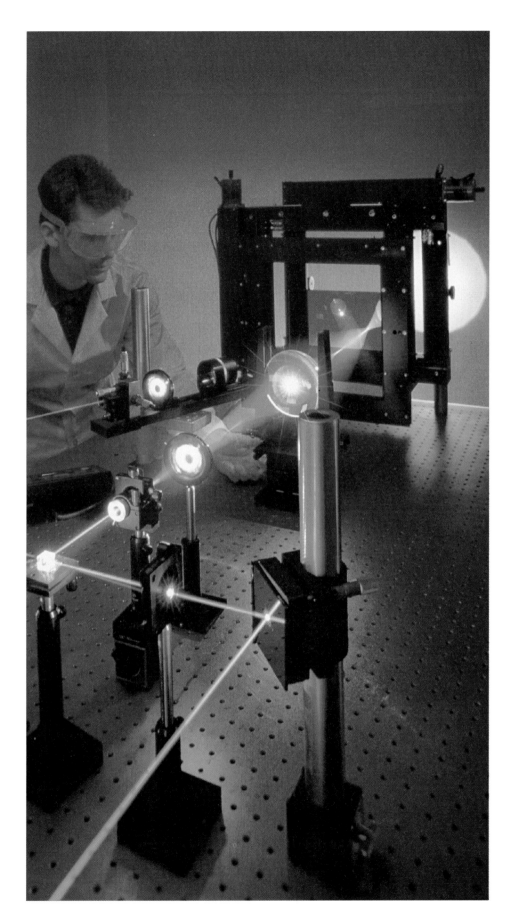

Above

In the late 1960s Dennis Gabor did much of his work in the CBS television laboratories. He made up the word "hologram" to describe his method of creating a picture that appears to have depth. *Holos*, from the Greek, means "complete" and *gram* means "written". A hologram captures information that is absent from a normal photograph.

Left

A technician adjusts an argon laser beam used to expose holographic-sensitive plates. Since the invention of the laser in 1960, new uses for holography continue to be discovered.

Carlo Rubbia

Carlo Rubbia shared the 1984 Nobel Prize in Physics with Simon van der Meer, both of the European Centre for Nuclear Research near Geneva (now called the European Laboratory for Particle Physics). The award was "for their decisive contributions to the large project, which led to the discovery of the field particles W and Z, communicators of weak interaction".

Rubbia wrote the following for this book:

"The twentieth century marks the discovery and exploration by man of the microscopic world, that of the atom and beyond. This has proved to be a surprisingly rich world, far from the homothetic repetitions that philosophers from past centuries could only imagine.

"Not only did successive layers of the unravelled structure of matter prove to be different, not only were there two new types of interactions at work to shape elementary bricks into ever more complex structures, but even more important was the realization of the quantum nature of the phenomena that prevail when one enters this microscopic world. The quantum view, although quickly accepted on the grounds of its operational usefulness, took quite some time to become a full part of our mental framework. While constraints set by the quantum theory seemed at first unduly to limit our ability to know the world ever better, the opposite view now prevails. We now think that quantum indeterminacy, by opening the new world of virtual phenomena, sheds new light on old questions such as the nature of the vacuum and the way the effect of forces can be felt at a distance. By exciting the vacuum with energy – as per the early twentieth-century conquest of Special Relativity – physicists can now create any sort of matter, including the very unstable one that prevailed during the very early universe.

"The driving force behind the exploration of this microscopic world was and remains human curiosity *vis-à-vis* the unknown. It is all the more remarkable that it has proved to be crucial to important questions affecting the macroscopic world.

"What is likely to happen in the future? Our idea of the vacuum is becoming more and more complex and is at the focus of contemporary physics research. According to a currently held view, it would be similar to a physical medium, and its properties could explain why some particles have mass. Why do we have weight? This is a question which the efforts of particle physicists in several countries world-wide is expected to solve in the coming decade.

"At the turn of the last century, scientists felt that physics was nearly completed and only missing details would have to be added. We should learn from history that it would be unwise to think that we shall soon have a working Theory of Everything. It is very probable that nature still has surprises in store for us."

As this century draws to a close, mankind becomes increasingly aware of the fact that our planet is rather small and by consequence finds it more and more difficult to provide the means and resources for a population still increasing. It will be crucial for the future of humanity, not only to develop proper ways of co-existence, but also to learn how to administer and share the resources the earth provides, in order to preserve the wonderful and delicate biological balance which makes this planet so precious and unique.

R. L. MÖSSBAUER, 1961

In the world of experimental physics, Carlo Rubbia is a
leader in the investigation of the smallest particles of
matter – quarks and neutrinos. It is believed that they may
prove to be the key to understanding how the universe
began, what it is made of, and where it is going.

Heinrich Rohrer and Gerd Binnig

1986

Is That a Microscope?

Gerd Binnig (right) says that he appreciates Heinrich Rohrer's "humanity and sense of humour" because it "restored my somewhat lost curiosity in physics".

Many Nobel Prizes in Physics have been awarded to the inventors of measuring devices that are of use only in laboratories.

When the 1986 Nobel Prize in Physics was awarded to the Swiss physicist Heinrich Rohrer and the German physicist Gerd Binnig for their design of the scanning tunnelling microscope, the spokesman for the Royal Swedish Academy said, "The scanning tunnelling microscope is completely new, and we have so far seen only the beginning of its development. It is, however, clear

Gallium arsenide is of great interest to the semiconductor industry. In this image provided by a scanning tunnelling microscope, individual gallium atoms are shown in blue, and the arsenic atoms are red. According to its creators, "The appeal and the impact of STM lie not only in the observation of surfaces atom by atom, but also in its widespread applicability, its simplicity, and its affordability."

that entirely new fields are opening up for the study of the structure of matter. Binnig's and Rohrer's great achievement is that, starting from earlier works and ideas, they have succeeded in mastering the enormous experimental difficulties involved in building an instrument of the precision and stability required."

The device examines the surface of a solid material with a sharp tip. A voltage is then applied between the tip and the surface. If the distance between the two is small enough, electrons will "tunnel" – "seep" might better describe what happens – from one to the other. That flow of current can then be measured. By moving the tip over the sample and monitoring the current, it is possible to map the atom-sized hills and valleys of the surface.

While developing this new piece of equipment, the scientists' biggest problem was noise. On 16 March 1981, they recalled in their Nobel lecture, they worked at night, "hardly daring to breathe from excitement, but mainly to avoid vibrations . . ." They concluded their lecture with, "We should not like to speculate where it will finally lead, but we sincerely trust that the beauty of atomic structures might be an inducement to apply the technique to those problems where it will be of greatest service solely to the benefit of mankind."

Today, scanning tunnelling microscopes are part of the equipment found in laboratories all over the world. In addition to inorganic substances, they are being used to study DNA and virus particles.

K. Alex Müller and J. Georg Bednorz

1987

The latest chapter in the long, sometimes maddeningly slow, search for a high-temperature superconductor was played out in an IBM laboratory in Switzerland. K. Alex Müller, a Swiss physicist, and German-born J. Georg Bednorz, who is knowledgeable in both solid-state physics and chemistry, came up with a new material made of barium, lanthanum, copper, and oxygen. Their accomplishment earned them the 1987 Nobel Prize.

The story of superconductivity began more than seventy-five years ago in a laboratory at the University of Leiden in the Netherlands. Heike Kamerlingh Onnes, professor of experimental physics, managed to achieve temperatures lower than anyone had believed possible. He then discovered that at four degrees above absolute zero, some metals lost their electric resistance. Resistance is a severe limitation in wire because it causes the wire to heat up. Not only does this heating waste energy, but it causes the material to deteriorate. When motion is reduced by cooling, resistance normally decreases. Onnes called this "superconductivity". The scientific world was fascinated, and in 1913, Onnes was awarded a Nobel Prize.

It was not until 1957, however, that John Bardeen – who shared a Prize in 1956 for his work on the transistor (see page 102) – and two of his students at the University of Illinois, Leon N. Cooper and J. Robert Schrieffer, provided an explanation. When a material is not superconducting, the electrons move in every direction, bumping into one another at random and draining energy. In a superconductor, electrons flow in unison without loss of energy. Bardeen, Cooper, and Schrieffer were awarded a Nobel Prize in 1972.

The important temperature in the quest for superconductivity is seventy-seven degrees Kelvin (zero degrees Kelvin is absolute zero). This temperature is like the sound barrier or the four-minute mile of superconductivity. It is the temperature of cheap, easy-to-handle liquid nitrogen. Anything that works only at a lower temperature is effectively useless – it is too difficult and expensive to achieve and maintain such low temperatures. The figure for the Müller and Bednorz material was thirty degrees Kelvin. Since they were awarded their Nobel Prize, others have discovered more effective compounds.

Above seventy-seven degrees Kelvin, if it is ever achieved, lies a world of science fiction, in which there is unlimited cheap power. The magnetically levitated trains for super smooth and rapid rides, and the ultrafast computers that will be possible with superconductivity are still in the future; the search goes on.

Left
K. Alex Müller (right) and J. Georg Bednorz went out of
their way to keep their discovery quiet. They published
their paper about their ceramic oxide substance that was
a superconductor in an obscure German journal because
they had hoped to have "a few more years to continue
our work in peace".

Above
One of the unusual qualities of a superconductor, first
discovered in 1933, is that a magnetic material placed
above it will hover on a cushion of magnetic repulsion.
This superconductor, at the IBM Swiss Research
Laboratory, is acting as a perfect mirror to the magnet,
causing it to levitate.

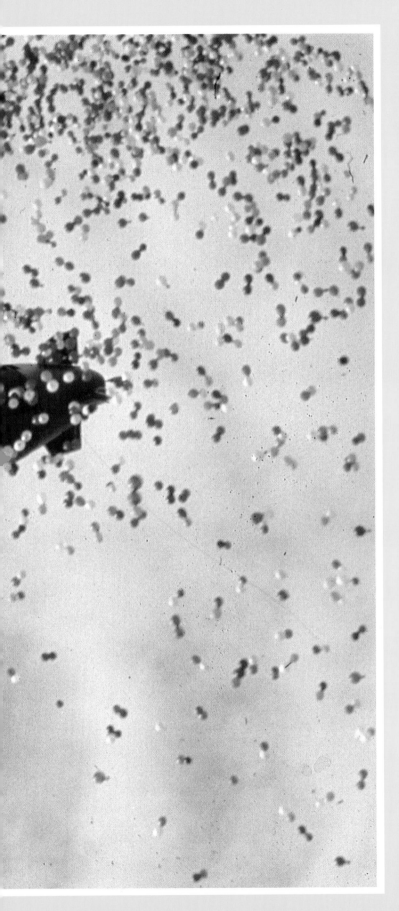

3 CHEMISTRY

With the discovery of helium, the dangerous and highly flammable hydrogen then used in balloons and lighter-than-air ships could be replaced by this safer gas. Rich sources of helium were found in mineral deposits.

Introduced by Richard Wolkomir

At about the time work started on the Suez Canal, and Queen Victoria began wearing widow's black, a Rotterdam physician's son was sneaking into his school's laboratory on Sundays to experiment with poisons and explosives. When administrators ended young Jacobus Henricus Van't Hoff's bootleg research, he transferred operations to his home, taking a businesslike approach by charging spectators a fee, which went toward new solvents and beakers.

Van't Hoff was to become the first Nobel Prize winner in chemistry in 1901, but not for his homemade eruptions. Rather, it would be for what an assistant at his Amsterdam laboratory described as "something mystical, something uncanny in the air".

As a child, Van't Hoff had won prizes for singing and piano-playing. He later said that if he had not turned to the poems of Lord Byron, his professors at Leyden University would have turned him into "a dried and shrivelled scientific conglomerate". Van't Hoff studied at a Bonn laboratory, grew despondent when a young woman studying there committed suicide, and wrote a Byronic poem about her – "Thy glory and thy suffering are past." He moved to a Paris laboratory, where another student noted that "He was so quiet that nobody paid much attention to him." But Van't Hoff had something on his mind, and it turned out to be atoms.

He was contemplating the carbon atom. At the time, chemists knew that the carbon atom can "attach" itself to four other atoms, as if it had four little "hands". What chemists did not know was the position of the "hands" around the atom. Van't Hoff decided it was at the four corners of a regular tetrahedron. This was the start of a new branch of science, stereochemistry, which deals with the spacial arrangements of atoms in molecules, and the effects of those arrangements on the molecules' properties. Van't Hoff's decision was brilliant, but in 1874 science still wore whiskers. The reaction Van't Hoff received was merely silence.

He considered quitting chemistry and even thought of emigrating to Australia, but he ended up teaching at a veterinary college in Utrecht. Then an illustrious Leipzig professor took it upon himself to lambast the young upstart for having "no taste for exact chemical research". Said the professor: "He has thought it more convenient to bestride Pegasus, evidently hired at the veterinary stables, and to proclaim in his *Chemistry in Space* how, during his bold flight to the top of the chemical Parnassus, the atoms appeared to him to have grouped themselves throughout universal space." Van't Hoff immediately photographed the saddest nag in the veterinary stable and pinned the picture to his laboratory wall, labelled "Pegasus".

It was the bewhiskered era's last shot. More alert minds, however, did take notice, and by the age of twenty-six Van't Hoff was professor of chemistry at the University of Amsterdam. Great works lay ahead; science's probing of atoms and molecules had opened the door to a new era of research.

Chemistry, the study of substances and their interactions probably is the oldest of sciences. It started when men in mammoth pelts first lit a fire. We know that one branch of chemistry, metallurgy, was extant at least five millennia ago, because archaeologists excavating a 3,200 BC Egyptian tomb found a copper frying pan. And in Greece, about 400 BC, Democritus pointed towards modernity by positing a universe of indivisible atoms and void. The progress in chemistry, however, became mired in alchemy, an amalgam of mysticism, rascality, and self-bamboozlement. True chemistry finally got up steam only about 1600, when Jan Van Helmont analysed vapours emitted by burning wood, naming them "chaos", which in Flemish is *gas*. But by 1900, that "something uncanny" which Van't Hoff's assistant noted had taken hold – chemistry began to fulfil alchemy's wildest dreams.

Alchemists sought eternal youth, and that particular elixir still is on biochemistry's agenda, but tweaking the innards of atoms has given chemists strange new powers. They can transmute soot into diamonds. They can even assemble atoms into molecules nature never imagined, from life-saving medicines to a flexible transparent sheeting that lightly adheres to itself and excels at wrapping sandwiches. Chemistry now fuels our 747s, extrudes fibres for our drip-dry shirts, purifies our water (and sometimes pollutes it), sparkles our sinks, fluffs our hair, lights our nights, and so pervades our days that we never notice what the last century of research has wrought.

Van't Hoff himself went on to demonstrate that molecules dissolved in a solution behave analogously to gases, helping to launch the new discipline of physical chemistry. That discovery enlisted him in the Ion Wars, set off by a chunky young Swede from Wijk.

Svante Arrhenius was the son of an estate manager. As an Uppsala undergraduate, he had been known mainly for partying. But as a doctoral student in Stockholm, he worked late into the night, running electric currents through beakers containing various liquids and analysing the gases that bubbled out. Here was a conundrum. Electricity will not pass through distilled water. It will not pass through a block of salt. But dissolve the salt in the water and the current flows. Nobody knew why.

After two years of beaker watching, Arrhenius came up with a rock-the-boat theory. The English chemist Michael Faraday had thought that tiny particles might carry electricity through a solution, and he had named his hypothetical particles "ions", meaning "wanderers". But no one knew what ions might be. Arrhenius's two years of experimentation gave him an idea. "I could not sleep that night until I had worked through the whole problem," he later said. In a solution, Arrhenius theorized, a salt such as sodium chloride (table salt) divides into its component atoms, in this case sodium and chlorine. However, these atoms retain the electrical charge that held them together as molecules. They are the ions.

Critics scoffed. If salt dissolved into sodium and chlorine in water, where was the greenish gas chlorine? Arrhenius argued that charged ions are not the same as uncharged atoms. Reactions in solutions, he said, were between ions, not atoms. He was proposing a new chemistry of ions.

In presenting his doctoral thesis to the august – and stuffy – committee of professors, Arrhenius tamed it to avoid shaking hidebound minds. Even so, he noted glumly that the professors seemed to regard him as a "stupid schoolboy". Finally they awarded his degree *in spite* of his dissertation. Stung, Arrhenius sent his theory to Wilhelm Ostwald, at the polytechnic school in Riga, who received it on the same day that his wife gave birth to a daughter and he got a stabbing toothache. "It was too much for one day!" Ostwald said later. "The worst was the dissertation, for the others developed quite normally."

Arrhenius went on to collaborate with both Ostwald and Van't Hoff, forming what amounted to the Three Horsemen of Ions. "Let us attack them," declared Ostwald. "That is the best method." The argument raged for years. In the end, the Ionians won. In 1903, Arrhenius received the 1903 Nobel Prize and in 1909 the Prize went to Wilhelm Ostwald.

The alchemists' philosopher's stone has turned out to be a smear of electrons around a pulsing pit of neutrons and protons. It has taken nearly a century of chemistry to probe that primal speck's interactions, and to see what might be done with them. But the universe's basic brick sizzles enough to light a city or incinerate it, and some probers have been seared.

Marie Sklodovski grew up in a Poland ruled by Russia's tsars, who forbade use of the Polish language in newspapers, schools, and churches. Secret police were everywhere. Marie was a high school physics professor's daughter, who grew to be a blond young woman with intense blue eyes. Mendéleyev, the Russian deviser of the periodic table of elements, saw her mixing chemicals in her cousin's laboratory in Warsaw and predicted she would be a great chemist. But Marie became a revolutionary. In 1891, at age twenty-four, she fled a police crackdown and settled in an unheated garret in Paris. She knew science was closed to women, but she enrolled at the Sorbonne anyway, paying tuition by washing bottles and tending the laboratory furnace.

Marie then met a thirty-five-year-old researcher, Pierre Curie, who once had written: "Women of genius are rare, and the average woman is a positive hindrance to a serious-minded scientist."

"I wonder, Monsieur," replied Marie, "where you can have imbibed your strange notions of a woman's limitations?"

It was not long before Pierre wrote to her: "It would be a lovely thing to pass through life together hypnotized in our dreams: your dream for your country, our dream for science. Together we can serve humanity." They were married in 1895, lived on *centimes*, and unexpectedly found themselves chasing mysterious rays.

In 1896, William Röntgen had described his discovery of X-rays. Then, due to a lucky accident and a sharp eye, Henri Becquerel discovered that uranium ore emits rays strong enough to cloud a photographic plate. The ore pitchblende, he found, emits even stronger rays. Having noticed Marie Curie's prowess in the laboratory, he asked if she and Pierre would study the pitchblende. It meant abandoning their current research, but Marie was certain that pitchblende contained an unknown element.

The Curies borrowed money to fund the research, and the Austrian government sent them a donation of a ton of pitchblende sand, which was deposited in their yard. Like alchemists in their improvised lab, the Curies boiled down sand from the great mound to filter out impurities. Pierre shovelled chemicals and Marie stirred bubbling vats with an iron rod nearly her own size. "We lived in a preoccupation as complete as that of a dream," she later said.

Work was interrupted by the birth of a daughter, Irène, but, a week later Marie was back in the workshop. Sometimes, as the years passed and the pitchblende heap dwindled to just 100 pounds, the Curies toyed with giving up.

But Marie said that "it was in that miserable shed that we passed the best and happiest years of our lives". Pierre turned down a physics chair at the University of Geneva to continue the work. Finally, from a bit of bismuth salts extracted from the pitchblende, Marie isolated a substance resembling nickel. She named the new element "polonium", in honour of her native Poland. The Curies, however, were sure that pitchblende held further secrets.

Two years of painstaking extraction performed by repeated crystallizations followed. One night, the couple walked out to the shed and saw the "feebly luminous silhouettes" of their fluorescing bottles. "They were like earthly stars – these glowing tubes in that poor rough shack," Marie wrote. Finally, they came to the end: a few crystals. It was another new element, which they called "radium".

Radium was powerful. New chemical theories would spring from it as if it were an intellectual fertilizer. Pierre Curie's fingers were virtually paralyzed from exposure.

Along with Becquerel, the Curies received the 1903 Physics Prize for their work on radiation, the money going to pay their debts for the research. Although poor, whatever of the valuable radium the Curies accumulated they donated to hospitals. They were interested only in their research, their two daughters, and each other. Then, in 1906, on his way home from the university, Pierre was knocked down in the street by a horse-drawn cab and killed.

"Pierre is dead, Pierre is dead," was all Marie said. A few weeks later she returned to the laboratory. She was given Pierre's university chair, the first woman to hold a Sorbonne professorship. For her first lecture, the gathered dignitaries ranged from scientists like Lord Kelvin to France's president. As one spectator described it: "On the stroke of three an insignificant little black-robed woman stepped in through a side door, and the brilliant throng rose with a thrill of homage and respect. The next moment a roar of applause burst forth. The timid little figure was visibly distressed and raised a trembling hand in mute appeal. Then you could have heard a pin drop."

Marie's aim was to isolate pure radium. In 1910, she finally passed a current through radium chloride. At the negative electrode, which was made of mercury, an amalgam formed that Marie heated in a silica tube filled with nitrogen. Mercury vapour boiled off, leaving white globules – pure radium. For this, she won a second Nobel Prize in Chemistry in 1911.

Later, helped by her daughter Irène, she worked on the use of X-rays in medicine. In 1934 Marie Curie died of leukaemia caused by the radiation that had crippled Pierre's hands, and to which they both had devoted their careers.

Irène and her husband, Frédéric Joliot, went on to create new radioactive elements. Irradiating aluminium foil, they produced radioactive phosphorus. They also created radioactive nitrogen and silicon. In 1935, Irène and Frédéric Joliot-Curie received the Nobel Prize in Chemistry. But once again radiation exacted its price and in 1956 Irène also died of leukaemia.

Chemistry has its faustian side; for a fingerhold on the philosopher's stone scientists may release unforeseen

Alfred Nobel was a chemist. Today his laboratory in Karlskoga, Sweden, is a museum.

forces: synthetic fertilizers that grow lush wheat can pollute; chemicals in refrigerators may destroy the earth's ozone shield; warring governments wield ghastly chemical weapons. Chemists, however, merely provide us with information, and we use it as we will. Besides which, a century of Nobel Prize-winners have bequeathed us fabulous tools.

Nobel laureates have produced medicines: Heinrich Wieland (Germany, 1927) and Adolf Windaus (Germany, 1928) studied cholesterol, leading to drugs for heart disease. Others – Walter Haworth (Britain, 1937), Paul Karrer (Switzerland, 1937), Dorothy Mary Crowfoot Hodgkin (Britain, 1964) – uncovered the structures of vitamins C, B2, A, and B12. Sir Robert Robinson (Britain, 1947) detailed alkaloid structures, leading to antimalarial drugs. Robert B. Woodward (United States, 1965) synthesized quinine. Frederick Sanger (Britain, 1958, 1980) enhanced the lives of millions of diabetics when he pieced together the architecture of the insulin molecule, leading to synthetic insulin.

Artturi Virtanen (Finland, 1945), developed a technique for adding dilute acids to silage, preventing fermentation that destroys stored fodder. His work has been vital to farms in regions where the winters are long and cold. Irving Langmuir (United States, 1932), who began as a child mixing iodine and ammonia with his brother to create an explosive went on to create the modern electric light bulb filled with an inert gas.

Chemistry has even opened a window on the past. When did the first humans arrive in the Americas? When were the Dead Sea Scrolls written? Willard Libby (United States, 1960) helped archaeologists to answer such questions when he discovered that all living things contain a kind of clock in the form of the radioactive isotope carbon 14. At the moment any plant or animal dies, the radiocarbon it contains begins to decay. Because scientists know the rate at which radiocarbon decays, they can measure the radioactivity remaining, for example in a bit of charcoal from a prehistoric campfire, or threads from an ancient garment, and can calculate when the firewood was cut, or the cotton was plucked.

At the beginning of this century, chemists such as Van't Hoff and Arrhenius were probing the nature of atoms and molecules. After the quantum revolution, chemists focused on how atoms *form* molecules electronically by sharing electrons, and geometrically by creating molecules' shapes. Twentieth-century chemistry has had two other major themes: synthesis, or the building of new molecules, and – especially in recent years – the melding of chemistry and biology.

Paul Sabatier (France, 1912), added hydrogen to organic compounds. His findings led to pharmaceuticals, perfumes, detergents, and margarine. Polymer research by the 1963 laureates, Karl Ziegler (Germany), and Giulio Natta (Italy), produced new plastics, including polypropylene and polyethylene.

Frederick Sanger (Britain), Paul Berg (United States), and Walter Gilbert (United States) shared the 1980 prize for helping to create the field of recombinant DNA, or gene "tinkering". That technology may lead to factories where vats of genetically altered bacteria turn out valuable drugs and hormones. The possibilities are endless. Bacteria implanted with vanilla plant genes, for instance, might ooze low-cost vanilla.

In 1987, Donald Cram (United States), Charles Pedersen (United States), and Jean-Marie Lehn (France) won the Prize for creating synthetic enzymes; one possibility might be super-cleansers that scrub pollutants from soils and water. The 1988 Prize went to Robert Huber, Johann Deisenhofer, and Hartmut Michel (Germany), for studying photosynthesis, the process by which plants convert light into food. Their work could lead to solar cells that act like artificial plants.

As 1981 Chemistry laureate Roald Hoffmann, who has published two books of poetry based on science, says of the molecular scene – "It's a rich, agitated world down there."

Chemists, Hoffmann says, are the molecular world's "driven natives". They are rearrangers of molecules, and makers of new molecules. "It is a remarkable activity that is at the heart of chemistry, that puts chemistry close to art," he says. Where the molecular world's scientist-artists are going, he believes, is hard to predict: "The web of knowledge builds, never as directly as ideologies of scientific method would have it, but perhaps more richly, more consistent with our humanity."

R.W.

William Ramsay

At the Museum of Neon Art (MONA) in Los Angeles the "Mona Lisa" wears an electrified smile and a green toaster spits out kinetic orange sharks. Clearly, neon has come a long way since William Ramsay, a Scottish chemistry professor, isolated the inert gas ninety-three years ago.

Born into a family of devout Calvinists, Ramsay grew up wanting to be a minister until he became fascinated by science while an undergraduate at the University of Glasgow. In all Ramsay discovered five atmospheric gases: argon, helium, krypton, neon, and xenon. Said his presenter at the 1904 Nobel Prize ceremony: "The discovery of an entirely new group of elements, of which no single representative had been known with any certainty, is something utterly unique in the history of chemistry."

In terms of saving lives, helium, which soon replaced the highly flammable hydrogen used in dirigibles and balloons, was Ramsay's most valuable discovery. However, artistically at least, neon was an even greater contribution. Shortly after the turn of the century, a French inventor was trying to find an inexpensive way to provide oxygen for hospitals. In the process he found that when neon is injected into tinted or phosphorus-coated tubes and charged with electricity, it can take on any number of gem-like hues. The city sky at night was never to look the same again.

In 1912, France became the first country to exploit neon's potential as an advertising medium when a Parisian barber put up a neon sign on the Boulevard Montmartre. A decade later a Los Angeles car dealer visited Paris and a light bulb – or, in his case, a pulsating glass tube – went on in his head. On his return to California he adorned his car lot with two neon signs, each outlined in blue with the word "PACKARD" in orange. Within a few years, there were glowing messages the length and breadth of the continent.

Throughout the United States neon put some razzle-dazzle into the lack-lustre years of the Depression. However, after the Second World War, as plastic became more prevalent, neon's popularity died out. Then, ten years ago, MONA opened, and neon was fashionable again. Vintage motel billboards, burned–out topless bar signs, and outmoded movie marquees, once destined for the scrap heap, were painstakingly salvaged and restored.

Perhaps William Ramsay, alone in his chemistry lab, had a premonition – a hot pink and turquoise vision of the future – when he decided to name his colourless, odourless discovery the Greek for "new".

It is ironic that Nobel's century should have begun with the notion that discovery was at an end, but it is fitting that it should close with a new understanding of the centrality of our relationship to nature, and consequently of our relationship to one another as nature's guests.

JOHN C. POLANYI, 1986

In 1898 William Ramsay liquefied fifteen litres of argon gas and allowed it to boil, a process called fractionation. The first "fraction" to boil off contained neon; the last contained krypton and xenon, which are both heavier than argon.

Chemistry has been evolving over the years towards an increase in complexity and in diversity, from molecules to materials, from structures to architectures, from properties to functions. Thus, beyond the molecule one sees the emergence of a supramolecular chemistry, a chemistry of organized assemblies, of systems and of functions. In addition to the exploration of the interface with molecular biology, there lies the promise of exploring abiotic, non-natural species which possess a desired chemical or physical property. All this opens wide the door to the creative imagination of the chemist at the meeting point of chemistry with biology and physics, expressing the basic essence of chemistry: not only to discover but to invent; like art, to create!

The impact of science on society is raising more and more insistently the question of its responsibility. The scientist is first of all responsible to the truth and only thereafter to the world at that particular moment in history. Ethics is a relative notion and ethical evaluations change with time and location. Pursuit of knowledge and truth must supercede present consideration on what nature, life or the world are or should be, for our vision of today can only be a narrow one, and we have no right to switch out the lights of the future.

JEAN-MARIE LEHN, 1987

Hong Kong at night is a blaze of neon colours, as is New York's Time Square and Las Vegas's Strip. An electric discharge through neon, mixed with mercury or krypton, produces intense light at low temperature and low cost. Fluorescent lamps also use inert gas.

Adolf von Baeyer

Although Adolf von Baeyer did not invent blue jeans, he did create the dye that makes them blue. Even as a child he was intoxicated by indigo's "strange behaviour and peculiar odour".

Adolf's brilliance as a chemist revealed itself early. At twelve years old he discovered a new sulphide of copper. He studied chemistry at the University of Heidelberg under Robert Bunsen, who had just invented his famous burner. At age twenty-five Baeyer got a modest teaching position at a technical academy in Berlin. There he began experimenting with uric acid, from which he derived a substance he called barbituric acid in honour of a girlfriend whose name was Barbara.

At thirty Baeyer began investigating the chemical properties of indigo, an obsession that would occupy him for nearly twenty years. He discovered accidentally that by heating the dye with finely divided zinc metal he could disclose its chemical skeleton. He became the first to manufacture the dye artificially, which caused a sensation among organic chemists. In 1883 Baeyer announced he had found the location of every atom in the indigo molecule.

Based on Baeyer's work, a synthetic indigo eventually was made from aniline and acetic acid. This development had worldwide repercussions. By the end of the nineteenth century, German chemical factories – many staffed by Baeyer's former students – were edging out the huge indigo plantations; in Bengal alone some half a million acres had been used for raising the indigo plant.

Baeyer's discoveries also led to the

One of Adolf von Baeyer's former students, who was also a Nobel Committee member, wrote, "Baeyer has worked in all possible fields of organic chemistry. Everywhere his work has broken new ground. There is scarcely one of his innumerable papers which does not contain some original idea or some new method."

production of other dyes, including a purple indigo derivative containing two bromine atoms that is identical to that secreted by certain snails.

At the age of forty Baeyer became professor of chemistry at the University of Munich, where he remained until his eightieth year, teaching virtually all of Germany's top chemists. So extraordinary were his accomplishments, that on his fiftieth birthday Baeyer was granted a hereditary patent of nobility, a privilege that allowed him to add the prefix *von* to his name.

In 1905 Baeyer won a Nobel Prize for "his researches on organic dyestuffs and hydroaromatic compounds". When illness prevented him from attending the presentation ceremony, the German ambassador to Sweden served as his stand-in. A member of the Nobel Committee noted that even at the age of seventy Baeyer had "an unbelievable thirst for work". Indeed, he continued investigating the structure of molecules for another decade. When he finally retired, he was offered lucrative consulting jobs with various chemical firms. However, Baeyer refused to have anything to do with the commercial application of his work, or to make any profit from his discoveries.

Richard Willstatter, fellow chemist and Nobel laureate, once recalled Baeyer's face as expressing "clarity, repose, and mental strength". He added that, "the blue eyes were expressive, penetrating, brilliant". It is a shame Willstatter did not specify the exact shade of Baeyer's remarkable eyes.

Could the cowboy have conquered the American West without blue jeans? The trousers, which became a worldwide uniform for men and women during the 1960s, get their colour from Baeyer's discovery of synthetic indigo dye.

Marie and Irène Curie

_1911, 1935_   _Two Generations_

Pierre Curie, Marie's husband, was killed in an accident on a Paris street in 1906. Ahead of her lay a long and distinguished career as a research scientist. She became the first woman to teach at the Sorbonne, and turned her efforts towards trying to isolate pure radium. In 1911 she was awarded a second Nobel Prize "in recognition of her services to the advancement of chemistry by the discovery of the elements radium and polonium, by the isolation of radium and the study of nature and compounds of this remarkable element".

Her older daughter, Irène, accompanied Mme Curie to Stockholm for the ceremony. Twenty-four years later, Irène and her husband Frédéric Joliot were awarded a Nobel Prize in Chemistry "in recognition of their synthesis of new radioactive elements", artificial isotopes that act as "tracers" in the diagnosis of certain diseases.

During the Second World War, Mme Curie showed army medical officers how to use radiology to find shrapnel, and helped outfit ambulances with portable X-ray equipment. After the War she worked with students, and promoted the medical use of radiology.

At the dedication of the Institut du Radium, which Mme Curie struggled to build, she described her new laboratories as "holy dwellings". She said, "They are the temples of the future, of wealth and well-being. It is there that humanity grows bigger, strengthens and betters itself. It learns there to read in the works of nature, works of progress and universal harmony, whereas its own works are too often those of barbarity, fanaticism and destruction."

Marie Curie, here with daughters Eve and Irène, had enormous persistence; once she decided what a problem was, she solved it. Eve grew up to become a concert pianist and to write a biography of her mother; Irène became a scientist like her parents.

However, Mme Curie could not afford the radium to use in her laboratories. American women raised money and bought one ounce for her, and Marie Curie sailed to the United States in 1921 to accept the gift, and to receive eleven honorary degrees. The latter occasions turned out to be painful because the long sleeves of the silk academic robes irritated her hands, severely damaged by radiation.

Marie Curie died on 4 July 1934 of leukaemia. Of his friend, Albert Einstein had said, "Marie Curie is, of all celebrated beings, the only one whom fame has not corrupted."

Above
Not only did the work of the Joliot-Curies advance pure science, but, as the Nobel Committee predicted, "physiologists, doctors and the whole of suffering humanities hope to gain from your discoveries remedies of inestimable value". During the Second World War, Joliot smuggled his supply of heavy water to England, where it was used by the British to try and develop an atomic weapon.

Right
The study of renal flow in human kidneys is made possible by introducing radioactive elements into the system. Artificial isotopes act as "tracers" to help in the diagnosis of certain diseases. These indicators show up, even in the smallest quantities, in X-rays.

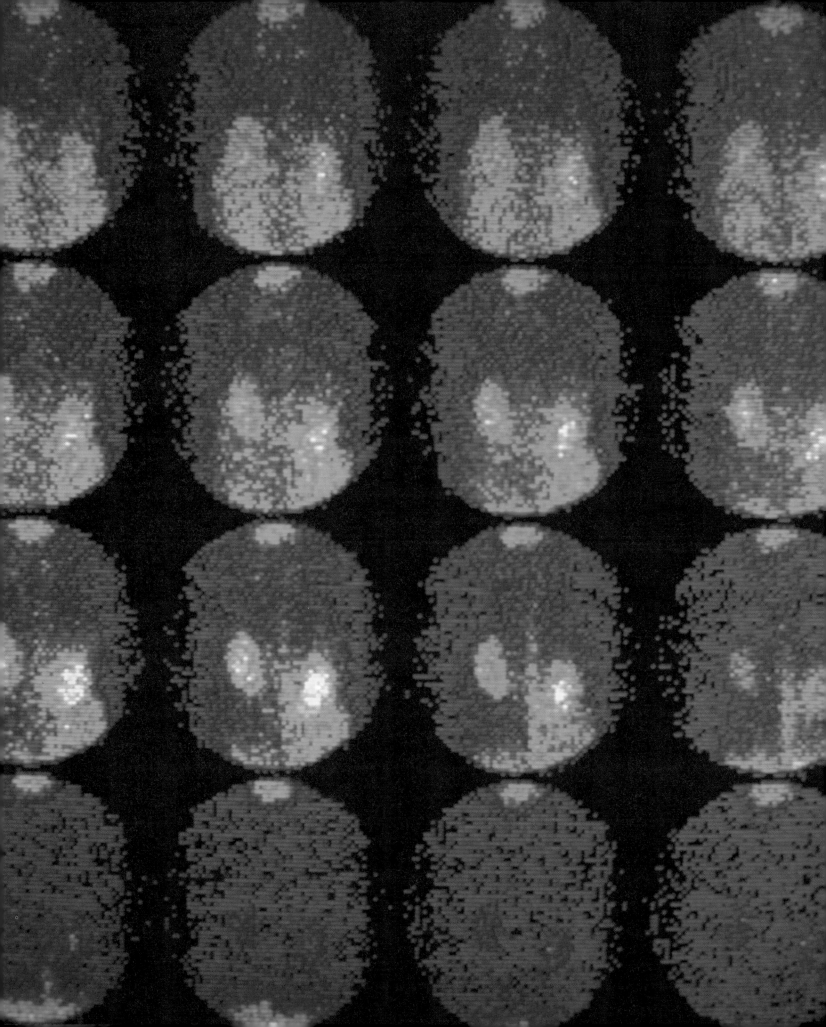

Paul Sabatier

Hydrogenator

The margarine on the table, the perfume behind her ear, and the detergent in the washing machine became possible when Paul Sabatier, a French chemist, began hydrogenating organic compounds. Edible fats, lingering scents, and deep-cleaning suds are just three of the hundreds of applications of Sabatier's process in use today, mostly in the preparation of pharmaceuticals.

Sabatier took up organic chemistry in the 1890s. He became interested especially in the catalytic processes involved in hydrogenation, through which unsaturated organic compounds become saturated. Unsaturated compounds can combine chemically; saturated ones usually do not. At the time, standard catalytic agents were expensive – platinum and palladium. Sabatier was able to produce a fully hydrogen-saturated compound using relatively inexpensive nickel as the catalyst. In his method, nickel forms a fleeting association with hydrogen, and with an unsaturated substance that then receives the hydrogen into a more permanent bond.

Soon after it was discovered, Sabatier's process was applied to convert low-melting fats into more saturated, higher-melting, and thus "hardened", substitutes for butter. It was a discovery of immense practical value.

Sabatier continued to be devoted to theoretical research, and so took out only a few patents on his discoveries.

For his work, Sabatier was awarded the 1912 Nobel Prize. In his Stockholm lecture, he said, "For the last fifteen years, this idea of mine on the mechanism of catalysis has never left me, and it is to the inferences drawn from it that I

As a boy in southern France, Paul Sabatier had a lively curiosity and teachers noted his keen intelligence. He was a hard-working student who said, "I study most the subject I like least." His Nobel Prize was shared with the French chemist Victor Grignard.

owe all my useful results. Theories cannot claim to be indestructible. They are only the plough which the ploughman uses to draw his furrow and which he has every right to discard for another one, of improved design, after the harvest."

Let us hope that the high intellectual capacities of humans can also be brought to bear to help world societies understand that unless the current excessive level of economic exploitation is replaced with sustainable economics, the future of our finite world will be rather dismal, despite all of its inspiring scientific and technological advances.

JEROME KARLE, 1985

Right
Perfume has been made for centuries from lavender fields such as this one in Norfolk, England. Sabatier's discoveries played a key role in modern perfume production.

Richard Willstatter

1915   *Plant Pigments Pioneer*

"Of genius there is no dearth," Richard Willstatter once said, "but character is a rare article." The German chemist had both.

As a young child in Nuremberg, Richard showed such extraordinary promise in mathematics, literature, and languages that he was recommended for one of the most prestigious schools in Munich. The school, however, turned him down because he was Jewish. Undeterred, Richard decided he must narrow his interests to "a one-sided life occupation," and opted for chemistry. He obtained his PhD in 1894 at the age of twenty-two.

An intellectual with a profound feeling for his Jewish heritage, Willstatter was to encounter more and more virulent forms of anti-Semitism. In 1924, for example, while professor of chemistry at the University of Munich, he discovered that a colleague whom he had appointed was turning down Jewish applicants for teaching positions. Willstatter promptly resigned in protest.

After Hitler came to power, everything worsened. Willstatter, by then one of the most renowned organic chemists in the world, was offered research and teaching jobs in the United States and Great Britain, but unwisely turned them down. At the end of 1938 he was ordered to the Nazi concentration camp Dachau, but when the police came to arrest him, his housekeeper managed to keep them from searching the garden where Willstatter was hiding.

A few months later he was captured by the Gestapo while attempting to escape from Germany by rowing across Lake Constance. This time the Swiss ambassador interceded on his behalf, and Willstatter was allowed to go on to Switzerland. There, a former student gave him the use of a villa near Locarno, where he remained until his death in 1942, ten days short of his seventieth birthday.

It was Willstatter's belief that "life is definitely a chemical process to which the passkey is the study of enzymes". In 1905, while teaching at the Federal Institute of Technology in Zurich, he began using nettle leaves to study the role of chlorophyll in photosynthesis, the process in plant cells whereby the energy of sunlight transforms carbon dioxide and water into sugar, starch and oxygen. At the time it was thought that a single plant could have numerous kinds of chlorophyll. Willstatter demonstrated that there is only one basic chlorophyll structure, consisting of two nearly identical components: blue-green chlorophyll "a" and yellow-green chlorophyll "b". This meant that photosynthesis uses a universal set of biochemical reactions.

Willstatter did not receive his 1915 Nobel Prize – "for research on colouring matter in the vegetable kingdom, principally on chlorophyll" – until 1920 because all award ceremonies were suspended during the First World War.

Although a mountain-climbing accident had left him exempt from military service during the First World War, Willstatter contributed to the war effort by developing a gas mask that used a triple layer of active absorbents.

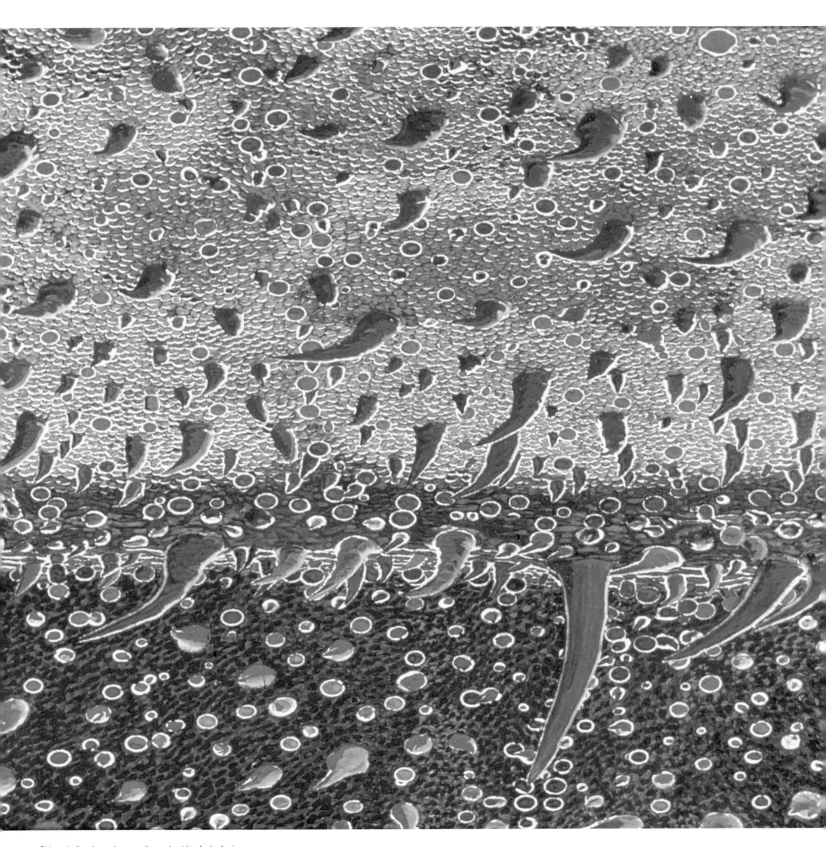

Chlorophyll – shown here on the underside of a leaf – is the green colouring matter in plants. Willstatter's major contribution to chemistry was the discovery that there is only one basic chlorophyll structure.

Walter Haworth and Paul Karrer

What has six carbon, eight hydrogen, and six oxygen atoms, is arranged in a five-sided ring, and has three short branches? Why, vitamin C, of course.

In the early 1930s Walter Haworth, a chemistry professor at the University of Birmingham in England, began investigating what was then known as hexuronic acid. Nobel Prize-winner Albert Szent-Györgyi previously had isolated the substance from paprika as well as from animal adrenal glands. By 1932 Haworth had not only established its molecular structure, but, in recognition of its ability to prevent and cure scurvy, had renamed it ascorbic acid, or vitamin C.

In 1937 Haworth received the Nobel Prize for his work with vitamin C and carbohydrates. The presenter of the award pointed out that by synthesizing vitamin C, Haworth had made possible its artificial production, " . . . a thing of very great importance in the case of vitamins which do occur in nature only in a state of very great dilution".

Haworth's interest in chemistry had been sparked when, as a fouteen-year-old boy in Lancashire, he dropped out of school to work in a linoleum factory managed by his father. He became so fascinated with the dyes the factory used that he found a tutor and got himself admitted to the University of Manchester, where he graduated with first-class honours in chemistry.

Like his fellow 1937 Nobel Prize-winner, the Swiss chemist Paul Karrer, Haworth began doing vitamin research after years spent working with polymer carbohydrates. In 1930 Karrer, director of the Chemical Institute in Zurich, formulated the structure of beta-carotene, a compound in carrots, finding it consisted of two symmetrical parts, each the mirror image of the other. Knowing that carotene is converted by the human body into vitamin A, Karrer extracted the substance from fish oil and established its molecular configuration as well: twenty carbon, thirty hydrogen, and one oxygen atom arranged in a six-sided ring, with three small molecules attached at two points, and a long zigzag chain attached at a third point. This turned out to be one-half of the beta-carotene molecule fastened to a molecule of water. While Haworth was the first person to synthesize a vitamin (vitamin C), Karrer was the first to describe the structure of one (vitamin A).

Karrer went from working with vitamin A directly to vitamin B2. Taking 100 tons of whey, he managed to extract a minuscule amount of the yellow water-soluble pigment that at the time was called lactoflavin. He deduced its formula, and in 1935 synthesized what was to become known as riboflavin, or vitamin B2.

In 1938, a year after receiving the Nobel Prize for his investigations into carotenoids, flavins, and vitamins A and B2, Karrer synthesized vitamin E, and immediately after did the same with vitamin K.

Both Haworth, who died on his sixty-seventh birthday, and Karrer, who lived to be eighty-two, were respected by their peers as much for their kindness as for their brilliance, and both left the world very much vitamin-enriched.

The important scientific discoveries in the first half of this century have supported the incredible evolution of science through the generalized understanding of nature. However, now that we are in a time when successive occurrence of revolutionary discoveries can hardly be expected, it would be better to hope for advancement in the opposite direction. This means that we should strive to understand the special properties of nature.

It would be interesting, for instance, to study how the generality of mathematics is specialized in nature, or how a general physical property can be actually realized in the field of chemistry. To analyze how special substances with biological qualities are to be located among the generality of chemistry is an already apparent field of science.

It should be evident that new sets of values are required for conducting scientific research. It can be stressed that the recognition of specificity in nature is essential to future science and culture. May the value of science continue to be kept universal by the strenuous effort of humankind!

KENICHI FUKUI, 1981

Artturi Virtanen

A lifelong resident of Helsinki, chemist Artturi Ilmari Virtanen was well acquainted· with the long and dark winters of northern Europe. Grass and clover had to be stored in silos for months, during which time there was so much bacterial decay that as much as fifty percent of the fodder's nutrients were lost. Dairy cows that ate the silage produced milk and butter greatly lacking in vitamins A and B12.

At the age of twenty-six Virtanen became director of the Valio Laboratory of the Finnish Co-operative Dairy Association, where he began to look for ways to prevent stored crops from decomposing. The method he developed, called AIV after his initials, essentially involved adding hydrochloric and sulphuric acids to the fodder to prevent protein breakdown and fermentation. Cows that ate acid-preserved silage suffered no ill-effects, and delivered nutritious, good-tasting milk.

The AIV process was first tried on Finnish dairy farms in 1929. The results were so promising that other European countries soon started using it, and so eventually did cattle-ranchers and dairy farmers in the United States, although in modified form.

In 1945, Virtanen, then director of the Biochemical Research Institute in Helsinki, won the Nobel Prize "for his research and discoveries in the field of agricultural and nutrition chemistry,

After winning the Nobel Prize for finding a way to preserve fodder, Artturi Virtanen continued in research and in 1948 became president of the State Academy of Science and Arts in Finland. He also served on the United Nations Commission on Nutrition.

and particularly his method of preserving animal fodder''.

In the late 1950s Virtanen embarked on another research project to see whether cows fed a protein-free diet could still deliver nutritious dairy products. He believed that a cow's digestive system could take the nitrogen compounds in urea and ammonium salts and synthesize them into the amino acids in milk. His theory proved correct.

In colder climates, when hay and other feed has to be stored in silos for months, bacterial decay can cause as much as fifty percent of the nutrients to be lost. Virtanen's method, first tried in 1929, added hydrochloric and sulphuric acids to prevent fermentation. Today the process is used in a modified form all over the world.

Linus Pauling

Linus Pauling is the only person ever to win two unshared Nobel Prizes. Now ninety, he is once again a figure of controversy, as he was in the 1950s. Critics are not convinced by his theory that vitamin C is effective in warding off the common cold, in preventing cancer, and in curing AIDS. Pauling insists that it is. At his Linus Pauling Institute of Science and Medicine in Palo Alto, California, he has a staff of fifty trying to prove that he is right.

For forty years and more, Pauling has been an outspoken opponent of atomic weapons testing. In 1954 President Eisenhower announced that atomic energy should be limited to peaceful purposes, and discussions with the Soviets began. In March of that year, the United States set off a hydrogen bomb in the Pacific Ocean. It was 600 times more powerful than the atomic bomb dropped on Hiroshima, which had released energy equivalent to 20,000 tons of Alfred Nobel's explosive. Delegates from the four most powerful nations met in West Berlin to discuss atomic weaponry. The Soviets asked that those countries possessing nuclear bombs pledge never to use them.

That same year, Pauling was awarded the Nobel Prize in Chemistry "for applying the quantum theory to chemical bonding". He increased his efforts to end weapons-testing, and joined fifty-one other Nobel Prize-winners – mostly scientists – in issuing an alarming statement: "By total military use of weapons feasible today, the earth can be contaminated with radioactivity to such an extent that whole peoples can be annihilated . . . All nations must come to the decision to renounce force as a final resort of policy. If they are not prepared to do this, they will cease to exist."

It was the McCarthy Era and Pauling, denied his passport, appeared before a Senate Committee, swearing under oath that he was not a Communist, a crypto-Communist or a theoretical Marxist. One senator remarked that it was his impression that "it was the Communists who had followed Pauling's line". The scientist's passport eventually was returned. Later, Pauling told a young audience, "I believe that no human being should be sacrificed to the project of perfecting nuclear weapons that could kill hundreds of millions of human beings, could devastate this beautiful world in which we live."

Pauling's dogged efforts to halt atomic testing earned him the Nobel Peace Prize in 1962. He said in Oslo:

"We are privileged to have the opportunity of contributing to . . . the abolition of war and its replacement by world law. I am confident that we shall succeed in this great task; that the world community will thereby be freed not only from the suffering caused by war but also, through the better use of the earth's resources, of the discoveries of scientists, and of the efforts of mankind, from hunger, disease, illiteracy, and fear; and that we shall in the course of time be enabled to build a world characterized by economic, political, and social justice for all human beings and a culture worthy of man's intelligence."

I received the Nobel Prize in Chemistry just for doing work that I enjoyed. I had been having a good time carrying on chemical research. I valued the Peace Prize more because to me it meant that working for world peace had become respectable. This was, of course, a reflection of the difficult time that my wife and children and I had gone through during the McCarthy period.

The world in which we live is a wonderful place, the mountains and the oceans and the trees, and the animal life like the sea elephants down on the beach here just below my house, the quail out in the meadows, even the cows eating the grass — they are wonderful. Every human being should have the opportunity to appreciate and enjoy the wonders of the world. We should all work for a world in which the amount of human suffering is kept to a minimum. We need to work together to achieve a world in which scientists are striving to overcome disease, to decrease the amount of suffering. This is the way we should be spending our billions of dollars, not on militarism.

LINUS PAULING, 1954, 1962

Linus Pauling, who used molecular models to explain his theories, has said, "We may ask what the next step in the search for an understanding of the nature of life will be. I think that it will be the elucidation of the nature of the electromagnetic phenomena involved in mental activity in relation to the molecular structure of brain tissue."

Willard Libby

Ora and Eva May Libby were California apple ranchers with little education and five children. One of their sons, Willard, wanted to become a mining engineer. His parents encouraged him to apply to the University of California at Berkeley, and once there he became fascinated with chemistry. Libby went on to get his PhD in the field of low-energy radioactive nuclei.

After the United States entered the Second World War, Libby, then a Guggenheim Fellow at Princeton University, was invited to work on the Manhattan Project. His task was to separate uranium isotopes, essential components of an atomic bomb, by gaseous diffusion. In the 1950s President Eisenhower appointed Libby to the Atomic Energy Commission, where he dealt with problems relating to radioactive fallout from atom bombs. Eventually Libby became a chemistry professor at UCLA, and director of the Institute of Geophysics and Planetary Physics.

Libby's most valuable contribution was his work with carbon-14, the radioactive isotope. In 1960 he was awarded the Nobel Prize for his method of using carbon-14 "for age determination in archaeology, geology, geophysics, and other branches of science".

Indeed, it did seem that not much had happened in the last 70,000 years or so on which Willard Libby could not pin a date. He calculated that North America's last ice age had not ended 25,000 years ago as geologists had once supposed, but 10,000; he determined the age of the linen in which the Dead Sea Scrolls were found wrapped; he dated charcoal for a Stonehenge campsite;

corn cobs from a New Mexico cave; and bread baked in Pompeii on the day Mount Vesuvius erupted.

Libby's technique involved measuring the amount of carbon-14 in animal and plant material. The carbon-14 found in the air is formed by cosmic rays colliding with atmospheric nitrogen. Since all animals eat plants, all take in carbon-14. (Only about one in one-trillion carbon atoms is radioactive.) When a plant or animal dies, it no longer takes in carbon-14. The longer a plant or animal has been dead, the less carbon-14 it contains. Since the time it takes for any given amount to decay is known – each carbon-14 atom lives an average of 8,000 years before it decays – it is possible to calculate the age of a plant or animal tissue by its concentration of carbon-14.

Libby tested the accuracy of his methods by examining artifacts whose exact ages were already known. One was the funerary boat of King Sesostris of Egypt; another was a redwood tree, whose age could be confirmed by counting its annual rings.

Libby was known for his wide-ranging scientific interests: everything from lunar research to civil defence to earthquake protection. But his key interest remained the radiocarbon dating of geological and archaeological events. As he said in his Nobel lecture, he believed that determining the age of a thing would "help roll back the pages of history and reveal to mankind something more about his ancestors, and in this way perhaps about the future".

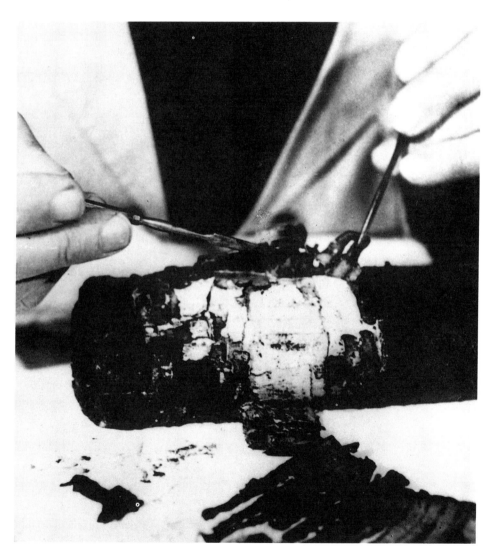

Left
During the 1950s, Willard Libby served on the Atomic Energy Commission. He was concerned with the problem of radioactive fallout from atom bombs. Earlier, he had worked on the Manhattan Project, the United States's programme to develop nuclear weapons.

Above
The linen wrapped around the Dead Sea Scrolls was used to determine their age. Libby built a special Geiger counter to prove his theory, and used the annual rings of redwood and fir trees to check its accuracy.

Frederick Sanger, Walter Gilbert, and Paul Berg

1980

Engineering the Future

Although each worked independently, the three scientists who shared the 1980 Nobel Prize for Chemistry all had a common goal: to discover the relationship between the chemical structure and the biological function of DNA, or genetic material. It had been known for almost three decades that the DNA molecule is arranged in the shape of a double helix. What the British biochemist Frederick Sanger, and the Americans Walter Gilbert and Paul Berg, focused on were nucleic acids, the so-called "rungs" that carry the code of genetic information in the twisted DNA "stepladder".

At the Nobel award ceremony, a member of the Royal Swedish Academy of Sciences pointed out that the work of the three biochemists "has already given benefits to mankind not only in the form of new fundamental knowledge but also in the form of important technical applications . . . "

One such application, the direct result of research done by Berg, was the manufacture of pharmaceuticals such as growth hormones and interferon, a protein that inhibits viral growth. Meanwhile, the techniques developed by both Sanger and Gilbert spawned an entirely new field: genetic engineering.

During the last decade, more than 1,000 drug companies have engaged in genetic research. Some recent achievements include poplar trees that have been altered genetically, enabling them to soar to maturity almost anywhere; pesticide-resistant corn and tomatoes; dairy cows that, thanks to a synthetic version of bovine growth hormone, have increased their milk output thirty percent; pigs with fifty percent less fat; rats that grow twice as big as their littermates; cloned cattle; "oncomice", or mice given a defective gene that makes them prone to breast cancer, providing a model for studying the disease.

Below left
As a young man, Frederick Sanger planned to become a doctor. He turned to biochemistry because "here was a way to really understand living matter and to develop a more scientific basis to many medical problems".

Below centre
Walter Gilbert met James D. Watson and Francis Crick at Cambridge when they were investigating the structure of DNA. In 1978 Gilbert founded Biogen, one of the earliest companies to specialize in genetic engineering.

Below
At first, Paul Berg's laboratory techniques caused scientists to fear that synthetic viruses might produce new, cancer-causing bacteria. Experiments were discontinued for a few years until it became clear that the controversy was unwarranted.

142

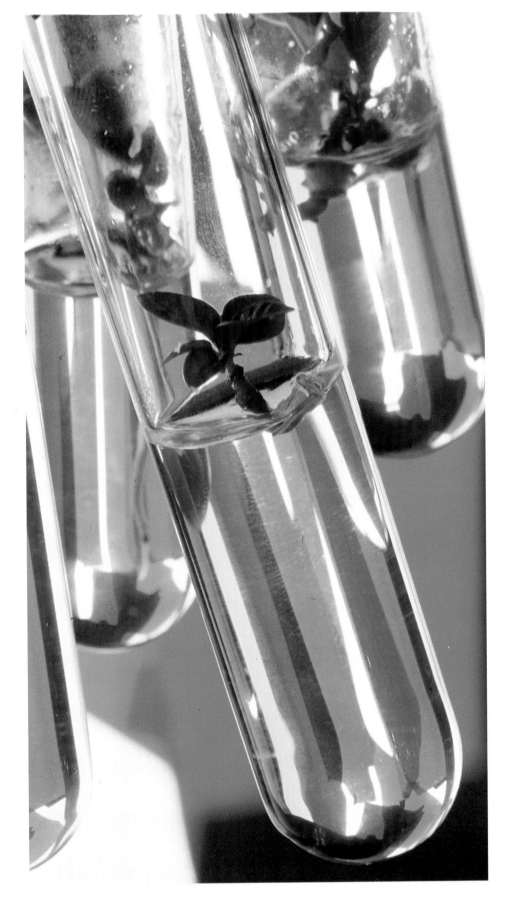

Another breakthrough that has a direct bearing on human disease is the ability of biochemists to extract trace amounts of rare naturally occurring substances and mix them with bacteria that then mass-produce crucial proteins in highly potent forms. This is then injected back into the body. Dwarfism is now being treated with human growth hormones; diabetes with human insulin instead of insulin taken from cattle and pigs; heart attacks and strokes with human protein that prevents blood clots. Eventually, it may be possible to extend the lives of AIDS patients by giving them temporary corrective genes that activate the immune system.

Today both Gilbert and Berg are still researching the molecular structure of genes at their respective universities. Sanger, now in his seventies, is one of the few scientists to have received two Nobel awards. In 1958 he was cited "for his work on the structure of proteins, especially that of insulin". In his Nobel lecture that year, Sanger expressed the hope that his findings on insulin would open the way to similar studies of the changes that proteins undergo in disease, so that his efforts might be "of more practical use to humanity". In the years since, Berg and Gilbert, and Sanger himself, have all helped to make that dream a reality.

Young seedlings, developed from tissue cultures, grow in test tubes. This technique enables prolific and rapid propagation of plants, and has also been used to free crops of virus infection.

Roald Hoffmann

Roald Hoffmann, who shared a Nobel Prize in 1981, won the award for his theory "concerning the course of chemical reactions". He is currently at Cornell University, and wrote the following for this book:

"In the twentieth century, science and technology transformed the world. The effect of science was surely felt before, in Alfred Nobel's time. But not until this century did the man-made and woman-made, the synthetic, the unnatural, truly contend with nature. Is this a time to praise or a time to fear?

"The world that men and women entered before there ever was such a thing as chemistry was not a romantic paradise, but a brutish, inimical environment in which men hardly outlived forty and women died earlier in childbirth. That natural world was transformed by our social institutions, our art, our science – but certainly not by science alone. We do not kill female children, nor keep slaves, nor let the sick die – all practices some societies once thought natural.

"Even though we have such a long way to go, we have changed our nature. Our lives are improved by detergents and synthetic fibres, and by a social web of human, constructed support. Our lives are enriched by Mozart and the Beatles, bringing to us a world of synthesized, transformed beauty and satisfaction.

"Yet we also use our transforming capacity destructively – to annihilate a quarter of the species in this world, to hurt our brothers and sisters. It is we who do this; there is no hiding behind a 'they'. This seems to be our dark side. We have a problem in finding a balance, with not letting our transforming nature run away; we seem to have difficulty in co–operating with our own world.

"In the tradition I come from, the Jewish tradition, there is a concept that is relevant to this theme of natural/unnatural. It is *tikkun*. The word literally means repair – of a shoe, but also of a soul, of the world. The sense is of change by human intervention. So the word's meaning shades over to transformation. *Tikkun olam* – the transformation of the world by human beings – is more than a salvaging; it is a making of our future consistent with what we are given.

"Friends, it is not given to us not to make new things – be they molecules, a sculpture, or desegregation plans. We are sentenced by our nature to create. But we do have a choice, to fashion this world in consonance with the best in us. Or the worst. One can doubt about whether our transformations are of human value. But there can be no doubt as to what they should be."

Roald Hoffmann was born in Poland, and in the Second World War his family was forced into a labour camp. In 1942, his father smuggled the boy and his mother out, and they hid in a schoolhouse attic for the rest of the War. The Nobel Committee said of Hoffmann's accomplishment, "From your theoretical work new tools have emerged of the greatest importance for the design of chemical experiments."

These days, when a discovery is made, the public usually asks what harm it will do. It is true that in an overpopulated world, any discovery of really significant proportions is likely to do harm as well as good. We must therefore carefully weigh benefit and harm against one another.

It is also true that the more we know, the less of it can be applied without danger. That, however, closes the circle. The smaller the fraction of knowledge that we are allowed to apply, the more we have to know. As with any living being, where establishment of equilibrium means death, if the growth of knowledge ceases, it will be the end of culture and society.

MANFRED EIGEN, 1967

Herbert A. Hauptman

Dr Herbert A. Hauptman shared the 1985 Nobel Prize with Jerome Karle "for their outstanding achievements in the development of directing methods for the determination of crystal structures". Dr Hauptman wrote the following about his speciality for this book:

"Anyone at all familiar with the history of science must surely marvel at the wonderful accomplishments of the masters – for example, Archimedes, Galileo, Newton, and Einstein, to name only a few. Yet, just as surely, one would have to marvel as well at the extraordinary pace of scientific progress in the twentieth century, and the pace appears to quicken with each passing year.

"The history of my own science, X-ray.crystallography, is not atypical. It is one of the sciences where it is possible to pinpoint the exact moment of its creation. It was in 1912 in Munich when the German physicists Friedrich and Knipping, at the instigation of Max von Laue, performed the landmark experiment which demonstrated the scattering of X-rays by crystals. Although it was soon recognized that this experiment provided the key to the determination of molecular structures, no one could possibly have anticipated the phenomenal progress which this science was destined to make in the next seventy-five years. Nor, even more importantly, could anyone have guessed the crucial role which the field of X-ray diffraction would play in a variety of disciplines – chemistry, physics, mineralogy, materials science, biology, and the other life sciences, as well as in mathematics. Thus, one may now understand the physical properties of materials in terms of molecular structure, or deepen our understanding of the course of chemical reactions by knowledge of the structures of the reactants.

"Again, by relating the molecular structures of biologically interesting materials to their biological activities one gets a better understanding of life processes. In this way one may, for example, design drugs – which will have specified properties and a minimum of adverse side-effects – more intelligently than would otherwise be possible. In short, greatly improved therapies for the prevention and cure of disease are now realized with ever increasing frequency, all a consequence of the watershed experiment of von Laue, Freidrich and Knipping less than eighty years ago.

"Another aspect of the growth of the science of X-ray diffraction which should also be stressed is the role which mathematics played in its development. The routine determination of the structures of the so-called small molecules, those consisting of fewer than some 200 non-hydrogen atoms, has been made possible by the creation of the "direct methods" which enable crystallographers to go directly from the observable diffraction pattern to the crystal or molecular structure. The development of the direct methods themselves is critically dependent on an appropriate mathematical machinery.

"In summary, then, the science of X-ray crystallography, born in this century, is seen to lie at the intersection of many fields of scientific endeavour. It has not only itself benefited from this interaction but has also contributed in essential ways to the further development of these diverse disciplines."

Herbert A. Hauptman's hobby of constructing polyhedrons from stained glass requires skills similar to those used in his work on molecular structures: the ability to think in three dimensions, and to calculate with enormous precision.

Donald J. Cram

1987

Donald J. Cram, who shared the Nobel Prize in 1987, realized that a certain molecule, called crown ether because it is shaped like a ring or bracelet, used the "hole" in the middle to "grab" other compounds. For example, in the human body this molecule will "seize" a protein molecule from a meat sandwich, and then break the chemical bonds of that protein molecule, converting it into human muscle. A fellow scientist explained the feat: "This is the first chemical step towards understanding an area called molecular recognition."

For The Nobel Century, *Dr Cram looks back on our century and forward to the year 2000:*

"I was born in 1919, but since my awareness of memory and consciousness of the world did not commence until about 1925, my firsthand experience of the twentieth century spans about sixty-five years. I was raised by people well acquainted with, and shaped by, the first quarter of this century, and in a rural setting (Vermont) far from the mainstream. The values of the period from 1900 to 1925 inculcated during my maturation gave me more than a little acquaintance with that time. My sixty-five-year love affair with reading books, particularly those dealing with social anthropology and history, has left me with some basis of comparison of our century with prior centuries. As a scientist trained by research experience in the semi-empirical field of organic chemistry, I have learned to differentiate between what is known, what is partially known, what is ambiguous, and what is unknown. My final qualification for commenting on the twentieth century is an optimistic approach to anticipating certain things that will happen in its last decade. If I have a faith, it is that many experiments will turn out well, and that the human species has the choice and, by and large, the will and inclination to exercise that choice, roughly in the direction of serving collective interests.

"The twentieth century above all has been the 'century of science'. Scientists have discovered and expanded the knowledge that has allowed engineers, inventors, doctors, and business people to put chemical and physical tools in our collective hands that have revolutionized the lives of about half the people in the world. Many in the other half aspire to acquire these tools for themselves. These tools removed much of the harshness from the human experience, preserved our offspring, extended our lives, provided time for education, and gave us more control over our environment than ever before.

"In previous centuries, death paid many visits to the average family, particularly with respect to infants. Now tools are available to provide life expectancies at birth of as much as seventy years. The green revolution allowed this planet to feed a rapidly expanding population. Acceptable birth control methods are now available to control that expansion. Many diseases have been completely eradicated, and many more can be controlled. We have instantaneous audible and visual communication, and fast transportation. We have computers that leverage our intellectual output, that help us model and monitor physical phenomena, and that calculate the formerly incalculable. The genetic codes have been broken and the genes, themselves, are being located and repaired. 'No-win weapons' have kept us out of world wars for nearly half a century. Atom splitting can provide unlimited amounts of energy.

"Before the finish of this century, I predict that AIDS will be curable, the immune system will be well understood and subject to stimulation, and faulty genes will be repairable. New ways of storing and recovering energy will be available for fuelling transportation in lightweight vehicles. Some forms of cancer will be curable. New ways of purifying water will be available. Much more biology will be reduced to chemistry and physics, and thereby subject to rational control and correction.

"Advances in science made these things possible: practical people reduced the attendant knowledge to use, and entrepreneurs brought the products to receptive public marketplaces. Although each link in the chain is necessary, a faith that such things as those listed above are possible and desirable had to precede their realization. The twentieth century could well be thought of by future historians as the age when science went to work for the general welfare. The Nobel Awards did much to stimulate and celebrate those changes for the better."

Donald Cram's approach to science, according to one associate, is characterized by "enthusiasm and novelty". Some fifty of his PhD students have spread his ideas throughout the international chemistry community. Many chemists studying molecular recognition have spent some time in Cram's laboratory.

This polarised light micrograph shows crystals of AZT (azidothymidine), the antiviral drug used to treat AIDS and HIV patients.

Elias J. Corey

In his laboratory at Harvard University, Elias J. Corey makes something valuable out of almost nothing. His great invention, which won the 1990 Nobel Prize, is a technique for finding, among millions of possibilities, the simplest steps for assembling complex organic molecules. The Royal Swedish Academy of Sciences noted that "organic synthesis, that is the production of complicated organic compounds using simple and cheap starting material, is one of the prerequisites of our civilization". Shortly after he heard that he had won the Nobel Prize, Corey made a few comments about his work:

"In nature, there are hundreds of millions of different molecules, and in each living person there are millions of molecules whose interaction and whose functions basically allow the life process as we know it.

"In the twentieth century, medicine has made tremendous advances so that for many illnesses, a physician can prescribe a medicine to effect a cure. Almost all of those medicines are comprised of synthetic compounds discovered by chemists and mass-produced in factories for the pharmaceutical industry.

"Most medicines today are dependent on synthetic, organic compounds because these are very precise substances: they can change the course of a disease; they can remove its symptoms; and they can cure. Antibiotics are used to treat infection, and most antibiotics in use now are synthetic. They are made not by nature but by humans. They are manmade compounds, and chemical synthesis is involved in every step of their development.

"When a research project begins, molecules are synthesized according to some theory or idea that they might have an appropriate biological activity – for instance, to kill certain micro-organisms. They are tested, and if they *do* have that biological activity, then those molecules are selected for clinical studies and large-scale manufacture. At almost every step in that process, synthetic chemistry is essential.

"Synthetic chemistry is really at the heart of chemistry; and chemistry, especially the chemistry of carbon compounds, is the basic language of all life."

Right
This electron micrograph shows a single bacterium (lower centre) in the process of division and the remains of a second (top) which has undergone lysis (bursting) due to the effects of antibiotics.

Below
At the Stockholm banquet in December 1990, Elias J. Corey (left) was seated next to Queen Silvia of Sweden. On her other side was professor Lars Gyllensten, Chairman of the Board of The Nobel Foundation.

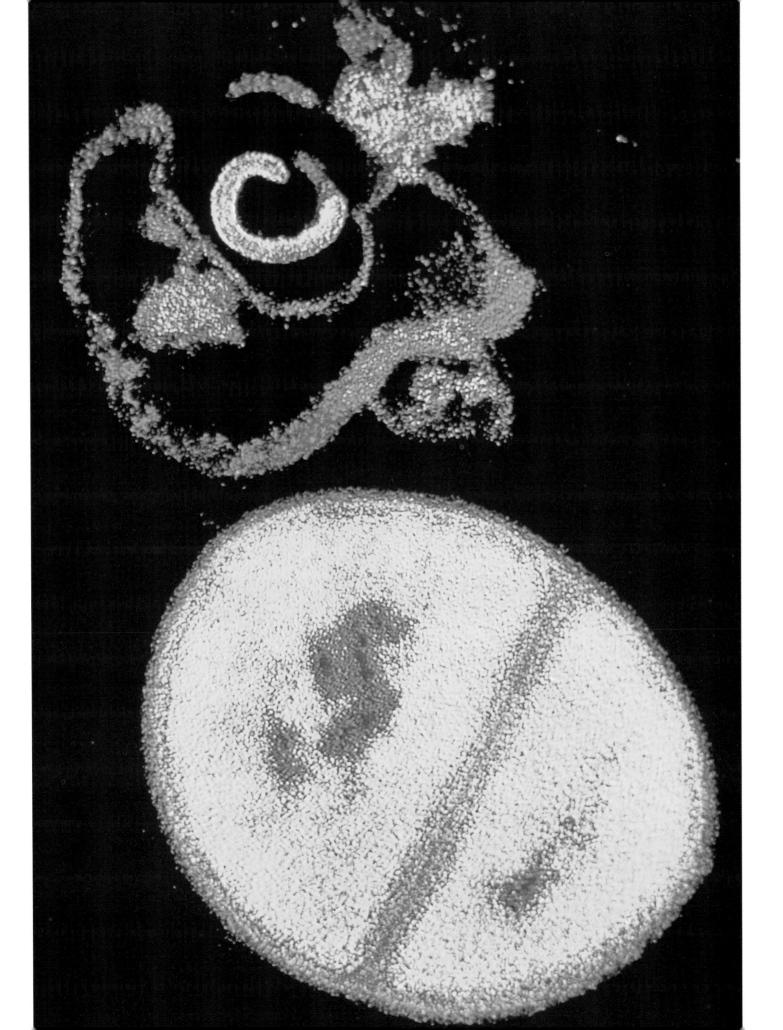

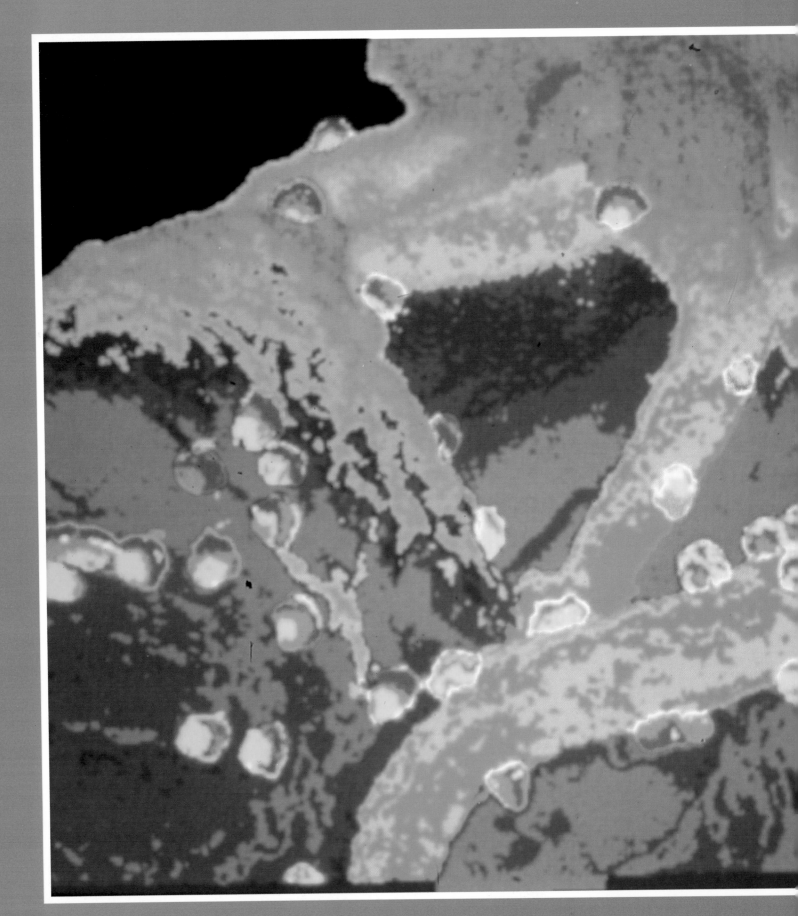

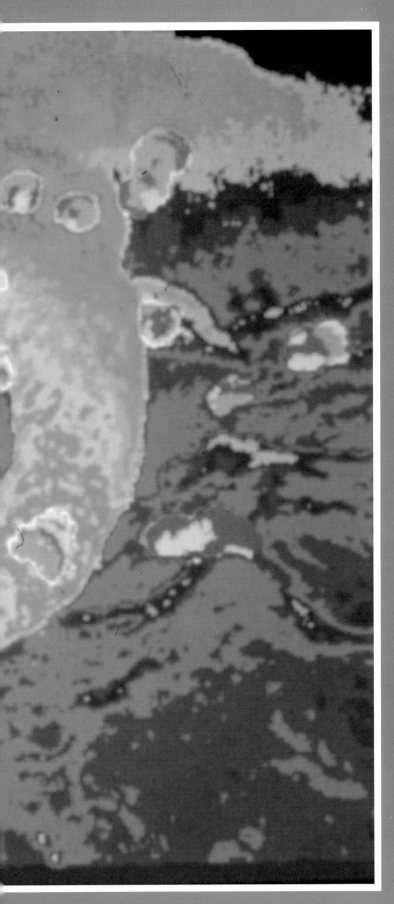

4 PHYSIOLOGY
OR
MEDICINE

A microscope provides a colourful image of the HIV virus.

Introduced by Douglas Gasner

On Christmas night, in 1891, a little girl lay dying of diphtheria in a Berlin clinic. Dr Emil von Behring injected an experimental antitoxin derived from the diphtheria bacillus into the child. The girl's swift recovery seemed a miracle. Within three years, 20,000 children in Berlin had been inoculated with a vaccination against diphtheria.

For this remarkable achievement Behring was awarded the first Nobel Prize in Physiology or Medicine in 1901. Along with a Japanese scientist, Shibasaburo Kitasato – who was unfortunately left out of the Prize – Behring showed that a substance called antikoper could protect the body against bacteria. That substance is now known as antibody, and Behring used it to turn the tide against the child-killer diphtheria.

Experimenting first on guinea pigs, which were to become the prototypical research animal, Behring found that after being given injections with weakened diphtheria germs, the guinea pigs' blood manufactured a substance to combat the toxins – an antitoxin. Behring injected this into other guinea pigs that had been exposed to full-strength diphtheria. They did not succumb to the disease, proving Behring's theory that toxins could be neutralized.

For the rest of the century the course of immunology was determined by the work of Paul Ehrlich and Elie Metchnikoff, the second of only two Russians who have won Nobel Prizes in Physiology and Medicine (the first went to Ivan Pavlov in 1904 for showing how the digestive system worked). Metchnikoff discovered the second half of the immune story: that white blood cells could fight bacteria. Ehrlich, who perfected the diphtheria antitoxin, proposed that bacterial toxins are bound to receptors on the surface of certain cells in the bloodstream, and in this lock-and-key fashion are ''grabbed up'' and taken out of action.

The first glimmer of understanding about how the human immune system works began in 1797 with Edward Jenner's vaccinations against smallpox. Early in this century, the Nobel Prizes went to scientists who, like Behring, had done much of their work in the previous decades. They were determined to conquer the infectious diseases that

were taking a vast toll in human lives. Few families escaped one or more of the dreadful illnesses: tuberculosis, malaria, syphilis, cholera, childbirth fever, gangrene, leprosy, influenza, dysentery, and diphtheria. Despite the fact that bacteria and other micro-organisms had been studied since the early days of the microscope 200 years earlier, scientists were just beginning to understand that these tiny ''bugs'' could cause fatal diseases. The prevailing theory was that infection came from the air.

When new, more powerful microscopes were trained on the fluids and discharges of diseased bodies, there was a flurry of discoveries. Bacteria were shown to be the cause of certain infections, offering doctors a new line of attack to focus on the organisms, rather than palliatives directed at symptoms.

The leading cause of death in Europe at the time was tuberculosis, and its cause was the first to be understood. Robert Koch, a German physician and bacteriologist, announced in 1882 that he had isolated the bacterium that triggers tuberculosis. He was given the Nobel Prize in 1905, and in his Nobel lecture said that ''quite an important beginning has been made''.

The methods Koch invented for his experiments are still used today in medical microbiology, but while his techniques for culturing micro-organisms persist, it is an assistant who probably is better known. G. R. J. Petri devised the shallow, round glass dish in which Koch grew his bacteria. Koch's efforts to grow and identify bacteria helped spawn the field of microbiology.

Biology is the science that underlies all the Nobel Prizes in Physiology or Medicine. It is a search by men to learn all they can about living beings – especially about themselves.

Unlike physics, discoveries in biology are not set in motion by grand upheavals in theory. They proceed, for the most part, in small steps. So far, the only exceptions have been in the work of Gregor Mendel, the founder of genetics, and Charles Darwin, founder of the theory of evolution. Their discoveries changed forever the way we look at ourselves; unfortunately their dramatic theories were proposed

Above
Women manufacture penicillin in an ultra-modern factory at Speke, Liverpool, in 1954.

before the Nobel awards were being presented.

Mendel and Darwin laid the foundation for molecular biology, the study of such molecules of life as DNA, the substance of genes. Research in molecular biology has produced a biological revolution, a huge burst of understanding and insight into the inner workings of the human body. More Nobel Prizes have been awarded in molecular biology – eleven – than in any other field of Physiology or Medicine.

Mastery over much of the microbe world through the use of antibiotics – the bolstering of the immune system, fighting cancer, treating heart disease, and transplanting organs – have all led to Nobel Prizes. So have the discoveries of vitamins and such hormones as insulin.

Other Nobel Prizes have been given to scientists who explained how our eyes see and our ears hear, how our limbs move and our skin is able to feel. A veritable cascade of chemical messengers carry signals to and fro, bringing us information on everything we perceive in the world about us.

Researchers developed doctors' tools as diverse as the electrocardiogram, which charts the beat of the heart on paper or on a monitor, and computerized (CAT) scanners, which show the inside of the skull. Other scientists were singled out for Nobel Prizes because they unlocked the secrets of the cell, that sac of protoplasm that is the foundation of life. They found the answers to such questions as why members of the same family share certain traits; how the food we eat is changed into energy; and how a complete human being develops from its inconspicuous beginnings.

Still more discoveries that earned Nobel Prizes included blood-typing, which put transfusions on a scientific basis and greatly enhanced the safety of surgery. Tissue-typing was expanded, and increased the success of organ transplants. Monoclonal antibodies, the product of hybrid, half-immune, half-cancer cells, provided the basis for the most sensitive of all tests for detecting certain malignancies and infectious diseases, such as AIDS.

The exploration of cell biology began in earnest after the development of the electron microscope in the 1930s. In 1969, Max Delbrück, Alfred D. Hershey, and Salvador Luria were awarded a Nobel Prize for their observation of the way viruses attack living cells. In 1974, George E. Palade, Christian de Duve, and Albert Claude were given a Nobel Prize for providing the first detailed views of the cell structures known as organelles, the warehouses and factories of the chemical processes of life.

The idea that microscopic organisms could cause illness led to efforts to stop them with chemicals that would kill the organisms without harming normal body cells, or with serums that would boost the body's defences.

The development of antibiotics produced astonishing advances in medical treatment. German bacteriologist Gerhard Domagk's sulpha compounds challenged the invincibility of staph and strep bacteria, for which he was awarded a Nobel Prize in 1939. In 1945 the award went to Alexander Fleming, Ernst Chain, and Howard Florey for penicillin, and in 1952 to Selman Waksman for streptomycin. This capped medicine's fifty-year conquest of a large part of the microbial world.

As the "wonder drugs" were discovered and developed, the great mystery of biology – how the substances that Mendel had called "factors" carry traits and pass them on – began to be revealed. When it finally came, the crucial discovery was as unexpected as any major finding in biology – an imaginative leap, helped along with knowledge from the X-ray crystallography branch of physics, and the chemical bonding branch of chemistry.

The secret lay in a code, the genetic code. The key to breaking it came from a twenty-four-year-old American, James Watson, who was working in the Cavendish Laboratory in Cambridge, a hotbed of atomic physics. Watson's collaborator was Francis Crick, a former physicist.

Max Delbrück, who was instrumental in solving another part of the gene puzzle, compared the construction that

Watson and Crick devised to a "child's toy that you could buy at the dime store". It was an assembly of coloured balls and sticks put together over fifteen months of intense activity. It was also the model for DNA, the famous double helix, which splits apart and pulls in complementary chemicals to form an exact duplicate of itself – the long-sought repository of hereditary information. The secret code itself was revealed by the arrangement of five nitrogen-carbon-based chemicals called bases, any three of which were coded for a particular amino acid, the building blocks of proteins.

The groundwork for this discovery, which brought the 1962 Nobel Prize to Watson, Crick and Maurice Wilkins, for his X-ray crystallography of DNA, was laid down by earlier researchers who were also rewarded by the Nobel Committee. Thomas Hunt Morgan made discoveries about the role played by chromosomes in heredity, and received the 1933 Nobel Prize. Hermann Müller was given the 1946 Nobel Prize "for discoveries concerning genetic recombinant and the organization of the genetic material of bacteria". The

1959 award went to Severo Ochoa and Arthur Kornberg "for their discovery of the mechanisms in the biological synthesis of ribonucleic acid and deoxyribonucleic acid".

All those scientists were needed to establish the principles of modern genetics: that chromosomes, the strand-like fibres in the nucleus of cells, carry genes, and that genes transmit hereditary characteristics and direct the assembly of proteins within other parts of the cell outside the nucleus.

The discovery of the structure of DNA opened wide the field of molecular biology. In 1965, François Jacob, André Lwoff, and Jacques Monod found that genes not only code for proteins, they also regulate how much or how little protein a cell makes. In 1968, Robert Holley, Har Gobind Khorana, and Marshall Nirenberg were rewarded with a Nobel Prize because they showed how the gene's "language" assures that amino acids are inserted into protein molecules in the correct order. In 1975, David Baltimore, Howard Temin, and Renato Dulbecco received a Nobel Prize for finding out how the genetic code of certain viruses, like the one that causes AIDS, interacts with the genes of cells. In 1978, Danièl Nathans, Hamilton Smith, and Werner Arber were given the Nobel Prize for finding enzymes that "slice" DNA at specific locations – a discovery that led to genetic engineering.

Then, in 1983, Barbara McClintock, whose work on corn plants thirty-five years earlier had been the first to show that chromosomes exchange genetic information, received a Nobel Prize, and in 1989 the prize went to J. Michael Bishop and Harold Varmus, who had found that normal cells contain genes that can cause cancer if they malfunction.

This burst of creativity was perhaps the most productive two-and-a-half decades in biology ever experienced by mankind. When it reached its climax, all the major details about what the gene is – how it duplicates itself, how it expresses itself by making proteins and enzymes, and how it undergoes change through mutation – had been exposed.

Each step described above was based on knowledge that had been gained earlier, but occasionally a door opens on to the unknown. Consider the unexpected finding of Christiaan Eijkman, a Dutch physician who was working at a military hospital in Java at the turn of the century. Beriberi, a debilitating nerve disorder, was epidemic. Eijkman thought that it might be caused by bacteria, and in an experiment in which he fed chickens a diet of processed, polished rice from the hospital kitchen, produced symptoms similar to those of beriberi in humans.

Late in the experiment, his chickens unexpectedly recovered. Eijkman found they had been fed unpolished rice because a new cook refused to give the birds the same polished rice that was served to the military personnel. Eijkman reasoned there was something necessary to proper health in the unpolished rice that was not in the polished grain; subsequent trials with his chickens proved him right. The original mistake in the chickens' feeding regime led to the 1929 Nobel Prize, shared with Frederick Hopkins, for the discovery of deficiency diseases and the role of vitamins in preventing them.

Or consider another case involving Daniel Gajdusek, an American paediatrician and virologist. While doing research on viruses in Australia, Gajdusek heard about a strange disease that affected a Stone-Age tribe in the highlands of eastern New Guinea. He went to live among them, studying the fatal brain disorder they called *kuru*, which progressively incapacitated its victims.

Gajdusek realized that the symptoms of *kuru* were similar to those seen in a disease of sheep – scrapie – and he recognized that the disease was spread among the tribesmen through ritual cannibalism – they honoured their dead relatives by eating their brains. This led to Gajdusek's discovery of a new type of human disease caused by a new kind of infectious agent, a slow virus. He was awarded the 1976 Nobel Prize.

Unlike the discoveries of Gajdusek and Eijkman, most advances in biology are the result of a careful, pointed journey along a dark and winding route – like the one that established the principles of modern genetics. That was the route Francis Crick set out on when he turned from physics to biology. In his application for a research grant he wrote in 1947 that his work "might be called the chemical physics of biology". Crick was interested in the division "between the living and non-living".

In the century ahead, there are still cures to be found, and aspects of life, such as longevity, to be explored. Some basic questions in biology also remain: How did life begin? How do immature cells in the embryo become an eye or a hand? How does the brain learn to remember, and why does it seek an understanding of itself?

If scientists find the answers to these questions, there is always the possibility of another door opening on to something else unknown.

D.G.

Ronald Ross and Charles Laveran

1902, 1907   *In Pursuit of Malaria*

Long before malaria had a name, it had a reputation: it was the unseen agent of death described by Hippocrates in the fourth century BC, and the plague of French Legionnaires in the nineteenth. Even today – more than 100 years after its cause was discovered in an Algerian hospital – malaria, which takes its name from the Italian for "bad air", continues to infect 300 million people a year in the underdeveloped nations of the world. Between one and two million die, many of them African children. About ninety million new cases occur annually in more than 100 countries. In India alone, the annual death toll of this preventable killer is one million.

Early observers of malaria were quick to connect the outbreaks of fever and delirium with swampy or wet areas. The English called it "marsh poison", and the eighteenth-century Italian physicians who gave it its name had in mind the "bad air" that rose from the marshes around Rome.

How victims became infected remained a mystery until the discoveries of two colonial military careerists, one a French biologist, the other an English physician. Together they laid bare the cycle of parasitic invasion and incubation in which humans figure as unwitting secondary hosts.

Charles Louis Alphonse Laveran was a second-generation military medical investigator. He was sent to Algeria by the French army at the age of thirty-three to study malaria. In November 1880, while investigating the blood of a soldier suffering a malarial relapse, Laveran detected something new: in a previous sample from the same patient, Laveran had seen only crescent shapes;

in the new sample he saw only spherical bodies; and, to his amazement, they moved independently in the blood. "At the periphery of this body," he later wrote, "was a series of fine, transparent filaments that moved very accurately and beyond question were alive."

What Laveran saw was the malarial parasite, a protozoon – a one-celled animal rather than a bacterium as previously thought – in the second phase of its asexual reproductive cycle. It lives in red blood corpuscles, and Laveran's fellow scientists held its existence totally improbable. Not until 1885 was Laveran's discovery fully accepted by his peers, and the bacterial theory of malarial infection was abandoned.

It was another ten years before malaria's next riddle was solved by a poorly trained medical investigator, who would rather have been writing poetry.

Born in Nepal to a British Army officer and his wife, Ronald Ross hoped for a literary career but to satisfy his father trained as a physician and joined the Indian Medical Service in 1881. After a decade of indifferent doctoring and frustrated writing, Ross turned his attention to the question of how malaria was transmitted. On a visit to England in 1894, he was shown a sample of these protozoa by a doctor who shared with Ross a theory that malaria was transmitted from an infected person to an uninfected person by mosquitoes.

Although he was years behind the scientific community in his knowledge of slide preparation and blood-cell classifications, Ross examined one type of mosquito after another. He bred his own to insure they were malaria free, fed them blood from malarial patients, then dissected them to analyse the condition of their stomachs. Two years into his search, Ross found pigmented cysts in the stomach lining of the *Anopheles* mosquito, the first clear evidence that the parasite matures in the bodies of mosquitoes and is transmitted by them. The theory had turned out to be right. Ross immodestly assumed this had "solved the malaria problem". Of course it had not, but it had solved one of the central mysteries. Five years later, in 1902, Ross received the Nobel Prize for his diligence.

Laveran's Nobel Prize came five years later in 1907, honouring both his discovery and his continued work "on the role played by protozoa in causing diseases".

Left
Charles Laveran studied fresh blood drawn from living malarial patients, rather than the dried stain-samples used previously. In this way he was able to prove the existence of a malarial parasite in the blood stream of infected people, although his discovery was not immediately believed by his peers.

Below
Ronald Ross spent the last twenty years of his life working at the School for Tropical Medicine in Liverpool, at the British War Office, and then at the Ross Institute of Tropical Hygiene in London. He campaigned for mosquito destruction as the way to eradicate malaria.

Above right
The female *Anopheles* mosquito is the carrier of malaria, which resists new drugs almost as quickly as they are discovered. Resistance to chloroquine, the standard treatment, has become almost as widespread as the disease.

Right
This diagram from the Shell film "Malaria" shows how some *Anopheles* mosquitoes become infected by drinking the blood of someone with malaria, and subsequently pass the disease on to other people.

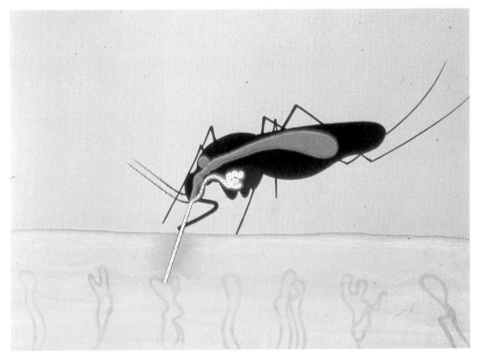

Robert Koch and Selman Waksman

1905, 1952

The Ancient Scourge

Darkling I listen; and for many a time
I have been half in love with easeful
*   Death,*
Called him soft names in many a mused
*   rhyme,*
To take into the air my quiet breath . . .

Tuberculosis, the so-called white plague, has been traced back to the Stone Age in Europe, and tubercular lesions have been discovered in Egyptian mummies dating to 3,700 BC. As recently as the nineteenth century, an estimated one-seventh of the world's population died from TB. One of them was the poet John Keats, who wrote the lines quoted above.

Two men – Robert Koch and Selman Waksman – received Nobel Prizes nearly half a century apart for their work in helping to eradicate the dreadful disease.

One of thirteen children, the German physician and bacteriologist Robert Koch grew up to be an avid chess player, an admirer of Goethe and a brilliant scientific investigator. Koch's first triumph was proving that the anthrax bacillus was the cause of anthrax, a disease affecting sheep and cattle, and sometimes humans. His discovery provided proof that bacteria could cause disease.

Koch next turned his attention to consumption, or tuberculosis. In 1882 he delivered a paper to the Berlin Physiological Society announcing that he had identified a tangible bacterium, *Mycobacterium tuberculosis*, as the causative organism. The finding showed beyond a doubt that tuberculosis was transmissable. It was Koch's most significant achievement.

Koch continued his research, and in 1890 announced that he had found a cure for tuberculosis. He was quickly proved wrong; in fact, the compound he had isolated, tuberculin, caused severe toxic reactions in the patients to which it was given. However, tuberculin did prove effective in diagnosis, particularly in bovine tuberculosis, and helped Koch to be awarded the 1905 Nobel Prize.

Another major breakthrough was made by the soil microbiologist Selman Waksman. Born in the Ukraine, Waksman emigrated to the United States in 1911 at the age of twenty-three. His first stop was a New Jersey farm, owned by relatives. The experience of farm life, he later said, inspired him to look to the soil "for an answer to the many problems that had begun to puzzle me about the cycle of life in nature".

By 1943 Waksman had been appointed professor of microbiology at Rutgers University. That same year a local poultryman brought some chickens to Waksman's laboratory; the farmer believed his birds had picked up an infection from something in the barnyard dirt. Waksman was able to identify the micro-organism causing the chickens' illness as a mould of the genus *Streptomyces*. He and his research team went on to show that streptomycin, an extract of this mould, was a powerful antibacterial agent.

In 1944 Waksman tested streptomycin on ten tubercular guinea pigs. All of them improved. Streptomycin was first used successfully on a human being on 12 May 1945. The antibiotic became commercially available in 1946, and was found to be extremely effective

against bacteria, particularly *Mycobacterium tuberculosis*, that were resistant to penicillin and sulpha drugs. When given streptomycin, patients with pulmonary tuberculosis coughed less, their lung lesions began to heal, their temperature returned to normal, and bacteria counts in their saliva declined. Waksman coined the term "antibiotic", meaning "against life", for those chemicals obtained from micro-organisms that kill bacteria.

Waksman's discovery of streptomycin won him the Nobel Prize in 1952. The presentation speech praised him as "one of the greatest benefactors of mankind". However, despite all the advances in treatment and prevention, tuberculosis is still the world's most prevalent communicable disease. Some two million people die from it each year, most of them in underdeveloped countries.

Scientific discoveries and their recognition by Nobel juries depend on chance, alertness to opportunities and "taste". In 1942, while studying the life cycle of bacterial viruses (phages), I was prompted to inquire into the mode of origin of bacterial mutants resistant to phages. The outcome of this inquiry opened the field of bacterial genetics, which provided the foundations of molecular biology – and all that followed.

SALVADOR E. LURIA, 1969

Above
Here, children study their lessons and catch the sun at a sanatorium in the German Alps in the 1920s. Death from tuberculosis began to decline in the mid-nineteenth century due to better hygiene, diet and rest.

Right
Robert Koch, on board ship with his wife, was a scientific experimenter of genius. The country doctor was inspired by the work of Louis Pasteur – and by his wife, who pointed out that microbes proliferated on discarded meat, which prompted Koch to try blood serum for growing bacilli.

Left
Selman Waksman worked as director of the Institute of Microbiology at Rutgers University. The streptomycin that he discovered is active against almost all organisms that penicillin works against, and many against which penicillin is impotent.

Paul Ehrlich

The Magic Bullet

Although he shared the 1908 Nobel Prize with Elie Metchnikoff "for their work on the theory of immunity", Paul Ehrlich's greatest contribution to medical science came later.

The son of a Jewish innkeeper, Ehrlich was born in a small German town in 1854. After receiving his medical degree, he studied the use of various aniline dyes to stain micro-organisms selectively. Ehrlich became a disciple of Robert Koch, the discoverer of the bacterium that causes tuberculosis, and provided Koch with an improved method of staining tissue cells and bacteria.

In his early thirties Ehrlich contracted tuberculosis during a laboratory experiment. With his wife and two young daughters he went to Egypt for two years to convalesce. When Ehrlich returned to Germany recovered, Koch appointed him head of his Institute for Infectious Diseases in Berlin.

Ehrlich continued experimenting with immunology, showing how antibodies form in the blood to neutralize the cause of a disease. His demonstrations that antibodies can be produced only by chemical interactions between antigens and cells led to his Nobel Prize in 1908.

A workaholic who enjoyed reading Sherlock Holmes stories, Ehrlich spent nearly a decade playing detective himself. He wanted to track down what he called "the magic bullet", a chemical substance that could "disinfect" a human being without destroying healthy tissue.

The affliction he focused on was syphilis. Near the end of the fifteenth century, Europe had been ravaged by an epidemic of the venereal disease that caused millions of deaths. Mercury had been found to lessen the symptoms, but there was no cure.

In 1901 Ehrlich began systematically testing derivatives of atoxyl, a highly toxic arsenic compound, hoping to find one that would work against the spirochete, the micro-organism that causes syphilis. Developed by German dye chemists, atoxyl had been shown to kill spirochetes. In 1909, after screening 605 compounds, Ehrlich finally found what he had been looking for: number 606 was effective in destroying syphilitic lesions in mice, guinea pigs, and rabbits. Ehrlich named the synthetic preparation Salvarsan from the Latin *salvare* ("to save"), and the German *arsen* ("arsenic"). In 1910 Ehrlich announced he had found a cure for syphilis, and the following year Salvarsan was tested on humans. It worked.

As a "magic bullet", however, Salvarsan left much to be desired. It did go straight to its target, the spirochete, but the intravenously injected compound was difficult to regulate: too small a dose and the spirochete rapidly would build up immunity, too large a dose and the patient could lose an arm.

In 1912 Ehrlich introduced compound 914, or Neosalvarsan, which proved much more reliable. Still, the bad press over Salvarsan – it had caused some fatalities – and the horrors of the First World War took their toll: Ehrlich died of a stroke in 1915 at the age of sixty-two.

Above
Hollywood made a film about Ehrlich's "Magic Bullet" starring Edward G. Robinson. One of Ehrlich's supporters for the Nobel wrote, "There can be no doubt that since the death of Pasteur, Ehrlich has been the foremost worker in the entire domain of immunology."

Right
In one experiment Ehrlich injected methylene blue dye into the ear vein of a rabbit and watched it spread slowly through the animal's bloodstream. The age of chemotherapy, a word that Ehrlich coined, was born.

Karl Landsteiner

Whether or not Karl Landsteiner read Shakespeare, he seems to have taken the advice given to Macbeth to "Be bloody, bold, and resolute", which helped in his discovery of human blood groups. Besides bringing him a Nobel Prize, Landsteiner's work made possible the safe transfusion of blood, thereby saving millions of lives.

If an incompatible blood type is used for a transfusion, antibodies in the recipient's plasma attack antigens in the red cells of the donor, making the cells clump together, or agglutinate. This allergic reaction can take the form of hives or asthma, or it can send the recipient into severe shock, sometimes resulting in death. Another danger is that as the cells clump and break up, their pigment, haemoglobin, is set loose, eventually blocking the kidneys. This, too, can be fatal.

Shortly after the turn of the century, Karl Landsteiner demonstrated that there are two antigens, A and B, in human red corpuscles. Each person has either A or B, both (AB), or neither (O). The 46.6 percent of those people with O-type blood are sometimes referred to as universal donors because their blood has no antigens for antibodies to attack. In the case of transfusions, each blood group must be matched with another appropriate group; for example, blood cells with A factor can be transfused with A or O, but not with B or AB.

Landsteiner spent most of his life in Vienna, his birthplace, studying immunology. He gained a great deal of information by performing no fewer than 3,639 post-mortems at the University of Vienna's department of pathological anatomy. Not surprisingly, this

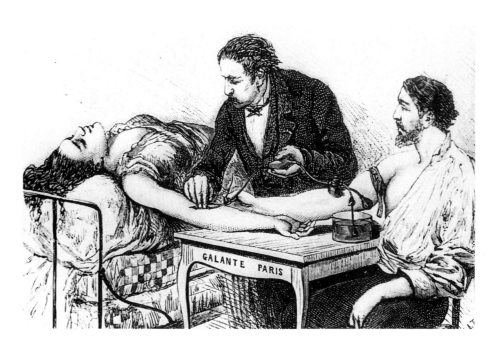

led to his promotion to chief dissector at a Viennese hospital. Eventually Landsteiner joined the staff of what is now Rockefeller University in New York City, and became an American citizen.

In his 1930 Nobel lecture, Landsteiner said of his human blood groupings: "The surprising thing was that agglutination, when it occurred at all, was just as pronounced as the already familiar reactions that take place during the interaction between serum and cells of different animal species."

Ten years later, the interaction between different animal species would figure in another momentous discovery. Landsteiner, with his colleague Dr Alexander Wiener, injected red blood cells from a rhesus monkey into a rabbit and then tested the rabbit's serum –

In the early days of blood transfusions, a suitable donor, often a relative, was chosen. After the typing of blood became possible, the safe transfusion of blood from one human being to another was based on blood groups.

now teeming with antibodies fighting the incompatible rhesus cells – on human blood. This experiment resulted in their discovering that some eighty-five percent of mankind is Rh (rhesus)-positive; that is, their red cells clump together when blood containing this factor is introduced.

The Rh-factor, which is entirely unrelated to the ABO grouping, was quickly shown to be linked to jaundice, anaemia and haemolytic diseases in newborn infants. That is because a pregnant woman who is Rh-negative forms antibodies that

attack the blood-forming cells of an Rh-positive foetus.

Among Landsteiner's other contributions was his work in Vienna with polio. In a key experiment, he withdrew tissue from the brain and spinal cord of a child who had died of the disease, and injected it into the abdomens of rhesus monkeys. Days later the monkeys developed polio-like symptoms of paralysis. Since there had been no demonstrable bacteria in the dead child's tissue, Landsteiner concluded – correctly as it turned out – that polio is caused by a virus.

At fifty-seven, highly respected and full of honours, Landsteiner suffered a fatal heart attack while at work in his New York laboratory.

When Karl Landsteiner entered the field, immunology was just beginning to take form as a discipline. Landsteiner devised a simple method for dividing human blood into four groups, and reasoned that the differences in human blood could be used to distinguish one person from another.

Alexander Fleming, Howard Florey, and Ernst Chain

1945   *A Spore in a Petri Dish*

"There are thousands of different moulds and there are thousands of different bacteria," wrote Alexander Fleming, "and the chance that put that mould in the right place at the right time was like winning the Irish Sweep." That particular mould was to yield the most effective killer of bacteria in the history of medicine.

Penicillin was discovered by Alexander Fleming, a bacteriologist at St Mary's Hospital, London, in 1928. Towards the end of the Second World War, fanciful press reports began to appear about how the discovery had taken place; Fleming would collect these mythical accounts to amuse his friends. One of his favourites appeared in a church magazine, which said that one day at his laboratory the absent-minded Fleming had picked up an old sandwich and eaten it for lunch. Suddenly, the boils he had been suffering from disappeared! Fleming supposedly attributed his cure to the mysterious green mould on his sandwich – and the rest was history.

The truth is nearly as improbable: Fleming had been experimenting with staphylococcus germs, and had placed some Petri dishes of the germ on a window ledge. Returning from holiday, he noticed that the lid on one of the culture plates had moved accidentally, and his experiment had become contaminated by a patch of mould. Fleming took a closer look, and was astonished to see that the bacteria around the periphery of the mould were dissolving. The mould spore that had floated in through the open window was traced to a laboratory on the floor below. Fleming identified it as *Penicillium notatum*,

and so decided to name its chemical secretion penicillin.

Fleming conducted enough experiments to conclude that penicillin had potential use in the treatment of diseases caused by penicillin-sensitive micro-organisms. However, a paper he published on his findings was met with universal indifference in the scientific community.

Then, in 1935, Howard Florey, a professor of pathology at Oxford University, needed someone to head his department's chemistry research, and recruited Ernst Chain, a young biochemist at Cambridge University. Chain embarked on a systematic study of natural antibacterial substances, and came across Fleming's 1929 paper on penicillin. Chain and Florey decided to investigate. They obtained some of the *Penicillium notatum* that Fleming had preserved since 1928, and painstakingly coaxed it into producing enough crude penicillin with which to experiment.

By mid-1940 Chain and Florey were able to test the substance on mice infected with pus and gas gangrene bacteria. The mice improved so dramatically that even the usually taciturn Florey remarked, "It looks like a miracle." A year later the first clinical tests were conducted on humans with serious infectious diseases, and showed penicillin to be the most powerful chemotherapeutic drug known, while causing relatively little harm to the infected host.

At the time, Britain was being blasted by the blitz and all production facilities were being used for the war effort. Florey flew to the United States, which had not yet entered the War, and per-

suaded several pharmaceutical companies to devise techniques to mass-produce the much-needed drug. Penicillin was first used in the War on D-Day at Normandy in 1944, and it saved the lives of thousands of Allied troops thereafter.

In 1945 the Nobel Prize was awarded jointly to Fleming for his discovery of penicillin, and to Florey and Chain, for their role in its development. The Nobel recipients were an unlikely trio. Fleming was originally from Scotland, Florey from Australia, and Chain from Germany. Fleming, the oldest, was a man of few words. Chain once recalled that the first time Fleming came to Oxford University to see the work being done with penicillin he did not make a single comment.

The story of penicillin – even today it is not known exactly how the drug works – is one of a series of flukes. It was discovered by chance and developed by chance, and chance even played a role in the ability of the United States to produce large quantities of it during the War. While there are several thousand types of penicillium moulds, until 1943 only the strain that had appeared in Fleming's Petri dish in 1928 had been found to yield an active extract, and only in minute amounts. Then, one day a government researcher happened to notice a mouldy melon in a market. The mould turned out to be a strain of *Penicillium chrysogenum*, which, when cultivated in huge aerated tanks, produced 200 times more penicillin than the original *Penicillium notatum*. Fleming's mouldy sandwich was apocryphal; the mouldy melon really happened.

166

In the past, benefits obtained from the progress of science and technology largely counterbalanced the possible threats. Of course, fire has always destroyed, and the sword has always killed, but damage was relatively localized and limited. Today, and this is a new fact, we feel that the equilibrium of the biosphere and the future of the species are globally endangered.

JEAN DAUSETT, 1980

Alexander Fleming began his medical studies in 1901. He spent his entire career at St Mary's Hospital in London. While he did not immediately see that penicillin had a future as an antibacterial medication, he did suggest as early as 1928 that it might eventually have a use.

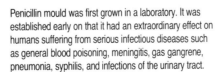

Penicillin mould was first grown in a laboratory. It was established early on that it had an extraordinary effect on humans suffering from serious infectious diseases such as general blood poisoning, meningitis, gas gangrene, pneumonia, syphilis, and infections of the urinary tract.

John F. Enders, Thomas H. Weller, and Frederick C. Robbins

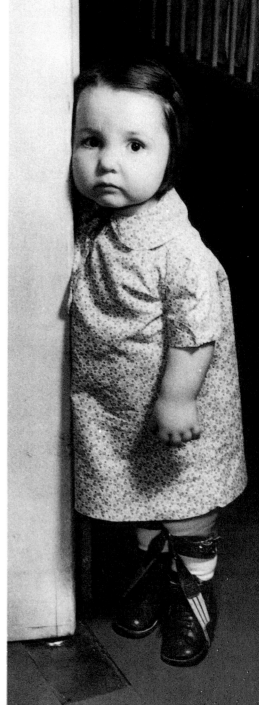

Sir Walter Scott's account of the moderately common childhood fever that left him lame at the age of eighteen months suggests that polio was well known in Britain as early as 1771. It was not until 1879, however, that a clinical description of the disease appeared in a medical text under the heading "Debility of the Lower Extremities".

The cause of polio was unknown, and would remain so until well into the twentieth century. By then – despite improved sanitary conditions that spared most infants from exposure to the virus – it had reached epidemic proportions in developed countries.

By the mid-1930s, the United States had experienced dozens of terrifying outbreaks of polio, and no cure was in sight. Virology was still a young branch of science, and although the polio virus had been isolated, it had been cultivated *in vitro* only with great difficulty, and in small amounts.

In 1947 the viral research team consisting of John F. Enders, Thomas H. Weller, and Frederick C. Robbins picked up where Enders and Weller had left off before the War. Polio at that time was not on the agenda. Enders, senior member of the group, and a PhD in bacteriology, shifted to the study of viruses shortly before the War. He had been persuaded to establish an infectious diseases research laboratory at Boston Children's Hospital, and invited Weller, who had been his assistant while a Harvard medical student, to join him. Robbins, a classmate of Weller's, soon followed.

The first project undertaken by the team was an attempt to culture mumps virus in chicken cells. It led to a pivotal innovation known as continuous culture. "Instead of transferring material from one culture to another after an interval of three or four days," they later wrote, "the tissues were preserved while the nutritive medium was removed." By continually adding new

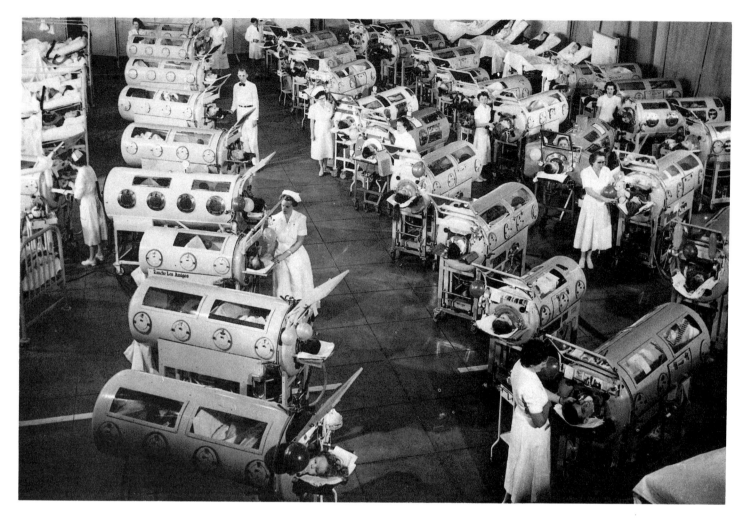

medium, they could maintain cells for as long as a month, allowing enough time to culture the slow-growing mumps virus. The threat of bacterial contamination, which for so long had complicated the culturing process, was eliminated by the postwar availability of penicillin and streptomycin, which killed off bacteria without damaging the test cells.

Following the successful cultivation of the mumps virus, the team moved on to the varicella, or chicken-pox, virus. Weller prepared host cultures using skin and muscle tissue taken from human embryos. The proximity of a rich supply of medium and a strain of Lansing polio virus in a nearby storage cabinet prompted an experiment of the sort that either makes history or is quickly forgotten. In 1949 the Lansing strain was introduced into the prepared tissue, where it proceeded to multiply. Overnight the rules of the game changed, and the way was cleared for

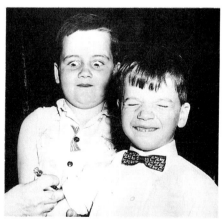

the development of a vaccine within a few years.

In 1954, as the United States undertook the first of many mass vaccination campaigns, Enders, Weller, and Robbins were awarded the Nobel Prize "for their discovery of the ability of poliomyelitis viruses to grow in cultures of various types of tissue".

Francis Crick, James Watson, and Maurice Wilkins

1962   *The DNA Triumph*

Francis Crick, a former Second World War researcher for the British Admiralty, was working on his doctorate at Cambridge University when twenty-three-year-old American James Watson arrived to study the structure of proteins. The two men got along, and set out to determine the structure of deoxyribonucleic acid, or DNA.

At a symposium in Italy, Watson met Maurice Wilkins, and learned that he and a colleague, Rosalind Franklin, had made X-ray diffraction studies of the DNA molecule.

In the spring of 1953, with Wilkins's and Franklin's photographs, Crick and Watson deciphered the structure of the storehouse of genetic information found in DNA. Watson's rickety six-foot model of the DNA molecule was made of wire, beads, and cardboard. It showed a double helix – a twisting ladder with rungs, which is the physical blueprint that virtually every organism uses to pass on genetic information.

Their work, widely hailed as one of the most important biological developments of this century, earned the men

Below left
According to James Watson and Francis Crick, the two parts of a DNA molecule split at the points of hydrogen bonding in the same way that a zip unzips. After the two men published their description of their model, they went their separate ways, although they have remained friends.

Below right
Maurice Wilkins subjected DNA samples to X-ray diffraction analysis, a process used to determine the chemical structure of molecules. In addition to his work on the structure of nucleic acids, Wilkins studied the structure of nerve membranes.

the 1962 Nobel Prize. In his presentation speech, A. V. Engstrom of the Karlinska Institute said that their discovery "opens the most spectacular possibilities for the unravelling of the details of the control and transfer of genetic information".

The breakthrough also set in motion at least two remarkable books. Watson's *The Double Helix*, published in 1966, was described by one critic as "an unexpected breeze of fresh air from a region men had thought of as stuffy and incommunicado, the world of pure science". It became a bestseller. Twenty years later, Crick published *What Mad Pursuit*, a memoir that includes a compelling account of the DNA discovery.

A third book, *Rosalind Franklin and DNA*, was written by Franklin's friend Anne Sayer, and is an angry attack on the way "Rosy" is portrayed in *The Double Helix*. Franklin died of cancer before the Nobel Prize was awarded, and

Sayer felt that Franklin had not received full credit for her contribution. In a gracious epilogue, added to later editions of *The Double Helix*, Watson says his initial impressions of Franklin, both professional and personal, "were often wrong".

In 1989 – thirty-six years after the double helix was described by Crick and Watson – researchers at the University of California's Lawrence Livermore Laboratory magnified the molecule one million times and found that it looks just as Crick and Watson said it would: like two bits of yarn twisted together.

Watson currently is director of the Cold Spring Harbor Laboratory on Long Island, New York, where a team of scientists are mapping the genome – all of the genes that make up the chromosomes in human cells. The project is expected to lead to major changes in the diagnosis, treatment, and prevention of diseases with a genetic origin.

From the model of the double helix, Crick and Watson saw immediately how exact copies of DNA could be made. Splitting the "ladder" down the middle produced two separate strings, which then formed new pairs that were duplicates of the original double helix.

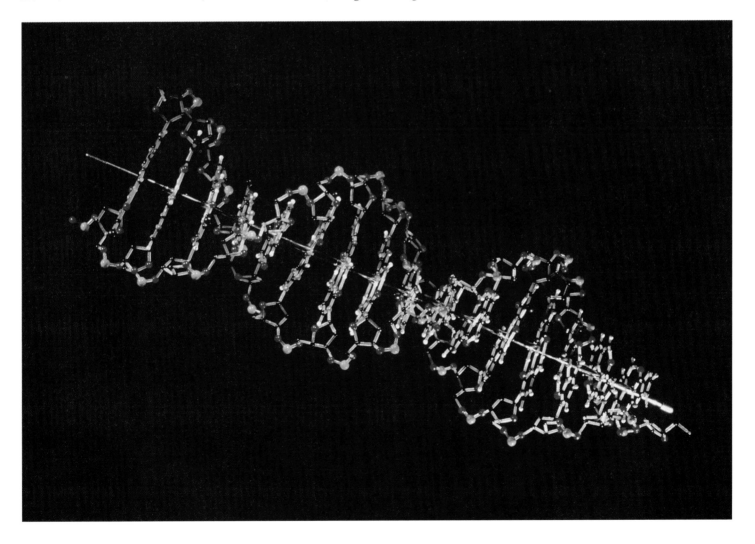

Konrad Lorenz, Niko Tinbergen, and Karl von Frisch

1973

Most childhood obsessions have a life-span of childhood toys: surviving, if at all, only in memory or in dim remembrance of the fascination they once held. In the case of the three men who shared the 1973 Nobel Prize, such an early passion not only endured past childhood, but shaped three lives of scientific distinction and great personal satisfaction.

Karl von Frisch and Konrad Lorenz were born seventeen years apart, both into Viennese medical families. They were sent as adolescents to the same school, and it was assumed they would follow their fathers into medicine. The greatest similarity in their lives, however, lay not in their early lives and families' expectations, but in what Lorenz later described as the "inordinate love of animals".

The young Von Frisch spent many hours observing and recording the movements of birds and animals, then submitting amateur scientific papers to popular journals. Lorenz's passion was ducks: his first discovery as a scientist was what came to be known as imprinting. "From a neighbour," he later recalled, "I got a one-day-old duckling and found, to my intense joy, that it transferred its following response to my person . . . my interest became irreversibly fixated on waterfowl, and I became an expert on their behaviour even as a child."

Several hundred miles away, another young boy, four years Lorenz's junior, had been seized by the same passion. The son of a grammar-school teacher living in the Hague, Niko Tinbergen discovered early that he preferred exploring the nearby North Sea coast-line, collecting sea shells, and observing birds, to sitting in a schoolroom. At the State University of Leiden, he did his doctoral dissertation – "a skimpy but interesting little thesis", he called it – on the homing behaviour of bee-killer wasps, which he had observed at his parents' summer home.

Over the next several decades, the interests of these three men converged. Having entered medical school to please his father, Karl von Frisch got a research project directed by a maternal uncle, a distinguished physiologist at the University of Vienna. Formally switching from medicine to ethology, Von Frisch became involved in the study of light perception and colour-changes in fish, receiving his doctorate for a thesis in that subject in 1919.

Lorenz, meanwhile, completed medical school and changed to zoology. Inclined at first to the behaviourist view that animal instincts are based on reflex responses to external stimuli, Lorenz was led to the opposite conclusion by his observation of continued mating behaviour in animals kept in isolation. Only after meeting Niko Tinbergen at a conference in 1936 did Lorenz begin to comprehend the potential reach of his findings. "We clicked at once," Tinbergen recalled long afterwards. "Konrad's extraordinary vision and enthusiasms were supplemented and fertilized by my critical sense, my inclination to think his ideas through, and my irrepressible urge to check out 'hunches' by experimentation."

Working together over many years, Lorenz and Tinbergen constructed a theory stating that the instincts do not originate simply in response to external

stimuli, but from inner impulses that are as distinct as a species' physical anatomy. As the author of such popular books as *King Solomon's Ring* and *On Aggression*, Lorenz became the far better known of the two men. He also drew more critical reaction, particularly in response to his assertion that aggression was but a "so-called evil", since despite its potential for destruction, it remains an essential instinct for the survival of species.

Together, the three "animal watchers", as Tinbergen called them, pushed back the narrow borders of ethology to tell us many important things about ourselves, the species that is both human and animal.

Left

Konrad Lorenz held strong views on many subjects. He favoured "families" in which several natural families developed close bonds, creating an extended group on which children could depend for close ties.

Below

Konrad Lorenz's research focused on waterfowl, such as these snowgeese. Lorenz stressed the importance of studying animals under near natural conditions.

The century following the first Nobel Prizes has seen greater changes in man's estate than any in previous history. Most of the changes have been a result of the advance of science, and the great majority have been for the better.

In the next century, science will bring many more surprises and advances that cannot be foreseen today. Whether they will be for better or worse will depend, not on scientists alone, but upon what use mankind as a whole decides to make of the power of its new knowledge. And to make the right decisions the public must understand science far better than it does today.

RODNEY R. PORTER, 1972

Howard M. Temin

The American virologist Howard Temin shared his Nobel Prize in 1975 for "discoveries concerning the interaction between tumour viruses and the genetic material of the cell". He wrote the following for this book:

"Many of the early Nobel Prizes in Physiology or Medicine were given to the great pioneers who studied infectious diseases and immunology. In many parts of the world, the knowledge of infectious diseases and immunology gained by these pioneers, combined with public health measures and a general increase in cleanliness, resulted in the end of infectious diseases as the major scourge of humanity. Following this decline in the importance of infectious diseases, the view developed that degenerative diseases were the major problem in the developed world.

"This view of infectious diseases as being under control was strengthened by the eradication of smallpox and its virus in the last decade. However, this view was overturned by the appearance of AIDS, caused by human immunodeficiency virus-1 (HIV-1), a virus with both RNA and DNA genomes – a retrovirus. HIV-1 is able to insert its genetic material into the genetic material of the host cells, to infect and destroy key cells of the immune system, and to vary its genetic material rapidly. When in the aftermath of World War II there were great societal changes and a great increase in intercontinental travel, HIV-1 was ready to cause a global pandemic.

"The World Health Organization estimates that by the year 2000 AIDS will be the tenth leading cause of death from illness in the world. Since deaths from AIDS are concentrated largely in people during their most productive years, their deaths will have an even greater impact on societies than the total numbers suggest.

"Despite the rise in AIDS, degenerative diseases remain the main cause of death in the world. During this century, knowledge of the genetic basis of many of these noninfectious diseases has grown. Now, with genetic engineering and new forms of genetic mapping, the molecular basis of many of these diseases has been established. The ability of retroviruses to insert exogenous information into cellular DNA has allowed some simpler retroviruses to be modified for use as vectors with the potential to ameliorate some of these genetic diseases. Attempts along these lines have begun, and many more are under development.

"Prevention and cure of human disease and postponement of death have been the great goals of physiology and medicine. However, the relative success of these endeavours has resulted in the present population explosion. This explosion is affecting the biosphere in ways that, in some parts of the world, could soon reverse the gains in health and extended life that have resulted from our increased knowledge of physiology and medicine. Unless population growth is controlled by other means, disease and death will control it. Our previous successes in improving human health and life will be undone unless we can meet this new challenge successfully.

"Retroviruses illustrate this duality. On the one hand, retroviruses are the cause of the twentieth century's last great human pandemic; on the other hand, retroviruses are the hope for a novel form of therapy for some human diseases."

Above
American virologist Howard Temin, with David Baltimore, discovered retroviruses, now known to cause a variety of diseases including acquired immune deficiency syndrome (AIDS), certain cancers, and hepatitis. He has also investigated how genetic information in the protovirus is able to transform a normal animal cell into a tumour cell.

Right
A single AIDS virus particle (roughly spherical, coloured red) is seen here budding from the plasma membrane of an infected T4 lymphocyte, a white blood cell.

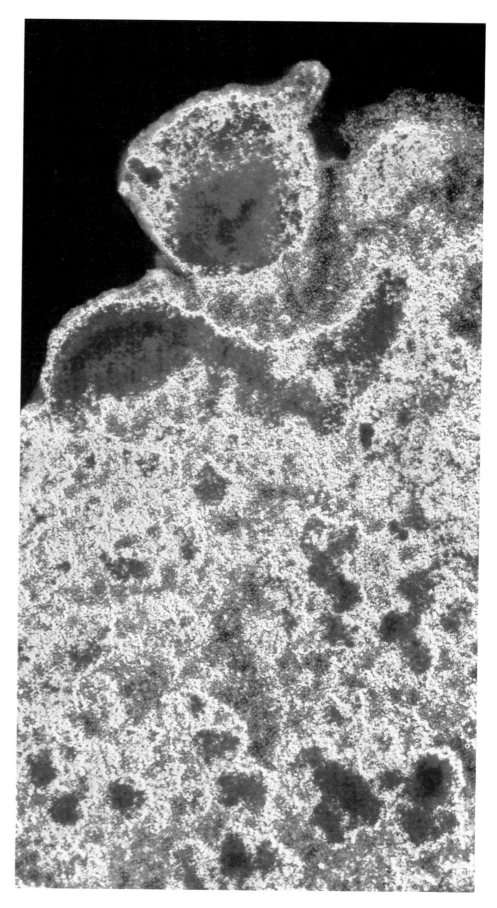

Rosalyn S. Yalow

Rosalyn Yalow shared the 1977 Nobel Prize "for the development of radioimmunoassays of peptide hormones". In her Nobel lectures, she said, "The first telescope opened the heavens; the first microscope opened the world of microbes." Radioisotopic methodology, as exemplified by RIA, has shown the potential for opening new vistas in science and medicine.

Dr Yalow considers herself a physicist turned biomedical-investigator. For this book she commented on the role of radioactivity in medicine:

"The twentieth century began with the awarding of the first Nobel Prize in Physics to Röntgen for the discovery of X-rays. Two years later Becquerel and the Curies shared the Physics Prize for the discovery of natural radioactivity. In 1908 Rutherford was awarded the Chemistry Prize for his work on the chemistry of radioactive substances, to be followed three years later by Marie Curie receiving a second Nobel Prize, one in Chemistry, for the discovery of radium and polonium. The 1930s were particularly exciting years for this field with the awarding of the Chemistry Nobel Prize to the Curie-Joliots for the discovery of artificial radioactivity, and of the Physics Nobel Prizes for the discovery of cosmic rays, to Anderson for the discovery of the positron and to Fermi, who had become a leading figure in the new science called 'nuclear physics'.

"The major progenitor for my career was Georg de Hevesy who received the 1943 Chemistry Prize 'for his work on the use of isotopes as tracers in the study of chemical processes'. In 1948 he published a remarkable book entitled *Radioactive Indicators: Their Application in Biochemistry, Animal Physiology, and Pathology*. As a trained nuclear physicist who had just taken a position in a hospital setting, I found this book an inspiration for my career which has been based on the use of radioisotopic methodology in medicine. I received the Nobel Prize in Physiology or Medicine for the development of radioimmunoassay, an *in vitro* technique that has been used in thousands of laboratories around the world to measure hundreds of substances in blood and other body fluids.

"The past half-century has seen the development of a new medical speciality, Nuclear Medicine, which employs radionuclides in multiple areas of medical diagnosis and therapy. It has been estimated that at present in the United States *in vivo* and *in vitro* radionuclide procedures are now employed in over one-third of hospital admissions as well as in extensive out-patient evaluations. Yet the use of radioisotopes in medicine, as well as nuclear power, is threatened by what has become an almost phobic fear of radiation at any level.

"Let us consider a few facts concerning the harmful effects of radiation. Among the survivors of the Hiroshima-Nagasaki bombings who received more than 0.1 Sievert (10 rem) radiation exposure, there appears to have been only a six percent increase in the number of cancer deaths compared to the number expected among those not exposed. Compare this increase with the data that indicate that about a third of cancer deaths in the United States are due to cigarette smoking.

"Treatment of an overactive thyroid with radioiodine 131-I is very common. It has been estimated that several hundred thousand people in the United States, including our First Lady, Barbara Bush, have received this treatment which on the average delivers about 0.1 Sv (10 rem) whole body exposure. A study of more than 30,000 hyperthyroid patients, of whom more than half were treated with 131-I and the others with surgery or drugs, reveals no difference between the two groups in the leukaemia rates. Yet data based on the atomic bomb survivors would have suggested that 131-I-treated hyperthyroid patients should have had a doubling of the leukaemia rate. The absence of increased leukaemia in the 131-I-treated patients indicates that the lower dose rate associated with 131-I therapy results in less radiation damage than the acute exposure associated with the nuclear bomb.

"For more than two decades, before determination of the concentration of circulating thyroid-related hormones was made possible by radioimmunoassay, the uptake of 131-I by the thyroid was the method of choice for evaluation of the activity of the thyroid gland. Several million people were studied in this way. The radiation dose to the thyroid averaged about 0.5 Sv (50 rem). A follow-up of a large group of such patients revealed that this radiation exposure resulted in no increase in thyroid cancer.

"All of us are exposed continuously to nature's radiation. Normal background radiation exposure due to cosmic radiation, or self-contained natural radioactivity, as well as the natural radioactivity in soil and building material, has been considered to be 1 mSv

(100 mrem) each year. Recently there has been some concern about exposure to natural radon and its daughter products. There are places in the world, in mountain areas or in regions where there is high natural radioactivity in the soil, where natural radiation exposure is ten-fold higher than usual, and adverse health effects have been investigated but have not been observed. Unfortunately the facts that I have just cited are not generally known by the public or even by most scientists.

"Receipt of the Nobel Prize gives the laureate a certain amount of visibility and credibility. I believe that it is part of my social responsibility to educate the public about facts such as those I have just described. Perhaps an education campaign by knowledgeable scientists will reduce the phobic fear of radiation and maximize its usefulness in the service of mankind."

While studying diabetes, Rosalyn S. Yalow helped to develop radioimmunoassay (RIA), a method that measures minute substances in blood plasma. The technique may be used to detect drugs, to screen blood donors for hepatitis virus, for the early detection of cancer, to measure levels of growth hormones, and to track leukaemia viruses.

Barbara McClintock

1983

Jumping Genes

In 1983, the Nobel Prize brought McClintock sudden fame, and photographers wanted pictures of her in her maize patch outside her laboratory in Cold Spring Harbor, New York. She said, "Being a woman has been a great benefit. There was no preconceived notion about what you had to do. You could just do your work."

Barbara McClintock is strictly a loner. Her thinking is totally original. And for her entire professional life she has studied the cell nuclei of a single plant – maize, or Indian corn. "As you look at these things, they become part of you," she once told an interviewer. "And you forget yourself. The main thing about it is you forget yourself."

McClintock is responsible for two vital discoveries in the field of genetics. The second won her a Nobel Prize, the first, some scientists say, deserved a Nobel Prize as well.

Born in 1902, as a child McClintock was a solitary reader and thinker. Although her father was a physician, he and his wife did not believe that girls should go to college. Barbara, the youngest of three daughters, went anyway, enrolling in Cornell's College of Agriculture in Ithaca, New York. As an undergraduate she began to study the genetics of maize, an organism particularly suited to investigation because its kernels are brightly coloured and variegated. For the last fifty years she has done her research at the Carnegie Institute of Washington in Cold Spring Harbor, New York.

As a graduate student, she devised a way to stain the ten pairs of chromosomes in each cell of maize to distinguish them under a microscope. In 1927, immediately after receiving her PhD from Cornell's Department of Botany, McClintock isolated a knob on the short arm of chromosome nine that allows chromosomes to exchange genetic material during meiosis, the process that leads to the formation of sex cells. Considered a crucial discovery in experimental genetics, it helped to

The theory of evolution stemming from Darwin is urgently in need of reassessment in light of recent biological findings. Among other things, spontaneous mutations must cease to be viewed as pure mistakes but rather must be recognized in a new world view as an indispensable part of steadily ongoing creation. This might help change our attitude towards genetic diseases.

WERNER ARBER, 1978

explain the diversity of characteristics found in organisms that reproduce sexually.

At that point, geneticists, McClintock included, believed that all genes within a single chromosome are immutable, which was one of the laws of heredity laid down by Gregor Mendel, the nineteenth-century Moravian monk and founder of genetics. Then, in the mid-1940s, McClintock demonstrated that genes are not stable after all.

She had observed that the patterns on twin sectors of maize seedlings were the inverse of one another. She also noticed that certain kernels had pigmentation that did not correspond with their genetic makeup. Suddenly, she had a profound insight, a phenomenon she has experienced many times: "When you suddenly see the problem,

something happens. You have the answer – before you are able to put it into words . . . I know when to take it seriously. I'm so absolutely sure . . . I'm just sure this is it."

Her realization was this: during the division of a single cell into sister cells, one gains what the other lost. In other words, not all genes behave alike. Certain genes can switch others on and off. These "switches" can move from place to place on a chromosome, and can even "jump" from one chromosome to

another. McClintock found her first "jumping gene" in the knob on the short arm of chromosome nine. Her discovery of transposable genetic systems led to her 1983 Nobel Prize, and has had enormous implications. For example, it explains how resistance to antibiotic drugs can be transmitted between different types of bacteria.

In her Nobel acceptance speech, McClintock said that cells "make wise decisions and act upon them". So does Barbara McClintock.

At a time when the science of genetics was just getting started, Barbara McClintock was at work in her laboratory thinking about how a small number of cells can grow into an entire organism. Her life has been devoted to fathoming the secrets of the cell's nucleus.

George H. Hitchings, Gertrude Elion, and James W. Black

Until the last quarter century, medical pharmacology had a history of happenstance and serendipitous discovery. From folk remedies to the contents of the modern physician's black bag, pharmacopia has consisted mainly of drugs accidentally "stumbled upon", rather than uncovered by a determined search. The three 1988 Nobel laureates represent a revolutionary break with that trial-and-error approach, replacing it with a goal-directed model that so far has proved hugely successful in the development of new drugs.

George Herbert Hitchings, Gertrude Elion, and James W. Black all came of scientific age in a world newly aware of the significance of nucleic acids in the formation and functioning of cell life. When Hitchings, born in 1905 and the most senior of the three, completed his doctorate in biochemistry at Harvard University in 1933, the three-dimensional model for DNA described by Watson and Crick was still twenty years in the future, but a sense of possibility in the study of RNA and DNA had made nucleic acids one of the hottest areas of biochemical research.

In the early 1940s Hitchings began a systematic review of the properties of specific drugs, in which compounds were selectively screened for their mechanism of action, rather than for their chance effectiveness. In 1944 he hired a young woman with a Masters Degree in biochemistry as his laboratory assistant. Because few scientists were willing to hire a woman to do research, Gertrude Elion had virtually no training in the field.

Elion had chosen a career in science after seeing her grandfather die of cancer. She soon ranked as an expert on nucleic acid synthesis, as she and Hitchings worked to discover ways to short-circuit, detour, and bamboozle murderous organisms through the rearrangement of harmless ones.

"The idea," Elion explains, "was to change the building-blocks slightly, just enough, perhaps, to fool a cancer cell or a bacteria or a virus into taking them up and then find that it's stuck and it can't get rid of them or utilize them and so can't multiply. That was really the basic theory."

Hitchings's and Elions's first hint of success was their discovery of diaminopurine, which appeared to prevent nucleic acid synthesis in cancer cells and micro-organisms. In 1948 the drug was tested in leukaemic patients. Although it successfully induced short-term remissions, it also produced nausea, vomiting, and bone-marrow suppression. The two researchers went back to search for more refined interceptors, and in 1953 developed thioquanine and 6-mercaptopurine, both of which showed significant activity against cancer. Continuing to tinker with 6-MP, Elion eventually directed the development of a closely related drug, allopurinol, for the treatment of gout, and pointed the way towards the use of 6-MP as an immune system suppressant, thereby making organ transplants between unrelated donors possible.

Elion's group later applied the same approach to the herpes virus, producing the drug acyclovir, the first to show any effect against the virus. Hitchings directed the development of pyrimethamine and trimethoprim, used to treat a range of bacteria and parasites, including malaria, as well as pneumocystis pneumonia, the most common of the infections suffered by AIDS patients in this hemisphere.

Following a parallel path of molecular research, the Scottish-born physiologist James Black spent a decade attempting "to understand how cells talk to each other" chemically. When he took on the job of senior pharmacologist in 1958, he had no training as a pharmacologist. What he did have was a storehouse of critical knowledge about how chemical messengers such as adrenaline and noradrenaline bind to the two major types of cell receptors in the organs of the body.

Black investigated how these messengers and receptors might be manipulated to produce a desired medical result. This led in time to the development of what came to be known as beta-blockers – substances that beat adrenaline to its target, and, by acting as false messengers, bring about the intended chemical reaction. Black eventually produced the drug propranolol, which is widely used in the management of angina, hypertension, arrythmia, and migraine. He later developed the drug cimetidine, which decreases the secretion of acid in the stomach, and thereby promotes the healing of peptic ulcers.

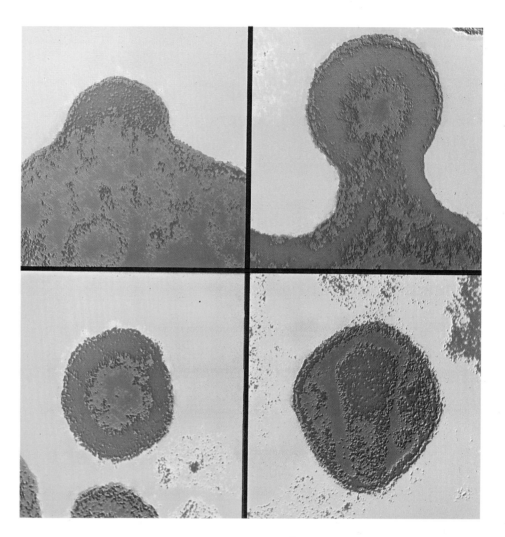

Right
This sequence of false-colour transmission electron micrographs shows the formation of a Human Immunodefiency Virus (HIV) particle, the causative agent of AIDS. Hitchings and Elion have been credited with laying the foundation for the development of AZT, an early weapon in the fight against HIV.

Left
In Stockholm in 1988, George Hitchings, Gertrude Elion, and James Black had their picture taken with Alfred Nobel. The drugs that resulted from their discoveries have become well-proven medications, and remain in the forefront for the treatment of many illnesses.

5 ECONOMICS

Gold bullion is a potent symbol of wealth. The first awards in Economic Sciences in memory of Alfred Nobel were made in 1969.

Introduced by Charles Mann and Mark Plummer

Surely no other intellectual discipline inspires the instinctive revulsion evoked by economics. Long before Engels denounced economists as hypocritical rationalizers of greed, its practitioners had grown accustomed to being regarded as the bearers of bad news. The bad news is not financial, but moral and spiritual, for economics rests upon the assumption that human actions can best be understood as unremitting attempts to fulfil individual self-interest in a world where nobody can get all he wants.

This was true from the early days of economics, when Adam Smith wrote *An Inquiry into the Nature and Causes of the Wealth of Nations* in 1776. Although Smith did not "invent" economics, he was the first to produce a comprehensive synthesis of what was then known, and he was the first to illustrate systematically how economic analysis could be used to shape public policy. It was useless, Smith wrote, to think of the mass of people as being motivated by the abstract ideas of the Good. "It is not from the benevolence of the butcher, the brewer, or the baker", he wrote, "that we expect our dinner, but from their regard to their own interest. We address ourselves, not to their humanity but to their self-love, and never talk to them of our own necessities but of their advantages."

Human beings, in the jargon of contemporary economics, are value maximizers. By "value", economists do not mean truth, love, or any of the commonplace virtues, but rather the ability of goods and services to satisfy human desire. Alas, desire is infinite, and the world is crowded and small. Unable to have everything, the individual has to make choices. Economics, as it is defined nowadays, is the study of those choices.

For a century and a half after Smith, economics was little more than a collection of sceptical observations about human behaviour. The province of talented amateurs such as David Ricardo, a stockbroker, and Thomas Malthus, a clergyman – Smith himself was a professor of moral philosophy – the field made generalizations about the unpleasant but necessary trade-offs in life.

In 1798, Malthus predicted the inevitable outstripping of the food supply by population. Ricardo, in turn, saw the subservience of workers as an ineluctable consequence of capitalism. "There is no way of keeping profits up but by keeping wages down," he explained, bluntly although not entirely correctly, in 1820. Such opinions were the reason that Thomas Carlyle, poet and wit, referred to the likes of Malthus and Ricardo as "Respected Professors of the Dismal Science".

By 1901, when Alfred Nobel's will established the Prizes, economics had become a profession, especially in the United States, England, Sweden, and Austria. But what those professional economists did, for the most part, was to speculate, proceeding from simplistic assumptions to conclusions verifiable only in the most rudimentary ways. This method produced some moderately useful insights about how markets worked, but it provided little empirical confirmation of economists' grander theories of nations and their wealth; economists learned why the price of oil rises and falls, for example, but rarely thought of applying this knowledge to a real world in which the price of oil was becoming ever more important.

This changed with the Great Depression of 1929. Economists suddenly found themselves called upon to explain what had happened and to delineate ways of pulling the industrial nations out of the mess into which they had fallen. During the next thirty years economics was revolutionized – an epoch of growth and creativity that was as exciting to economists as the first three decades of the century were to physicists.

Today the effects of the economic revolution are as present as the revolution in the sciences. Previously recondite terms like "inflation" and "cost-of-living adjustments" fill newspaper headlines, and rare is the nation without a council of economic advisers.

Recognizing the flowering of the discipline, the Central Bank of Sweden in 1968 established the Central Bank of Sweden Prize in Economic Science in Memory of Alfred Nobel. It is presented annually "to a person who has carried out a work in economic science of the eminent significance expressed in the Will of Alfred Nobel". Fittingly, it has generally been awarded to the surviving members of the generation that pioneered rigorous economic analysis in the years following 1929.

In the 1920s, economics revolved around a single concept, that of *economic equilibrium*. Economic behaviour is the product of an individual's attempts to find the best choice from among an array of possibilities; equilibrium is the result of that choice. It is the balance struck every time you go to the food shop and weigh the benefits of buying the fancy, extra-fresh bread you like (at a fancy price) against the benefits of purchasing the unexciting, house brand (with its lower price).

These balances shift constantly, as economists have already recognized. People have more or less money on hand and more or less of a yen for fancy bread. The most interesting question, economists thought, was: How would individuals react if circumstances changed? How much would the price per loaf have to rise to discourage buying? What would happen to the baker's willingness to make bread if the price of flour increased? Thus were formulated some of the "laws" of economics, such as the law of demand, which, as the world knows, suggests that the change in price of a good is inversely related to the amount purchased.

Equilibrium analysis permeated the profession, as did the emphasis on theories of individual consumers, businesses, and industries – the whole gamut of what we today call *microeconomics*. Studies of the workings of whole economics, or what is called *macroeconomics*, languished. Equilibrium-based microeconomics – to call it by its full, unlovely name – was a good focus for amateurs, for it could be pursued without much mathematics. Economists, in those long-ago days, had as much use for figures as their cousins in anthropology and political science.

This changed dramatically in 1932, when the United States Senate called on the economics profession, through the National Bureau of Economic Research, to provide estimates of national income: the dollar value of the nation's output of goods and services.

Simon Kuznets (Nobel, 1971) was given this task. Having escaped Leninist Russia in 1921 at the age of twenty, Kuznets ended up devoting his life to the production of such statistics. His labours were prodigious. Gradually, economists realized that for the first time they were acquiring the lifeblood of any empirical science: rivers of raw data that could be analyzed and explained.

Kuznets's national income accounts, as they became known, gave life to the infant field of macroeconomics, led by the most influential economist of the day, John Maynard Keynes. Beginning with his *Treatise on Money* in 1930 and culminating in his *General Theory of Employment, Interest and Money* in 1936, Keynes sought to move beyond the past 150 years of economics to what he called "classical"

economic theory.

As he put it, "The characteristics of the special case assumed by the classical theory happen not to be those of the economic society in which we actually live, with the result that its teaching is misleading and disastrous if we attempt to apply it to the facts of experience."

A superb literary stylist, Keynes made his case forcefully, even intemperately, savagely attacking his opponents. His wild words, he said, were "the assault of thoughts on the unthinking". In a stream of elegant phrases, he replaced the classical theory with one of his own, which sought to explain how a nation actually uses its resources: labour from its citizens, machines and equipment from its capitalists, and money from its bankers and government. Managing the aggregate demand for goods, Keynes argued, was the key to controlling economic well-being. The best way to do so, he said, was by government action.

Although pieces of the *General Theory* existed before its publication, Keynes put them together and encouraged governments to intervene in economic affairs. Life was breathed into the modern discipline of macroeconomics.

In a sense, Keynes's great influence was to make economic science seem less dismal. Although always a supporter of capitalism – it was amazing, he thought, that "a doctrine so illogical and so dull (as Marxism) can have exercised so powerful and enduring an influence" – Keynes believed that careful use of his ideas could stead the course of economic growth and temper some of the harshnesses of the free market. Humanity, according to Adam Smith, might not be able to depend on the benevolence of the butcher, the brewer, or the baker, but it could trust the benevolence and wisdom of the government economist. Little wonder that Keynesianism, as it came to be called, was adopted by nation after nation.

The argument over Keynes drew enormous attention. Less noted was another development, of equal or greater significance: the rise of mathematical methods in economics. In 1930 an international group of scholars established the Econometrics Society. Ragnar Frisch (Nobel, 1969) was one of its founders. As the name suggests, econometrics is measurement in economics.

The Econometrics Society sought to use mathematics and statistics to increase the level of rigour in the formulation and testing of economic theory. The end product, the founders of the Econometrics Society believed, would be a more practical science. During the Second World War, Frisch learned firsthand the consequences of a government with deranged economics beliefs – the Nazis believed that Jews controlled the economics, and he, a Jew, was imprisoned.

In post-war Norway, Norwegian trade unions followed the suggestions of econometricians and agreed to resolve labour disputes without strikes by incorporating into wage negotiations a recent econometric invention: the cost-of-living index. The index was developed under the direction of Frisch, who employed 100 students for the necessary data-gathering and calculations.

Similarly, Jan Tinbergen (Nobel, 1969) used the efforts of hundreds of students to develop models of the economies of the Netherlands in 1935 and the United States in 1939. For the Netherlands, at least, his efforts bore fruit; Tinbergen's ten years as director of the nation's Central Planning Bureau (1945-55) helped lay the ground for its post-war prosperity.

The trend towards increased use of mathematics found its most masterful expression, however, in the work of Paul Samuelson (Nobel, 1970), culminating in his *Foundations of Economic Analysis* (published in 1947, but based on his dissertation, which was written in the late 1930s). Samuelson showed his brilliance early – he was appointed a professor in the newly created economics department at Massachusetts Institute of Technology when he was just twenty-six.

For years, Samuelson was the towering figure in economics, introducing his rigorous approach to welfare economics, international trade, macroeconomics, and the theory of growth. With great intellectual daring, Samuelson borrowed freely from other disciplines, adapting the Le Chatelier principle, a highly complex mathematical description of thermodynamic equilibrium, into economics. (Most important was his consistent method of mathematically analyzing economics questions: characterize behaviour as the solution of a maxima-minima problem; find the equilibrium conditions to this problem; and then derive observable hypotheses about changes in the initial set of conditions that determine equilibrium. In this way, Samuelson argued, economics could produce meaningful, testable theorems.)

Because Samuelson's major work was about method, his influence permeates almost every aspect of contemporary economics. Unsurprisingly, he is often regarded by economists themselves as the most important practitioner of the dismal science in this century.

Samuelson began as a supporter of Keynesian thought, but his mathematical methods eventually led to its rejection. This rejection began simply enough, when economists decided to prove something that many in the discipline had long taken for granted: whether an economic system, characterized by free-wheeling competition, was, in truth, capable of producing the state of equilibrium envisioned by economists.

Imagine a town with many businesses, all having the marvellous ability to set up a factory or shut it down in an instant, and an equally large number of buyers, all with complete knowledge of the locations and virtues of each business. If economic equilibrium exists, the system will naturally gravitate to a set of prices that will entice the businesses to produce the exact number of goods demanded by the buyers at those prices.

Although this had been examined by earlier savants such as Leon Walras in the 1880s and Abraham Wald in the 1930s,

it remained for Kenneth Arrow (Nobel, 1972) and Gerard Debrue (Nobel, 1983) to lay out the general proof that a competitive economic system always reaches an equilibrium. They also established the principle, fundamental to modern welfare economics, that a competitive equilibrium is optimal from a social point of view – that is, that any move away from equilibrium will entail greater economic losses than gains – and that any optimal allocation of resources corresponds to a competitive equilibrium. In less formal terms, Arrow and Debreu showed that Adam Smith had been right when, two centuries earlier, he argued that an "invisible hand" leads individuals motivated by personal gain to create a situation that benefits society.

Kuznets's invention of the national income accounts gave economists the ability to test more advanced theories, including Keynes's famous consumption function – the propensity to spend rather than to save income. Keynes had argued that this propensity could be related in a simple way to income – in many cases, it is taken as a constant percentage – and that whatever form the relation took should remain the same over time. When national income accounts showed behaviour at odds with Keynes's assertions, economists began to think that the master might be wrong. Although a new theory of consumption was put forth by Franco Modigliani (Nobel, 1985), the most important attack came from Milton Friedman (Nobel, 1976), perhaps the most controversial economist since Keynes.

Based at the University of Chicago, where Samuelson got his undergraduate degree, Friedman was instrumental in the revival of what is known as the quantity theory of money. This theory later evolved into what is known as the monetarist school of macroeconomics.

Friedman noted that money itself was a commodity, something that was bought and traded like any other good, and that the demand for it should be just like the demand for any other commodity – a notion that suggested that the money supply, not demand, was the decisive factor in the growth of national income. According to Friedman, a change in the amount of money (currency, coins, and so forth) issued by the government may have short-run implications for unemployment or national output, but in the long run affects only the level of prices. If money flows too freely, as it all too often does, the only result is inflation. The wonderful world envisioned by Keynes, Friedman said, simply could not exist.

Curiously, this attack, and that of many other economists of the left and right who disparaged Keynes, had little immediate effect on the legions of political leaders who embraced his intellectual schema. Even as the economics profession drifted away from Keynes, President Nixon

Right
Financial markets fulfil an important function in modern economies, but the dealing rooms of New York, Tokyo and London could not exist without computers and instant worldwide communications.

argued in the 1970s that "we are all Keynesians now" – lending ironic emphasis to Keynes's remark that the "practical men" who run the world "are usually the slaves of some defunct economist". When Keynes wrote this, of course, he meant his predecessors. Now, alas, it could be applied to Keynes himself.

The one early trend in economics that has continued is the ever-increasing role of advanced mathematics. In virtually every field of economics, mathematical models dominate, sometimes without being tested at all. Two important examples are the rise of the theory of rational expectations and game theory, both of which draw complex conclusions from what seem like simple, commonsensical beginnings. Rational expectations conjectures that people use past performance to judge future conditions, and that this rule enables them to make predictions that are correct on average. This is much like the horse track, where the odds are determined by the bettors, the "market participants". Favourites who go off at 2-1 odds do not, of course, win all the time, but the odds will be "rational" if they win, over a long run, about half the time.

The theory has found important applications in macroeconomics, especially in what is called the Phillips curve. In 1958, A. W. Phillips, a British economist, found empirical evidence of a negative trade-off between unemployment and inflation: an increase in inflation was associated with a decrease in unemployment, and vice versa. Many thought this relation was causal, that changes in inflation *caused* changes in unemployment. A government that would tolerate a light dose of inflation could assure jobs for almost everyone. Far from being the untoward result of misguided government intervention, inflation suddenly became another Keynesian tool by which the government could control the economy. The monetarists, it seemed, were wrong.

Ten years later, Milton Friedman, the demon of the Keynesians, struck back. He questioned the theoretical basis for the Phillips curve, arguing that while such a trade-off might exist in the short run, unemployment in the long run should be unaffected by inflation and return to what Friedman called the "natural rate". His argument relied on the notion of rational expectations, and particularly that people have rational expectations about inflation: they use past patterns of inflation to predict future inflation. If inflation has been consistently low in the past, people looking for a job, currently counted as unemployed, will expect this trend to continue. If inflation then increases unexpectedly, job-seekers scanning the "help wanted" pages will find offers with wages that should have been made higher through inflation. Mistaking them for wages that are higher in some real, non-inflationary sense, job-seekers will rush out the following week to take those jobs, and unemployment will decrease.

This decrease will not last, Friedman argued, as expectations catch up with inflation. Weeks or months of help-wanted advertisements filled with increasing wages will inure job-seekers to the inflation rate, changing their expectations. Only a *change* in inflation, then, can produce a change in unemployment, not inflation per se. Even this relation breaks down if the changes in inflation themselves become more predictable. In this case, the Phillips curve breaks down completely; the trade-off vanishes, and inflation loses all power to affect unemployment.

The rational expectations approach eventually became another nail in the coffin of the Keynesian belief that government intervention could successfully manage the economy. Its theoretical implications were back in the 1970s, when both high inflation and unemployment appeared – an impossibility, according to the Phillips curve, but there it was.

This application of rational expectations was of the first importance, for it dealt with major problems of the real world. But the same mathematical elegance that allowed rational expectations to demolish Keynesian formulations has proven to be an irresistible lure to many economists. The post-Samuelson generation has taken the tools he pioneered and spun them off into ever more sophisticated equations about formal situations that have less and less to do with the mundane world of jobs and house payments and loaves of bread.

A principal offender in this regard, critics say, is game theory. Introduced to economics by John von Neumann and Oscar Morgenstern in *The Theory of Games and Economic Behaviour* (1947), game theory is based on the recognition that people try to take into account the probable actions of other people when they make their own decisions. If this interdependence is taken into account, one person may have opportunities to manipulate others into taking certain actions that increase the first person's welfare.

Game theory's greatest influence has been in the theory of imperfect competition, where firms are large enough in size or few enough in number to be able to affect the economic variables, such as output prices or input wages, that are taken as fixed in a perfectly competitive market. Although this application is promising, it has yet to match the earlier mathematical revolution which brought forth new theories *and* new empirical tests of those theories.

Indeed, some economists feel the discipline's fascination with abstract theorizing, such as game theory, is in danger of turning economics into a kind of recreational mathematical theology, its practitioners involved with calculating the economic equivalent of the number of angels that can dance on the head of a pin.

Not all of modern economics, of course, has gone in the direction of increased mathematics. The study by George Stigler (Nobel, 1982) of government regulation has led to the eminently empirical argument that intervention usually benefits a small group of economic interests at a cost to society overall. With such beliefs now dominant, the influence of economics today is almost diametrically opposed to that which emerged from the revolutionary work of the 1930s. Economic theory today is used more often to justify government abstention than intervention. Economists today are tearing down the institutions recommended by their predecessors.

The economic and political revolution in Eastern Europe, the de-regulation of markets, and the privatization of publicly owned industries – all are reflections of the increased belief in the importance of unconstrained markets in the successful operation of an economy.

The turnabout has not come without public reaction. To a public raised on images of the Good Samaritan, it seems positively wicked to recommend that a government should in many cases do nothing. The citizenry feels that such a course leaves them helpless against the workings of powerful economic forces. They are right, to some extent; economists now tend to believe that, in the long run and on average, people are better off without that protection. By leaving out positive images of intervention, economists are forced to argue that in most cases individuals, not public institutions, are in the best position to foster the collective good.

In some sense economics has come full circle. Today, economists still believe that, as Adam Smith said, individual self-interest may be the key to the prosperity of all. And, like Thomas Carlyle, their critics still find that notion repugnant.

Economists today do little to defend themselves. Like their nineteenth-century forebears, they seem increasingly uninterested in applying their ideas to the real world. They calculate and project ever-more rarefied models, and all too often are unconcerned about whether the models mean anything.

As the profession enters the twenty-first century, this may create a problem for the Nobel Memorial Prize Committee. As that first generation of revolutionary economists dies, the Prize Committee will eventually face a task already bemoaned by many economists: finding significant recent accomplishments to reward. For even as economists's pronouncements become ever more powerful in the council of nations, even as theories of the market help to topple nations in Eastern Europe, the discipline of economics may be slipping into insignificance.

C.M. & M.K.

Ragnar Frisch

1969   *Adding Mathematics*

As a young man Ragnar Frisch trained as a goldsmith, his family's trade, and was certified in 1920. He was studying economics at the University of Oslo at the same time, and later did graduate work in the United States, France, Great Britain, Germany, and Italy.

In 1925, when Frisch first began teaching economics at the University of Oslo, he decided that the subject was too "literary" and set out to make it more scientific by basing his theories on mathematics and statistics. He called what he was doing "econometrics", which is concerned with trying to estimate the impact of, for example, a tax increase or reduced work effort.

Frisch was also the first to use the term "microeconomics", which describes an individual's economic behaviour, and "macroeconomics", which describes the economic actions of a nation. One of his most important contributions is a model he created to explain business cycles. He showed that the acceleration effects of investment widen the swings in the business cycle, pushing it up faster and higher, but down faster and lower as well. His macroeconomic model illustrated how business fluctuations could be triggered by unexpected shocks such as a stock market panic, a war, or a dramatic increase in the cost of a basic material such as oil. His model reflected the short or long duration of genuine business cycles.

Although he was not especially political, Frisch was an outspoken opponent of the Nazis. During their occupation of Norway in the Second World War, he was imprisoned and shared a cell with a chemist, Odd Has-

sel; both men would be awarded a Nobel in the same year.

The first Alfred Nobel Memorial Prize in Economic Sciences, shared with Jan Tinbergen of the Netherlands, went to Frisch in 1969. The two men were cited by the Committee "for having developed and applied dynamic models for the analysis of economic processes".

Ragnar Frisch and his wife were greeted by torch-carrying students when they learned he had been awarded the Nobel Prize. In 1930 he was one of the founders of the Econometric Society, an international group of statisticians and mathematical economists.

The symbolic scene of the Great Depression of the 1930s shows men selling apples on a New York street. Frisch sought solutions to the problem of restarting production during a depression when low demand for products discourages potential investors.

Paul A. Samuelson

Paul A. Samuelson's Foundations of Economic Analysis, *published in 1947, is one of the most influential economics books of the century. He received the 1970 Nobel Memorial Prize for "the scientific work through which he has developed static and dynamic economic theory and actively contributed to raising the level of analysis in economic science".*

Samuelson wrote the following for The Nobel Century:

"Mine has been a long life in economic science. Since 1930 this subject has made quantum strides. We know more today because our data are better. We can be deeper in analysis because our computers are speedier and cheaper. The sophistication of our economic theories represents a quantum jump ahead of earlier stages of economic thought.

"Nonetheless economics remains an inexact science. Together with logic and mathematics, it still depends on the art of judgment. And, to be candid, my extrapolation of past and present trends of progress does not suggest any imminent convergence on precise truth.

"Was it proper, then, to establish in 1969 a new Nobel Award in Economics to complement the traditional Nobel Prizes established in Alfred Nobel's will? Yes, I think, is the answer – provided we realize that Economics will have to earn its role as a parallel honour to those awarded in Physics, Chemistry, Physiology or Medicine, Literature, and Peace.

"In my own case the 1970 trip to Stockholm was an undiluted pleasure. My family and colleagues applauded my good fortune and Freudianly I was not aware of much criticism concerning the 1970 choice of the Royal Swedish Academy of Science. Aside from the pat on the back for past achievements, receiving the Nobel Medal remotivated the following two decades of active economic research. If anything, my subsequent research findings have received too much rather than too little attention from the busy world of affairs.

"The lustre of that Nobel Medal gained in brilliance because of the illustrious economists singled out by the Nobel Committee since 1969. That the winners were generally old friends is of personal significance only, but it says something for the networking of scientists that the three dozen scholars singled out for celebrity should generally be old friends and acquaintances. (A cynic will naturally wonder whether there does not lurk within such a cosy system the perils of collegial nepotism and ideological cliques. Just as eternal vigilance is the price of liberty, so eternal alertness is the price of objectivity.)

"Before there was an Alfred Nobel Award for Economic Science there were geniuses and sages toiling in the vineyard of political economy. I have my own list of "Nobelists" from the past. They include: Adam Smith (1776), our fountainhead; John Stuart Mill (1848), our *wunderkind*; Karl Marx (1867), our heretic; John Maynard Keynes (1936), our brilliant innovator and policy sage; and, of course, many others over the last two centuries deserve all the laurel wreaths that can be given.

"As I sit thinking at my desk, I feel part of this great chain of scholarship. Knowing that the future is longer than the past, I am also conscious of creative researchers yet unborn who will carry forward the frontier of knowledge and whom I honour as co-workers."

Left
In his office at the Massachusetts Institute of Technology, the staff help the Nobel laureate to celebrate. According to the citation, Samuelson's life work has been to reveal the "role of maximizing principles in analytic economics". In the 1960s he was an adviser to President John F. Kennedy.

Below
Paul Samuelson's ideas have been considered enormously relevant in economics since the Second World War. The rapid flow of Japanese exports, like this automobile being unloaded in an American port, was responsible for raising Japanese incomes in relation to those in the rest of the world.

Milton Friedman

1976

Milton Friedman is known as "the dean of the Chicago school of economics". A highly controversial theorist, Friedman has been a prolific writer of books, a columnist for magazines and newspapers; he even hosted a television series called *Free to Choose*.

Friedman first stirred up controversy by suggesting that the United States do away with social security, the minimum wage, and issue educational vouchers so that parents could choose a school for their children. Other Friedman proposals that *have* been adopted include economic deregulation and a volunteer army. His proposal for a negative income tax has its advocates in government, but has not passed Congress.

In his 1957 book, *A Theory of the Consumption Function*, Friedman theorized that consumers do not make important purchases on present income but on their future, expected, "permanent" income. This is his most important contribution. Later Friedman demonstrated that long-run changes in the demand for money throughout the history of the United States were almost always because of changes in permanent income. His massive studies caused economists to take monetary issues more seriously than they had in the 1950s and 1960s.

The Nobel Prize was awarded to Friedman in 1976 for "his achievements in the fields of consumption analysis, monetary history and theory, and for his demonstration of the complexity of stabilization policy".

As a student at Rutgers University, which he entered on a scholarship at the age of sixteen, Friedman had as a teacher Arthur F. Burns, later chairman

of the US Federal Reserve System. In 1950 Friedman went to Europe as a consultant to the Marshall Plan. He thought there should be floating exchange rates, and said that the fixed exchange rate system set up at the 1944 Bretton Woods Conference would collapse. In the early 1970s, it did.

Friedman gained still more notoriety as one of President Richard Nixon's informal advisers. Some economists who disliked Friedman's recommendations about the role of government in economic matters protested when Friedman was awarded the Nobel Prize, but his prominent contributions to modern economic theory and research are widely acknowledged.

I began my study of economics in the 1930s, when the Great Depression made the prospects for capitalism and democracy look very uncertain. After the Second World War, capitalist democracies performed extraordinarily well. Production, trade, and living standards grew rapidly, with quite moderate cyclical fluctuations. Can the discipline of economics claim any credit for this improvement? I think the answer is moderately affirmative, because the field of macroeconomics, founded by John Maynard Keynes when I was a student, taught governments and central banks how better to use their fiscal and monetary tools. They helped to create an environment in which systems of popular governments and market economies succeeded, while despotic governments and command economies failed.

The challenges of the future are quite different: speeding economic progress for the vast populations of the poor countries of the world, and coping with the environmental effects of economic progress and population growth.

JAMES TOBIN, 1981

Milton Friedman has been an active member of the American Economics Association for thirty years, and served as its president in 1967. He has also been a senior research associate at Stanford University's Hoover Institution.

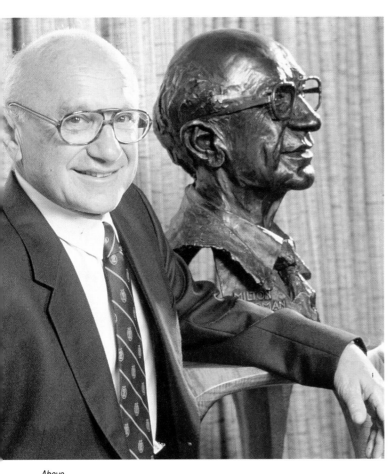

Above
In his Nobel lecture, Friedman said he rejected the Keynesian idea that there was a stable trade-off between the rate of inflation and unemployment. An inflationary monetary or fiscal policy might lower unemployment, but as workers and their companies became accustomed to a higher money growth, the price level would rise.

Right
Friedman met his wife, Rose Director, at the University of Chicago. She too is an economist, and they often collaborate. Parents of a son and a daughter, they have been married since 1938.

George Stigler

"Most economists", said George Stigler in his 1982 Nobel lecture, "are not the suppliers of new ideas but only demanders. Their problem is comparable to that of the automobile buyer – to find a reliable vehicle. Indeed, they usually end up buying a used, and therefore tested, idea."

In his work Stigler prefers a "literary" approach and avoids advanced mathematics. His style has been praised for its clarity, erudition, and elegance.

Over the years he has been concerned with production and distribution theories, with the impact of rent controls (he, like virtually all economists, believes they lead to poor construction and maintenance and housing shortages), supply and demand, industrial organization, the behaviour of industrial prices, and deregulation. *The Theory of Price*, which he published in 1947, has been a textbook for thousands of undergraduates.

Stigler has asked such questions as how much time and effort should a consumer spend trying to find the lowest price for a product? Until the costs, he found, of searching became more than the benefits of a cheaper price. Stigler theorized that uncertainty and ignorance on the part of purchasers could be reduced by information, but providing information costs money. His approach has had a major impact on advertising, on the understanding of purchasing behaviour and – most importantly and controversially – as an explanation for unemployment. A worker, for example, has poor information about the labour market and decides to wait for more job offers rather than take a current one. He

thinks there may be a job out there with a higher wage.

Stigler's theory of regulation was a key contribution. He argued that regulatory agencies tend to become the captive of the industries which they are supposed to regulate. Instead of serving the interests of the general public as intended, they become sympathetic to the industries and limit competition or approve excessive rates.

Stigler, who has a reputation as the world's authority on early economic history, was awarded his Nobel Prize in 1982 for his "seminal studies of industrial structures, function of markets, and causes and effects of public regulation".

The Third World, as it is sometimes called, is experiencing revolutions of many kinds – political, economic, cultural – but none more fundamental than the scientific revolution, which is inherent in all the others. Science affects all our ways of thinking about the world, both the physical world which, if I may make so bold, is easy to understand because it is regular and follows simple laws, and also the social world, which is more baffling and less predictable.

ARTHUR LEWIS, 1979

James M. Buchanan

James Buchanan's abiding interest in politics came from his family: his grandfather, John P. Buchanan, was once governor of Tennessee. The Depression, however, thwarted young James's plans to study law and to become a politician himself. Instead, he lived at home, milking cows to pay his tuition at Middle Tennessee State Teacher's College. He graduated first in his class, and was awarded a fellowship to study economics at the University of Tennessee.

According to Buchanan, the basic units of economics are individuals who are capable of making choices that will benefit the whole of society. His public choice theory is designed to predict how individuals will behave in their political roles – as voters, lobbyists, candidates, bureaucrats, judges and taxpayers. Economic theory explains the behaviour of individuals as buyers, sellers, producers, workers, investors, or entrepreneurs.

Buchanan has become a highly controversial figure among economists and has his detractors. The following comment on the twentieth century was written by him especially for this book:

"This century has witnessed the great experiments in collectivist organization and control of national economies, the experiments that are now universally acknowledged to have failed. Intellectuals and academicians everywhere, including political economists and social philosophers, are asking themselves why the "fatal conceit" that was socialism trapped so many minds for so long. Only as social scientists and social philosophers come to understand and to appreciate the creative potential that emerges in settings that minimize restrictions on individual liberty can effective reform, both in socialist and nonsocialist regimes, be designed.

"Individuals, both within and among nations, can live together in liberty, peace, and prosperity, but accomplishment of this purpose requires a generalized recognition of the limits imposed by the nature of man and his environment. Persons must, somehow, be brought into agreement upon the rules that define the social order in which they live.

"With the collapse of socialism, both as idea and reality, we are offered a once-in-history opportunity to create the constitutional order of a truly free society."

Left

James M. Buchanan, who has translated many economic papers from German and Italian, is advisory general director of the Center for Study of Public Choice at Fairfax, Virginia, an organization he helped to found. Its purpose is to extend economic methods and ways of thinking to the study of the political process.

Right

The voter plays a vital role in James Buchanan's theories, which link politics and economics. His Nobel citation said that his "foremost achievement is that he has . . . applied the concept of the political system as an exchange process for the achievement of mutual advantages".

6 LITERATURE

Edouard Vuillard's watercolour, "Woman Reading", evokes the pleasure which books afford.

Looked at empirically, the list of those "enobled" by the Nobel Prize for Literature offers a challenge to the historian. If he is true to his vocation, the historian's viewpoint cannot be strictly literary.

An examination of this interesting and varied group of writers suggests a classification under three headings. Although this may surprise some readers, the first and most obvious category is politics. By this I do not mean mere political activism but the nature of moral conviction. Secondly, and in a distinct minority, there are writers with religious preoccupations. The third category is the literature of identity, the search for "roots" — a particular place, an ethnic group or even a nation, any one of which may stir a writer's imagination.

To begin with politics. It is clear that for much of the century the Nobel Prize for Literature has gone to men of the Left, or rather from a certain element of the Left in the widest and most honourable sense of that term as a protest against social injustice. This is in the tradition of the Enlightenment or of our contemporary humanism. To take a typical example, the Swiss writer Carl Spitteler (1919) made his name with a book called *Imago*, a lively if somewhat trite critique of bourgeois traditions.

The same is true on a higher level of John Galsworthy (1932), a writer who, like Zola, took up the cry (never mind whether or not it is true) of the French Jacobins or Montagnards: "The rich are what they have always been — hard and pitiless." It is also true of the Italian poet Giosuè Carducci (1906). He was a republican, democrat and pro-revolutionary, often hostile to Catholicism or at least anti-clerical, even if in later years he came to write quite warmly of the monarchy. Anatole France (1921), a champion of internationalism who played an important role in the pro-Dreyfus campaign, also belongs in this group.

Noble at heart, or wishing to appear so, the Left intelligentsia vigorously opposed the carnage of the First World War. Two examples are Romain Rolland (1915) who courted considerable unpopularity with his pacifist collection *Au dessus de la melée* and, to a lesser extent, Martin du Gard

(1937). Their position was compounded after the war by a fairly widespread refusal among Nobel writers to compromise with dictatorships. The Spanish poet Juan Ramón Jiménez (1956) left for America in 1936 because of the Spanish Civil War. The Swedish novelist Eyvind Johnson (1974) was a bitter critic of authoritarian regimes who contrived to pillory them in novels devoted to witchcraft trials or filled with a retrospective hatred of the ninth-century Carolingian dynasty!

Anti-totalitarian writing could change into the restrained but classical anti-Fascism of the Italian poet Eugenio Montale (1975), and there was a strong allergy to his country's periodic despotisms in the work of the Greek poet and diplomat Giorgos Seferis (1963). Leftish trends also produced a Nobel Prize for George Bernard Shaw (1925), a Fabian socialist with a soft spot for the Soviet Union and, unfortunately, for the Stalinism of the 1930s.

Venturing a stage further, communism played a considerable part in the life and work of a number of Nobel laureates. The poetry of Pablo Neruda (1971) combines an extraordinary fluency with an unswerving fidelity to Marxist-Leninist ideology. On the other hand, commitment to communist regimes when one has to live under them may have a purely institutional character. The Yugoslav writer Ivo Andrić (1961), who wrote in Serbo-Croat, became a deputy in the legislative assembly of Bosnia-Hercegovina after the Second World War and, in this way only, an official figure in the Titoist system. But with the honourable exception of Andrić, the dangers to an artist of compromise are obvious. Mikhail Sholokhov (1965) appears to have indulged in plagiarism even in the best of his works. But the author of *And Quiet Flows the Don* was also the recipient of the Stalin Prize and thus was able to shelter behind his semi-official status.

In the West, the dangers of compromise have been less sinister. The possession of a party card in post-Fascist Italy was a ritual gesture for a member of the intelligentsia. It is of little consequence to the work of Salvatore Quasimodo (1959) who briefly enrolled in the Italian Communist Party at the end of the Second World War. The career of André Gide (1947) was more dramatic. For years, Gide was a contented fellow-traveller of the French Communist Party. The break came with the publication of *Retour de l'URSS,* in which he decided to eat his words and tell the truth about the wretchedness of Russian life. His former comrades never forgave him and even went so far as to attack him for his morals (Gide was homosexual), which he had never tried to conceal. In certain respects the much less well-known career of the Swedish poet and novelist Harry Martinson (1974) is similar to Gide's, from the initial sentimental attachment to communism to his final rejection of totalitarian repression.

Sympathy for the Left was also apparent in the Holy of Holies of the Existentialist Church which the Nobel jury singled out for distinction on two occasions after the Second World War, in Albert Camus (1957) and Jean-Paul Sartre (1964). Sartre declined the prize, having "joined the Resistance" as they said in those days, or at least *after* the liberation of Paris in 1944. It was a shrewd decision, allowing Sartre to maintain his credibility in a variety of eclectic causes beginning with Castroism and culminating later (while awaiting the final call) with Maoism, perhaps the Great Thinker's final indignity.

Camus, on the other hand, was close to communism in his youth and later was active in the French Resistance. He subsequently dissociated himself from regimes based on violence and persecution (those on the Soviet model and others in the Third World). At times — a little-known fact — Camus discreetly favoured a form of Atlanticism, to be seen here and there in his *Essais.* Contrary to the usual practice of the high-minded, therefore, Camus abandoned his impartiality and took up a position more sympathetic to the West than to the East.

The late 1960s brought a handful of heroes — or heralds — out of the cloisters and on to the barricades in both Europe and North America. Bertrand Russell (1950), by then in his nineties, led the intellectual opposition to the war in Vietnam and to nuclear weapons. The novelist Halldór Laxness (1955) protested at the US "occupation" of Iceland, comparable in his view to the Danish domination of the eighteenth century. A certain mysticism of the time sought spiritual nourishment in the works of Hermann Hesse (1946) from an earlier period.

To conclude on this category of Nobel laureates. Certain affiliates or fellow-travellers of the Socialist International (to one degree or another) were rewarded for their individual talents, which were often very considerable. They were not rewarded — let us be clear — for purely political activities. That includes some important figures from Germany: Gerhart Hauptmann (1912), the dramatist who introduced the collective hero (the struggling artisans in *Die Weber*); Thomas Mann (1929), symbol of moral resistance to Nazism; and Heinrich Böll (1972), champion of fashionable radicalism against Germany's right-wing press. Following

the same principles, we should include from the United States Sinclair Lewis (1930), scrouge of small-town American philistinism; John Steinbeck (1962), whose *The Grapes of Wrath* is an angry chronical of the miseries of the Great Depression; and Ernest Hemingway (1954), who enlisted transatlantic sympathy for the republican struggle in the Spanish Civil War. Similar criteria would single out two outstanding Latin American writers: Miguel Angèl Asturias (1967) who denounced the immorality of banana republics; and Gabriel García Márquez (1982), whose fictions of Macondo, the town of his imagination, have always connoted progressive social principles, sometimes too "progressive"!

None of this is to accuse the Nobel Committee of left-wing orthodoxy. Liberal or radical opinions have for very long been associated, almost unavoidably, with the writing of poetry and prose. The correlation is not easy to explain, but it exists. Perhaps we should simply say that although twentieth-century writers, good or mediocre, are not drawn from any particular socio-political milieu, they tend to belong to the Left. It may be regrettable, but it is a fact.

Conservatives have had their triumphs too, however. Churchill and Kipling both won the Nobel. Churchill (1953) was by then a statesman above factionalism. Kipling's award in 1907 came from the simple fact of his tremendous artistic achievement. With some reservations, we could say the same about Spain and some less significant writers: both the dramatist José Echegaray (1904) and his fellow Prize-winner Jacinto Benavente (1922) were reactionaries. Finally, and in a special category, there is Knut Hamsun (1920), the Norwegian novelist whose reputation for fine novels such as *Hunger* and *The Growth of the Soil* was disastrously compromised by his support for Nazism in his later years — a far cry from Churchill and Kipling indeed. In fact it is arguable that the Nobel Committee should have honoured a greater number of writers who, like Churchill, were dual personalities — both scholars and men of action. But individuals who combine such qualities are perhaps rarer than we think.

Today, the divisions between right and left, between reaction and progress, are fading; and the division between Fascism and anti-Fascism is so dated as to belong to a previous generation. It is the Nobel Prizes awarded to dissident writers that now compel our attention. It is enough to recall that awards made to Czesław Miłosz (1980) of Poland, Jaroslav Seifert (1984) of Czechoslovakia (a country whose president is a playwright) and even more those made to writers from the Soviet Union who were implacable opponents of totalitarianism such as Boris Pasternak (1958), Alexander Solzhenitsyn (1970) and Joseph Brodsky (1987). Pasternak's great novel *Dr Zhivago* was banned and he was obliged to decline the prize; both Solzhenitsyn and Brodsky sought refuge in the United States.

Politics and religion make strange, sometimes dangerous,

bedfellows. Moving from one to the other, however, to our second of three categories, we note the prominence given to Catholic writers by a prize born of Northern Protestantism. François Mauriac (1952), who was at one time regarded as the leading Catholic novelist, wrote of sin with delicacy and remorse. The papistic traditions peculiar to Poland and Ireland (and to Ireland's emigrants) produced a Nobel for Henryk Sienkiewicz (1905) and Eugene O'Neill (1936), for converts to Catholicism such as the Norwegian Sigrid Undset (1928), for sympathizers Henri Bergson (1927), strongly drawn to Catholicism in spite of his Jewish origins) and for straightforward spiritualists (Rudolf Eucken, 1908). Other religions are less well represented. T. S. Eliot (1948) is a particularly powerful presence; we know how greatly this poet was marked by his reception into the Anglican Church. Rabindranath Tagore (1913) must stand as almost the sole representative of the vast mystical and philosophical tradition of the Indian subcontinent.

But the capacity to enter into religion is passing from the West. Our third category, that of the literature of identity, is one which occasionally provokes wry amusement, sometimes well deserved, from literary critics like the historian Richard Cobb. It has, however, produced some masterpieces, albeit of unequal value.

Of course, it would be dangerous, even grotesque, to pigeonhole a writer according to the place of his or her birth. Luigi Pirandello (1934) had little to do with Sicily and Maurice Maeterlinck (1911) even less to do with Flanders. A purely negative approach, however, would not be appropriate either. Sardinia, at least to begin with, was the inspiration for the Italian novelist Grazia Deledda (1926).

Further to the north, several writers picked out by the Nobel Committee are too easily dismissed as provincial or jingoistic. They include the Swedish poet Erik Axel Karlfeldt (1931), associated with his native Dalkarl; Bjornstjerne Bjornson (1903), whose novels and plays of Norwegian life arguably had as great an influence on his country as the work of his mentor Ibsen; the Swedish essayist Verner von Heidenstam (1916), preoccupied with the Vikings, St Bridget, Charles XII and Nordic heroes; and the Danish essayist, novelist and poet Johannes Jensen (1944), a prophet of social Darwinism.

Far to the south of the Baltic and Schleswig-Holstein, other distinguished names stand out in a distinctive southern light. Frédéric Mistral (1904) sang of a boundless Provence; William Faulkner (1949) transformed the old, defeated American South into a *locus classicus* of world literature. At its best this art — tensioned between the particular and the general, between the established and the deracinated, the long hidden and the suddenly revealed — acquires a universal significance, combining ethnicity, religion and the sharpened sensibility typical of cultures in the process of disintegration and secularization.

This brings us, in the literature of identity, to the great Jewish writers of the twentieth century. They belong respectively to the English language (Saul Bellow, 1976), to the German (Nelly Sachs, 1966), to the Yiddish (Isaac Bashevis Singer, 1978) and to the Hebrew and Israeli (Shmuel Agnon, 1966). Tragedy is politics, André Malraux remarked, and Malraux never won the Nobel Prize. Indeed, political decisions — some criminal (Nazism and Stalinism), some positive and difficult, like the establishment of the State of Israel — have at different times respectively destroyed or liberated the Jewish people. Particularly for those who have written of the suffering of our century, the Nobel Prize is no act of providence but a tribute paid to a tragedy that affects us all. Let me conclude with the words of a Polish novelist who wrote literature of world importance in a language not his own and who also never won the Nobel Prize, Joseph Conrad: "All ambitions are lawful except those which climb upward on the miseries or credulities of mankind."

E. Le R. L.

On the eve of his ninetieth birthday, George Bernard Shaw meets his neighbours, Samuel and Clara Winsten, at his country home in Hertfordshire. Mrs Winsten, a sculptor, made a bust in bronze of her famous neighbour.

Rudyard Kipling

By the time Rudyard Kipling was forty-two years old he had published hundreds of poems, sixteen collections of short stories, two travel books, and four novels: a body of work that won him the 1907 Nobel Prize for Literature. Although he did not deliver a laureate lecture, Kipling did attend the ceremony in Stockholm, where a member of the Swedish Academy cited *Barrack-Room Ballads* (1892), which included his two most famous poems, "Gunga Din" and "Mandalay", as being "magnificent soldier-songs brimming over with virile humour". Conceding that some of Kipling's language was "at times somewhat coarse", the speaker pointed out that his style had an "invigorating directness", as well as "tenderness and delicacy of touch".

Born in Bombay in 1865, Rudyard Kipling was brought to England in 1871 at the age of six. He spent several miserable years as a boarder with his younger sister, which he recounted in *The Light that Failed* (1890). He then attended a secondary school that trained young men for Britain's finest military academies, however, none of these would take him because of his severe near-sightedness. In 1881 at age sixteen he returned to India, where he began writing stories and light verse for Anglo-Indian newspapers.

When Kipling moved back to England in his mid-twenties, his work already was being read throughout the British Empire. Many compared him to Charles Dickens, to which the Nobel Committee agreed: "Like Dickens he feels a keen sympathy with those of low degree in the community, and like him he can perceive the humour in trifling

traits and acts.''

Unlike Dickens, Kipling spoke fluent Hindustani, and set the scene of many of his books in the nineteenth-century India he had known as a child. In *Kim* (1901), generally considered his greatest novel, an Irish street-boy and a Buddhist priest wander together through the Himalayas in search of a holy river. Although Kipling's two *Jungle* books (1894/5) were also set in India, he wrote them in Brattleboro, Vermont, where he went to live with his American-born wife. New England was also to become the setting for his children's classic, *Captains Courageous*.

Kipling stayed in the United States only a few years, but his popularity while he was there was immense; on a visit from England in 1898, he developed pneumonia, and the newspapers printed daily bulletins on his condition.

In 1902 Kipling moved with his wife to a village in Sussex, where he would remain for the rest of his life, although he still travelled widely. That same year he published the *Just So Stories* (1902), full of such now-familiar fables as ''How the Camel Got His Hump''. Kipling, whose immense feeling for children was so evident in his work, had three of his own. Tragically, one of his two daughters died of pneumonia when still a little girl, and his son was killed in the First World War. Grieving over the loss of his son, Kipling immersed himself in politics. Closely associated with the right wing of the Conservative party, he spoke out strongly against home rule for Ireland, and against women's suffrage.

By the time he reached the age of seventy, Kipling perhaps had fulfilled the ideal he had expressed years earlier, to be ''ready, ay ready at the call of duty'', and then, when the call came – as it did in 1936 – to ''go to God like a soldier''.

Left

The humorous magazine *Punch* greeted Kipling's Award with this gently satirical portrait of him as ''a verray parfit Nobel knight ''.

Right

In 1889, when Rudyard Kipling arrived in London, he was hailed as the literary successor to Charles Dickens. He met and became a friend of King George V. Kipling is buried in the Poet's Corner of Westminster Abbey.

Above
Kipling's stories for children have been among his most lasting works. He is seen here telling one of the "Just So" stories he wrote for his "best beloved" daughter, Josephine.

Left
Kipling and his wife stroll in London. The former Caroline Balestier, Mrs Kipling was from Brattleboro, Vermont, where the couple lived after they were first married. Kipling wrote *Captains Courageous*, a sea adventure about New England fishermen, while living there.

Right
Cyrus Cuneo's portrait of the popular poet and storyteller surrounds Kipling with many of his creations including Mowgli, Kim and the Soldiers Three.

Rabindranath Tagore

According to an often-repeated story, Rabindranath Tagore, who was awarded the Nobel in 1913, insisted that his goat be given a room at his Stockholm hotel so he could have goat's milk whenever he wished. In fact, Tagore did not attend the ceremony, but sent a telegram from India that said, "I beg to convey to the Swedish Academy my grateful appreciation of the breadth of understanding which has brought the distant near, and has made a stranger a brother."

Rabindranath Tagore's father was a leader of a religious sect in nineteenth-century Bengal. Rabindranath, who was born in 1861, was educated at home, wrote his first poem at the age of eight, and at seventeen was sent to England to study.

When he returned to India, Rabindranath was sent by his father to manage the family estates in Bengal. During this time he wrote poems, novels, short stories, plays, composed musical dramas, dance dramas, and did numerous drawings and paintings. He also started an experimental school, and took part in the Indian nationalist movement. Tagore was a devoted friend of Gandhi.

In 1913 his incredible creative outpouring was rewarded by the Nobel Committee – its first award to an Asian – because of Tagore's "profoundly sensitive, fresh and beautiful verse, by which with consummate skill, he has made his poetic thought, expressed in his own English words, part of the literature of the West".

One of Tagore's most acclaimed poems is "Gitanjali: Song Offering" (1912). Here is a noted passage:

Where the mind is without fear
and the head is held high;
Where knowledge is free;
Where words come out from the
depth of truth;
Where tireless striving stretches
its arms toward perfection:
Where the clear stream of reason
has not lost its way into the
dreary desert sand of dead habit:
into that haven of freedom, let
me awake.

Two years after receiving his Nobel Prize, Tagore was knighted by the British. Later, in protest against British policies in India, he resigned the honour. Some of Tagore's short fiction, such as *Hungry Stones* (1916), *Broken Ties* (1925), and *The Housewarming* (1965) makes strong political comments on Indian social concerns. He died in 1941, but is still considered to be the most eminent contemporary Bengali poet.

Tagore's poetry was praised by T.S. Eliot as "a reminder of one thing and of forty things which we are ever likely to lose sight of in the confusion of our Western life, in the racket of our cities, in the jabber of manufactured literature".

Rabindranath Tagore wrote more than 3,000 songs, which people living in Bengali villages sang without knowing who the author was. Much of Tagore's poetry has never been translated into English; he wrote primarily in Bengali, encouraging other Indian authors to write in their own vernaculars as well.

Today the greatness of a civilized leader ought to be measured by the universality of his vision and his sense of responsibility towards all humankind. The developed world and the Third World are but one family. Each human being bears responsibility towards it by the degree of what he has obtained of knowledge, wisdom, and civilization. I would not be exceeding the limits of my duty if I told them in the name of the Third World: Be not spectators to our miseries. You have to play therein a noble role befitting your status. From your position of superiority you are responsible for any misdirection of animal, or plant, to say nothing of man, in any of the four corners of the world. We have had enough of words. Now is the time for action. It is time to end the age of brigands and usurers.

NAGUIB MAHFOUZ, 1988

George Bernard Shaw

1925 *The Artist-Philosopher*

Recalling his youth, George Bernard Shaw once remarked that it was a time "when I was almost unendurably brilliant". Indeed, Shaw lived ninety-four years, and remained almost unendurably brilliant right to the end.

Shaw is still the most written-about writer of the last two centuries; the first full-length Shavian critique, by H. L. Mencken, was published in 1905. During Shaw's lifetime, everyone from Frank Harris to G. K. Chesterton to Edmund Wilson – who compared him to Plato – tried to pin down his genius. Since his death in 1950, nearly 150 critical biographies have been published.

Although he called himself an "artist-philosopher", Shaw fulfilled an incredible number of other roles as well: Creative-Evolutionist; pacifist; leader of the Fabian Society; and reviewer of the fine arts (W. H. Auden called him "probably the best music critic who ever lived").

Primarily George Bernard Shaw was a dramatist. By the 1920s he was the world's best-known living playwright. His plays include such classics as *Arms and the Man* (1898), *Caesar and Cleopatra* (1901), *Man and Superman* (1903) (its famous discursive third act, "Don Juan in Hell", is often performed independently), *Major Barbara* (1905), *Androcles and the Lion* (1912), *Pygmalion* (1913), *Heartbreak House* (1919), and *Back to Methuselah* (1921). His only tragedy, *Saint Joan*, was written in 1925, four years after the canonization of Joan of Arc. It was also a year before Shaw won the Nobel Prize "for his literary work which is marked by both idealism and humanity, and whose sharp satire is often infused with a singular poetic beauty".

A non–believer in prizes – he called the Nobel Prize "a life belt thrown to a swimmer who has already reached the shore" – Shaw expressed his appreciation to the Swedish Academy but declined to attend the award ceremony. He used the prize money to create the Anglo-Swedish Literary Foundation, which financed good English translations of Swedish literature, especially the plays of August Strindberg.

Shaw's beginnings were nearly as unpromising as those of his immortal "dragon-tailed guttersnipe" Eliza Doolittle. He was born in Dublin in 1856, the third child and only son of an alcoholic civil servant who was always on the verge of bankruptcy. Shaw left school at the age of fifteen, and went to work in Dublin at an estate agency. A year later he moved to London. There, writing five pages a day, he turned out five novels, none of which were published. His first play, *Widowers' Houses* (1893), produced when he was thirty-six, closed after two performances. When success finally came, Shaw wrote of himself in the third person in a letter to the writer Edith Nesbit: "Shaw was an utterly ignorant man . . . He was a dis-

grace to his school, where he acquired little Latin & less Greek. He got no secondary education & came to London an unknown & obscure provincial. And this is the man to whom people attribute the omniscience, the knowledge of public affairs, of law, of medicine, of navigation &c&c&c which informs the plays & prefaces of GBS. Absurd!"

At the age of forty-two Shaw married Charlotte Payne-Townshend, an Irish socialist. The marriage, which lasted until her death forty-five years later, was reportedly never consummated.

Shaw spent his last years at his country house in Hertfordshire. In *Man and Superman*, a character seems to speak as much for the playwright as for himself when he says: "Were I not possessed with a purpose beyond my own I had better be a ploughman than a philosopher; for the ploughman lives as long as the philosopher, eats more, sleeps better, and rejoices in the wife of his bosom with less misgiving."

Thomas Mann

Born in 1875, the German novelist Thomas Mann spent his first sixteen years in Lübeck, a bustling commercial city on the Baltic Sea. The city became the setting for his first novel, *Buddenbrooks*, which was published in 1901 when Mann was twenty-six years old. It is a multigenerational chronicle that traces the slow decline of a wealthy bourgeois family. The German poet Rainer Maria Rilke called the book a fusion of the novelist's "colossal labour" and the poet's "gift of seeing". Mann's 1929 Nobel Prize was "principally for his great novel, *Buddenbrooks*, which has won steadily increased recognition as one of the classic works of contemporary literature".

Married and the father of three daughters and three sons, Mann was plagued throughout his life by his homosexuality. His novel *Death in Venice* (1912), in which a distinguished middle-aged artist is destroyed by a hopeless infatuation with a beautiful young boy, was influenced by Schopenhauer and Nietzsche. Written a decade after his other short classic, *Tonio Kröger* (1903), *Death in Venice* is considered one of the most brilliant novellas ever written.

With the onset of the First World War, Mann wrote a 600-page criticism of rationalist philosophy, entitled *Observations of an Unpolitical Man* (1918). He later reworked many of the themes in his novel *The Magic Mountain* (1924), in which patients at a tuberculosis sanitarium in the Swiss Alps embody the spiritual ills of pre-war Europe.

In 1930, a year after he won the Nobel Prize, the self-proclaimed "unpolitical man" turned profoundly political.

Mann delivered an impassioned "appeal to reason" in Berlin, calling for socialists and liberals to resist Nazism. He also published *Mario and the Magician*, an allegory in which a decadent hypnotist suggests such future dictators as Hitler and Mussolini.

When Hitler became chancellor in 1933, Mann and his wife, who was Jewish, were in Zürich. They decided not to return to the fatherland, and three years later Mann was stripped of his German citizenship.

In 1938 the family emigrated to the United States. Mann, who eventually became an American citizen, spent

In 1938, emigrating to the United States, Mann and his daughter and wife are greeted by photographers on board ship in a New York harbour. After the Second World War, Mann visited West and East Germany, but refused to live in his homeland. He spent his last years near Zürich.

three years as a humanities lecturer at Princeton University before moving to southern California. Throughout the Second World War he made frequent radio broadcasts to Germany denouncing Hitler.

Mann's Nobel presentation speech lauded him for wrestling with ideas and creating "painful beauty though . . . convinced that art is questionable". This Mann never ceased to do. He spent more than a decade working on a quartet of novels, *Joseph and His Brothers*, an ironic retelling of the biblical story from a modern viewpoint. Three years before his death in 1955, Mann moved back to Zürich where he wrote his last book, *The Confessions of the Confidence Trickster Felix Krull* (1954). The autobiographical parody is about a dazzling artist who, try as he might, cannot change the world. Mann thought it was his "best and most felicitous achievement".

Left
Thomas Mann's first novel *Buddenbrooks* was partly autobiographical. It tells the story of a wealthy, good-natured German family, who, when they lose their money, are destroyed.

Below
British actor Dirk Bogarde (right) starred in a film of Mann's famous novella, *Death in Venice*, directed by Lucino Visconti. The movie version made the main character a great composer. The story is about an artist's isolation and the impact of a hopeless love.

Pearl Buck

Only two Nobel Prizes were awarded in 1938. One went to the Italian nuclear physicist Enrico Fermi, the other to the American writer Pearl Buck. Hers almost didn't happen. The literature prize had been a three-way contest, with most selection Committee members favouring the Flemish storyteller Stijn Streuvels over either Buck or the German novelist Hermann Hesse. In the end it went to the most universally popular of the three "for her rich and truly epic descriptions of peasant life in China and for her biographical master-pieces".

Fermi's wife, Laura, was at the Stock-holm ceremony and observed the forty-six-year-old writer closely: "Plump and attractive in a soft evening dress, the train of which she had gracefully gathered around her, a pensive smile on her pleasant face, her hands demurely resting on her lap, Pearl Buck sat still: her stiffness was the outward projection of her bewilderment at the undemocratic manifestations of an Old World order and of her astonishment at being the object of such a manifestation."

The Committee's choice – Buck was the first American woman ever to win a Nobel Prize for Literature – caused a furore. American critics predicted face-tiously that next the Prize would go to such best-selling authors as Anita (*Gentlemen Prefer Blondes*) Loos or Margaret (*Gone With the Wind*) Mitchell. They were more right than they knew. Mitchell had indeed been proposed as a 1938 candidate, and the Literature Committee had given *Gone With the Wind* serious consideration.

During the course of her eighty years, Pearl Buck wrote as many works, including, in 1936, biographies of both her mother (*The Exile*) and her father (*Fighting Angel*). However, it was her story about a peasant family living in northern China, *The Good Earth* (1931), that was generally felt to be her master-piece and won the 1932 Pulitzer Prize. Published in 1931, the book was her third novel; the manuscript of her first had been lost in the late 1920s when her house in Nanking was ransacked during China's civil war; her second novel *East Wind: West Wind* (1930), a love story set in China, had been an immediate success.

Born Pearl Sydenstricker in Hillsboro, West Virginia, Pearl was an infant when her Presbyterian missionary parents moved the family to China's interior city of Chinkiang. Pearl spoke Chinese before she spoke English, and was tutored at home by a Confucian scholar before being sent to boarding school in Shanghai. Later she attended Randolph-Macon Women's College in Virginia.

In the words of a Nobel spokesman, it was Pearl Buck's mission to act "as interpreter to the West of the nature and being of China". She was most eloquent, particularly in *The Good Earth*, on the position of Chinese women. About Western women, however, she was just as outspoken. In *Of Men and Women*, published in 1941, the feminist-before-her-time wrote about coming to the United States to live: "Surprise followed upon surprise. Where I had expected in a free society to find women working everywhere as men worked, according to their ability, I found them actually less influential by far than women had been under the traditional scheme of life in China."

I did not have much to do and I had free time for writing and being foolish, I lived on tea, bread, and dreams. I was twenty-two years old. I was healthy, had only one suit, and boots with holes in them. I had faith in the world and a thousand bold projects in my mind. I wrote feverishly: dramas in ten acts, novels without end, stories in several volumes, poems. Then I tore up everything mercilessly and burned it.

W. S. REYMONT, 1924

For a true writer each book should be a new beginning where he tries again for something that is beyond attainment. He should always try for something that has never been done or that others have tried and failed. Then sometimes, with great luck, he will succeed.

ERNEST HEMINGWAY, 1954

Above
Pearl Buck and her second husband set up Welcome House, which sponsored the adoption of children of Asian-American ancestry. The Pearl Buck Foundation was funded by Buck's considerable earnings from her popular novels.

Left
Luise Rainer and Paul Muni starred in the film version of Pearl Buck's most popular novel, *The Good Earth*. It told of a Chinese peasant's life on a farm and of his trip to the city when starvation threatened. The story ended when the time came for him to be claimed by the good earth.

André Gide

A Man of Contrasts

André Gide, the French novelist, essayist, critic, and dramatist, tried his hand at every conceivable genre. His first book, *The Notebooks of André Walter*, about a young man (himself) trying to write a novel, was written in prose poetry. He wrote a number of brilliant *recits*, or narratives, including *The Immoralist* (1930) and *Strait Is the Gate* (1924). Gide claimed to have written only one novel, *The Counterfeiters*. Published in 1927, it brought him international recognition and caused Aldous Huxley to dedicate his novel *Point Counterpoint* to him. Gide also wrote a major study of Dostoyevsky. He wrote travel diaries – blistering attacks on social and political abuses – about the Congo and the Soviet Union. He translated Shakespeare, Conrad, Whitman, and Rilke, adapted Kafka for the stage, and co-founded the distinguished literary journal, *Nouvelle Revue Française*. More than sixty years went into his *Journals*. His work inspired a generation of French writers, among them André Maurois, who, meeting Gide after the First World War, described him as "a clean-shaven man whose features reminded one of certain Japanese masks, a face so striking as to be handsome".

An only child, André Gide was born in Paris in 1869. His father, a law professor at the Sorbonne, died when he was ten, leaving him at the mercy of an austere, Calvinist mother. At thirteen André fell in love with his cousin, Madeleine Rondeaux, three years his senior. It was a chaste love; the two spent hours reading aloud to each other.

Gide's first sexual experience, at the age of twenty-three, was with an Arab boy in Tunisia. After contracting tuberculosis, Gide returned to Paris where his mother nursed him back to health. Two years later in Algeria, Gide met Oscar Wilde to whom he attributed "the courage of my tastes".

In 1895, five months after his mother's death, Gide married his cousin Madeleine. Shocked by her husband's sexual proclivities, Madeleine Gide soon retreated to their estate in Normandy. Ironically, in 1923 Gide fathered a child by another woman. A year later he published *Corydon*, a theoretical justification of homosexuality in the form of a Platonic dialogue. He fully expected, and even welcomed, the public condemnation that followed: "I consider it much better," he said, "to be hated for what one is than loved for what one isn't." After spending much of their married life apart, Gide and his wife were reconciled several years before her death in 1938.

The presentation speech at the 1947 Nobel Award ceremony noted that "more than any of his contemporaries, Gide has been a man of contrasts". This was certainly true. Gide was a Frenchman who preferred North Africa. He was a Protestant who very nearly converted to the Catholic faith. He became a Communist in 1931 and denounced Communism five years later. He was frail and sickly all his life and yet lived to be eighty-one. His education, because of his poor health, was at best erratic. Yet Gide became what the deputy chairman of the Nobel Foundation called "the venerable master of French literature whose genius has so profoundly influenced our time".

In 1947, the year Gide won the Nobel Prize, he was too ill to attend the Award ceremony in Stockholm.

Mankind is not divided into a flock of individuals, people floating about in a vacuum, like cosmonauts who have penetrated beyond the pull of earth's gravity. We live on earth, we are subject to its laws and, as the Gospel puts it, sufficient unto the day is the evil thereof, its troubles and trials, its hopes for a better future. Vast sections of the world's population are inspired by the same desires, and live for common interests that bind them together far more than they separate them. These are the working people, who create everything with their hands and their brains. I am one of those authors who consider it their honour and their highest liberty to have a completely untrammelled chance of using their pens to serve the working people.

MIKHAIL SHOLOKHOV, 1965

André Gide was much celebrated in his old age. In 1950, a year before his death, he published the last of his four-volume journals which he had begun in 1889. They are considered unique in the world of literature.

T. S. Eliot

Born in St Louis, Thomas Sterns Eliot grew up in the United States but spent his adult life in London and became a British citizen.

Critics consider his "The Love Song of J. Alfred Prufrock", written while Eliot was at Harvard, and published in 1917 by Virginia and Leonard Woolf at the Hogarth Press, to have marked the beginning of modern poetry. Eliot married Vivien Haigh-Wood the same month as the poem's publication. During the First World War he taught, and then worked for Lloyds Bank. He became assistant editor of *The Egoist* in 1917, and published *Prufrock and Other Observations* the same year. In 1922 *The Waste Land* appeared, voicing the discontent of a disillusioned generation. Eliot left Lloyds in 1925 to become a director of Faber and Faber, the well-known publishing house.

Eliot's move towards the church and High Anglicanism can be seen in his poetry from 1927 onwards. His plays include *Murder in the Cathedral* (1935), *The Family Reunion* (1939), and *The Cocktail Party* (1950), among others.

Only a poet of the first rank could make an acceptance speech as graceful as the one Eliot delivered in Stockholm:

"To profess my own unworthiness would be to cast doubt upon the wisdom of the Academy; to praise the Academy might suggest that I, as a literary critic, approved the recognition given to myself as a poet. May I therefore ask that it be taken for granted, that I experienced, on learning of this award to myself, all the normal emotions of exaltation and vanity that any human being might be expected to feel at such a

moment, with enjoyment of the flattery, and exasperation at the inconvenience of being turned overnight into a public figure? Were the Nobel Award similar in kind to any other award, and merely higher in degree, I might still try to find words of appreciation: but since it is different in kind from any other, the expression of one's feelings calls for resources which language cannot supply."

Eliot was a reclusive, secretive man. When someone congratulated him on winning the Nobel Prize, his dour reply was, "The Nobel is a ticket to one's funeral. No one has ever done anything after he got it."

Left
T.S. Eliot as a young man, "Standing on the shore of all we know ", as his graduation poem of 1905 puts it.

Right
Eliot's portrait was painted in 1949 by Patrick Heron. He had told the Nobel audience in 1948, "I stand before you, not on my own merits, but as a symbol, for a time, of the significance of poetry."

William Faulkner

"Truths of the Heart"

The author of The Sound and the Fury *(1929),* As I Lay Dying *(1930),* Light in August *(1932), and other novels and short stories took his themes from his home state of Mississippi. Faulkner's tragic sense of life in the South after the Civil War was dark and melodramatic, but occasionally humorous as well. Other important works include* The Hamlet *(1940), and* Intruder in the Dust *(1948).*

His Nobel Prize acceptance speech is regarded as perhaps the most effective ever made there. It is reprinted here in its entirety.

"I feel that this award was not made to me as a man, but to my work – a life's work in the agony and sweat of the human spirit, not for glory and least of all for profit, but to create out of the materials of the human spirit something which did not exist before. So this award is only mine in trust. It will not be difficult to find a dedication for the money part of it commensurate with the purpose and significance of its origin. But I would like to do the same with the acclaim too, by using this moment as a pinnacle from which I might be listened to by the young men and women already dedicated to the same anguish and travail, among whom is already that one who will some day stand here where I am standing.

"Our tragedy today is a general and universal physical fear so long sustained by now that we can even bear it. There are no longer problems of the spirit. There is only the question: When will I be blown up? Because of this, the young man or woman writing today has forgotten the problems of the

human heart in conflict with itself which alone can make good writing because only that is worth writing about, worth the agony and the sweat.

"He must learn them again. He must teach himself that the basest of all things is to be afraid; and, teaching himself that, forget it forever, leaving no room in his workshop for anything but the old verities and truths of the heart, the old universal truths lacking which any story is ephemeral and doomed – love and honour and pity and pride and compassion and sacrifice. Until he does so, he labours under a curse. He writes not of love but of lust, of defeats in which nobody loses anything of value, of victories without hope and, worst of all, without pity or compassion. His griefs grieve on no universal bones, leaving no scars. He writes not of the heart but of the glands.

"Until he relearns these things, he will write as though he stood among and watched the end of man. I decline to accept the end of man. It is easy enough to say that man is immortal simply because he will endure: that when the last dingdong of doom has clanged and faded from the last worthless rock hanging tideless in the last red and dying evening, that even then there will still be one more sound: that of his puny inexhaustible voice, still talking. I refuse to accept this. I believe that man

will not merely endure: he will prevail. He is immortal, not because he alone among creatures has an inexhaustible voice, but because he has a soul, a spirit capable of compassion and sacrifice and endurance. The poet's, the writer's, duty is to write about these things. It is his privilege to help man endure by lifting his heart, by reminding him of the courage and honour and hope and pride and compassion and pity and sacrifice which have been the glory of his past. The poet's voice need not merely be the record of man, it can be one of the props, the pillars to help him endure and prevail."

On a day like today, my master William Faulkner said, "I decline to accept the end of man." I would feel unworthy of standing in this place that was his if I were not fully aware that the colossal tragedy he refused to recognize thirty-two years ago is now, for the first time since the beginning of humanity, nothing more than a simple scientific possibility. Faced with this awesome reality that must have seemed a mere utopia through all of human time, we, the inventors of tales, who will believe anything, feel entitled to believe that it is not yet too late to engage in the creation of the opposite utopia. A new and sweeping utopia of life, where no one will be able to decide for others how they die, where love will prove true and happiness be possible, and where the races condemned to one hundred years of solitude will have, at last and forever, a second opportunity on earth.

GABRIEL GARCÍA MÁRQUEZ, 1982

Left
Faulkner and his wife Estelle called their plantation home, near Oxford, Mississippi, "Rowan Oak". The author suffered from a serious drinking problem, and, even when the critical acclaim was enormous, his books earned very little money.

Right
William Faulkner moved to Oxford, Mississippi as a child. He learned to read before he started school, and began to write poetry as a teenager. Faulkner dropped out of high school, and, although he attended classes at the University of Mississippi, he never received a degree.

Sir Winston Churchill

"I notice that the first Englishman to receive the Nobel Prize was Mr Rudyard Kipling and that another equally rewarded was Mr Bernard Shaw. I certainly cannot attempt to compete with either of those. I knew them both quite well and my thought was much more in accord with Mr Rudyard Kipling than with Mr Bernard Shaw. On the other hand, Mr Rudyard Kipling never thought much of me, whereas Mr Bernard Shaw often expressed himself in more flattering terms." – Winston Churchill

Winston Churchill was born in 1874 at Blenheim Palace. His father was Lord Randolph Churchill, a descendant of the first Duke of Marlborough, and his mother was Jennie Jerome, the daughter of a wealthy American. Winston graduated from Sandhurst and worked as a journalist – and sometime soldier – in India, Spain, and the Sudan. He stood for Parliament and was defeated. He became a war correspondent, was captured by the Boers, and escaped. As an adventurous hero, Winston stood for Parliament again and won. He was twenty-six years old, and when he made his first speech as a member of Parliament, Queen Victoria was still on the throne.

Churchill had major leadership roles in both World Wars. In the Second, especially his speeches and two-finger "victory" sign defined the Allied spirit. Indeed, he won his Nobel Prize as much for the poetry and inspiration of his *War Speeches 1940-5* (1946) as for his historical works such as the massive *History of the English-speaking Peoples* (1956-8).

One of his many biographers called him "The man of the century", but Churchill was also described as a man of animal vitality, courage and egotism, rudeness and humour, brutality and compassion. He loved good cigars, caviar and fine brandy, and he could be famously sharp. "If you were my husband I'd poison your coffee," Mary Astor once said to him. "And if you were my wife I'd drink it," Churchill replied.

At the age of eighty, Churchill retired as prime minister, and ten years later he died. Once during his later years he was asked if he feared death. He said, "I am ready to meet my Maker. Whether my Maker is prepared for the great ordeal of meeting me is another matter."

Churchill was taken on a tour of Coventry Cathedral, a casualty of the blitz. He rallied Britain during the war with a famous speech: "We shall defend our island whatever the cost may be." In 1945 he visited the bombed-out ruins of the German Chancellery in Berlin.

A world hero, Churchill was paraded on an open car in Canada in 1943, where he attended a conference with the prime minister. In a speech in Fulton, Missouri, Churchill used the words "iron curtain" for the first time and added the phrase to the world's vocabulary.

Right
Sir Winston Churchill was awarded the Nobel Prize for Literature in 1953 "for his mastery of historic and biographical description as well as for brilliant oratory in defending exalted human values". The presenter said "that one is tempted to portray him as a Caesar who also has the gift of Cicero's pen".

Ernest Hemingway

1954   *The Big Guy*

He is the bigger-than-life legend of American letters. The hairy-chested, barrel of a man who boxed, drank too much, hunted big game in Africa, hung out with bullfighters in Spain, fished for the big one off Cuba, and married four times. Ernest Hemingway looked up Gertrude Stein in Paris and learned – perhaps from her – that the short, simple English sentence can be a powerful and effective tool for a writer.

From the beginning, places and events in Ernest Hemingway's life furnished the settings, and often the characters, for his novels. *The Sun Also Rises*, published in 1926, is about disillusioned Britons and Americans looking for the meaning of life in Paris and Spain.

In the First World War, Hemingway served as an ambulance driver in Italy, and the hero of *A Farewell to Arms* (1929) is an American serving with an Italian ambulance unit. The novel was a great critical and popular success.

In the late 1930s, Hemingway worked in Spain as a war correspondent during the Civil War. The hero of *For Whom the Bell Tolls* (1940) is a young American teacher in Spain fighting with the Loyalist guerrillas. The author's own Africa can be found in two of his best short stories, "The Short and Happy Life of Francis Macomber" and "The Snows of Kilimanjaro." *To Have and Have Not* (1937) was set in Florida where the author lived for a time, and *The Old Man and the Sea* (1952) was written about a fisherman's contest with a giant marlin off Cuba, where Hemingway lived outside Havana.

In 1950 – his first novel for ten years – he published *Across the River and Into the Trees*, about an older American man

who loves a beautiful young Italian woman. The critics were savage: *The New Yorker* profiled the great writer as a peevish, disagreeable, egotistical monster. This was followed in the same magazine by a parody, "Across the Street and Into the Grill". Hemingway had become fair game.

In 1960, Hemingway was suffering from poor health and depression. He was at his home in Ketchum, Idaho, when he put a shotgun to his head and fired both shells. Despite the reduced quality of much of his later writing, Hemingway's style – at its best direct, hard, brilliantly polished and effective – has had an incalculable impact on writing. He is widely translated into other languages, and interest in the man himself, as evidenced by the books that continue to be published about his life, is unabated. His reputation as one of America's greatest writers continues.

Left
Martha Gellhorn was a correspondent in Madrid when she and Hemingway met. She became his third wife in 1940, and they bought "Finca Vigia" outside Havana. During the Second World War, Hemingway armed his fishing boat to patrol Cuban waters for German submarines.

Above right
A grim-faced Spencer Tracy starred in the film version of *The Old Man and the Sea*. The Nobel Committee cited Hemingway "for his mastery of the art of narrative, most recently demonstrated in *The Old Man and the Sea*, and for the influence that he has exerted on contemporary style".

Right
Ernest Hemingway's house outside Havana was overrun with cats; he judged his visitors' characters by whether or not they liked his pets.

Albert Camus

Born in Algeria in 1913, Albert Camus was less than one year old when his father was killed in the First World War. Albert and his older brother were raised in Algiers by their illiterate Spanish mother, who worked as a housemaid. "I lived in destitution but also in a kind of sensual delight", said Camus, who recalled the sun, sea, and sky of the North African coast in many of his books.

Camus worked his way through the University of Algiers, where he studied philosophy; later he wrote his graduate thesis on the influence of Plotinus on Saint Augustine. An attack of tuberculosis cut short his plans for an academic career; instead he went to the French Alps, his first trip abroad, in search of a cure. Back in Algeria, recovered, Camus joined the staff of a newspaper and began writing for the theatre. At the age of twenty he married a morphine addict and joined the Communist Party; neither venture lasted more than a year.

In 1938, Camus, aged twenty-five, moved to France permanently. Inspired by his reading of Suetonius's *Twelve Caesars*, he wrote his most influential play, *Caligula* (1944). He also began his best-known novel, *The Stranger* (1942), and his greatest essay, *The Myth of Sisyphus* (1942). The themes found in the three works were to become lifelong obsessions.

Caligula deals with the irrational nature of man's fate. "Men die," the Roman emperor says, "and they are not happy." He proceeds through an orgy of murder to practice a freedom that knows no bounds. Finally, by destroying everything around him, he destroys himself.

Camus claimed that the myth of Sisyphus is a metaphor for man's futile and hopeless existence. "There is no fate," he wrote, "that cannot be surmounted by scorn." The book could not have been more timely; it was the darkest hour of the War, when atrocities committed by the Nazis contradicted any sense of a rational universe.

The Stranger has been called a dramatization of the ideas contained in *The Myth of Sisyphus*. Meursault, a young Algerian office clerk, accidentally kills an Arab with a revolver. He becomes a "stranger" to society by refusing to lie, to express a remorse he does not feel, to go along with convention. Sentenced to death, Meursault relinquishes hope, thereby gaining inner freedom.

During the War, Camus worked for a Paris-based underground newspaper, *Combat*, eventually becoming editor-in-chief. The books that followed, among them the novels *The Plague* (1947), *The Rebel* (1951), and *The Fall* (1956), and the story collection *Exile and the Kingdom* (1957), all dealt with his two major ideas: absurdity and rebellion. He also wrote, translated, or adapted a dozen plays, which, according to one critic, mirror "the metaphysical anguish of our age".

With his Nobel Prize money, Camus bought a house in southern France and began working on *The First Man*, which he told reporters in Stockholm would be "the novel of my maturity". The partly written first draft has never been published. In January 1960 Camus was returning to Paris from his house in the country when the car in which he was travelling crashed, and he was killed instantly.

Truth is mysterious, elusive, always to be conquered. Liberty is dangerous, as hard to live with as it is elating. We must march towards these two goals, painfully but resolutely, certain in advance of our failings on so long a road. What writer would from now on in good conscience dare set himself up as a preacher of virtue?
ALBERT CAMUS, 1957

Left
Albert Camus's fiction has been described by one critic as being about "the problems of innocence and guilt, responsibility and nihilistic indifference".

Right
Albert Camus (right) directed Catherine Sellers and Marc Cassot in a Paris stage adaptation of William Faulkner's *Requiem for a Nun*. One evening, when one of the leading actors was ill, Camus took a leading role.

Boris Pasternak

1958   *Patriotic Dissident*

Leonard Bernstein was in Moscow in 1959 conducting the New York Philharmonic when Boris Pasternak went backstage to his dressing room. As a young man, Pasternak had studied music – his mother was a concert pianist.

When the Russian author Boris Pasternak learned that he had won the 1958 Nobel Prize for Literature, he sent the Swedish Academy a telegram: "Immensely thankful, touched, proud, astonished, abashed." Four days later he sent the Academy another, regretfully declining the award.

During the intervening days, Pasternak had been branded in the Soviet Press as a "malevolent Philistine", a "Judas", and an "extraneous smudge in our socialist country". He had been expelled from the Soviet Writers' Union. He might even have been thrown out of the country had he not written to Premier Nikita Khrushchev pleading to be allowed to stay: "Leaving the motherland will equal death for me."

At the award ceremony, an announcement was made to the effect that Pasternak's refusal to accept the Nobel Prize did not alter its validity; the award had been for his "important achievement both in contemporary lyrical poetry and in the field of the great Russian epic tradition".

The book that had caused the furore was Pasternak's great Russian epic *Dr Zhivago*. The only novel Pasternak ever wrote, it followed Dr Yuri Andrevich Zhivago, poet and physician, through the First World War, the Russian Revolution, and into the Stalinist era. Pasternak had intended it to be a book "in which, as in an explosion, I would erupt with all the wonderful things I saw and understood in the world".

In 1957, after the novel had been rejected by the Soviet authorities for expressing "a negative attitude towards the revolution", it was published in Italian in Milan. By the end of 1958 it had been translated into eighteen languages, and would soon become a legendary motion picture. Not until 1988, thirty years after Pasternak's Nobel Prize, was an unabridged edition finally published in the Soviet Union.

Boris Pasternak was born in Moscow in 1890 to a highly cultured Jewish family. His father was a noted portrait painter, his mother a concert pianist. Young Boris grew up knowing the composers Scriabin and Rachmaninoff, the poet Rainer Maria Rilke, and the novelist Leo Tolstoy, whose image, he said later, "stalked me through life". Indeed, the spiritual quality and epic sweep of *Dr Zhivago* have been likened to Tolstoy's *War and Peace*.

After first studying music at the Moscow Conservatory and then philosophy at Warburg University in Germany, Pasternak returned to Moscow determined to devote his life to literature. He brought out his first collection of poems – *A Twin in the Clouds* – at the age of twenty-four in 1914. With *My Sister Life* (1922) he became known as one of

Russia's most distinguished poets. A contemporary described his verse as "a downpour of light".

Having broken his leg as a boy, Pasternak was barred from serving in the military during the First World War. Instead, he volunteered for clerical work in a factory in the Ural mountains, an experience that later appeared in *Dr Zhivago*.

As a poet, Pasternak got into trouble for refusing to restrict himself to proletarian themes, and throughout much of the 1930s he could not get published. Being multilingual he made a living translating Shakespeare, Shelley, Verlaine, and Goethe's *Faust* into Russian. His translations of *Hamlet, Othello, Mac-*

beth and others are highly valued in the Soviet Union. During the Second World War he composed patriotic verses and served as a war correspondent. He then returned to Peredelkino, a Soviet Writers' colony near Moscow, where he had lived with his second wife since the early 1930s.

After Pasternak's death in 1960 at the age of seventy, a biographer wrote: "Again and again in his poems and in the novel, Pasternak declares the supremacy of man and of the heart's affections over all the regimentation of dictatorship."

Even the name he gave his novel's protagonist, Zhivago, is the Russian word for "life".

Pasternak's father Leonid was a prominent artist, whose 1895 painting "The Night Before the Exam" sharply evokes the intellectual atmosphere of pre-Revolutionary Russia, and of Boris's youth.

John Steinbeck

In 1962, the year he won the Nobel Prize, John Steinbeck said in an interview, "The profession of book writing makes horse racing seem like a solid, stable business." Sixty years old, he knew whereof he spoke. As a young man, Steinbeck had dropped out of Stanford University twice, taken a series of odd jobs, and written short stories, none of which he was able to sell. His first novel, *Cup of Gold*, based on a real-life seventeenth-century pirate, was published in 1929 and received blessedly little attention. His second, *To a God Unknown*, a laboured synthesis of Jungian ideas and archetypal themes, got bad reviews. A play, *Burning Bright*, closed after thirteen performances. Steinbeck went on to write a number of other forgettable novels, including *In Dubious Battle* (1936), *The Wayward Bus* (1947), and *The Pearl* (1947). Over a period of twenty years he also wrote such modern masterpieces as *Tortilla Flat* (1935), *Of Mice and Men* (1937), *Cannery Row* (1945), and *East of Eden* (1952).

Ironically, even when Steinbeck was at the height of his powers, he seemed to have no conception of his own abilities. While writing *The Grapes of Wrath* (1939), arguably his finest work, he confided in his journal: "I am sure of one thing. It isn't the great book I had hoped it would be. It's just a run-of-the-mill book. And the awful thing is that it is absolutely the best I can do." The novel, which came out in 1939 and won the 1940 Pulitzer Prize, told the story of the Joad family, tenant farmers who in the depths of the Great Depression leave their home in the Oklahoma dust-bowl to look for work in California. Though the book became a bestseller, its author

was accused of being a Communist sympathizer who purposely exaggerated the deplorable living conditions of America's migrant workers.

The Nobel presentation speech pointed out that Steinbeck's "sympathies always go out to the oppressed, to the misfits and the distressed; he likes to contrast the simple joy of life with the brutal and cynical craving for money". Besides *The Grapes of Wrath*, this observation was particularly relevant to *Of Mice and Men*. Like many Steinbeck novels, it is set in the area around his birthplace, Salinas, California. The story involves an itinerant farmhand and his mentally retarded buddy, whose shared dream of owning their own small farm is destroyed by sadistic ranchers.

Throughout his life, Steinbeck showed extraordinary versatility. During the Second World War, he wrote an Army Air Corps training manual, *Bombs Away* (1942); after the war he sent dispatches from the Soviet Union to the *New York Herald Tribune*; he wrote the screenplay for the 1952 film classic, *Viva Zapata!*; he made a cross-country trip with his dog and turned it into the popular 1962 travel book, *Travels With Charley in Search of America*; he even wrote political speeches for President Lyndon Johnson. His final work, published posthumously, was *The Acts of King Arthur and His Noble Knights*, a modern retelling of the fifteenth-century *Morte d'Arthur*. The book harks back to his 1935 bestseller *Tortilla Flat*, in which episodic tales about a group of Californians echo

the Arthurian legends Steinbeck had read as a child.

Since his death in 1968, some of Steinbeck's work has come to seem naïve and ponderously allegorical. Still, a half-dozen of his books, as well as the excellent films they engendered, such as *The Grapes of Wrath* and *East of Eden*, live on, each celebrating what Steinbeck called in his Nobel acceptance speech, "man's proven capacity for greatness of heart and spirit".

Left
John Steinbeck escorts his wife to a New York film prèmiere. Critics noted that his work was marked by an underlying sympathy for all his characters, no matter how mean or pitiful they might be.

Above
In the late 1980s, Steinbeck's famous novel *The Grapes of Wrath* was given a much-praised stage production by a Chicago theatre group.

Right
On a tour of Europe, Steinbeck signs autographs for German police in Berlin. After the Nobel ceremonies in Stockholm, Steinbeck lost his award cheque. It turned up a few days later in a friend's purse.

Jean-Paul Sartre

1964

No Thanks

Jean-Paul Sartre is the only man to have declined the Nobel Prize of his own accord, as distinct from those who, like Pasternak, were pressured to do so by their governments. Among his reasons: He did not wish to be associated with any institution.

Sartre was born in Paris in 1905. His father died when he was an infant, and he was brought up in his mother's family. His grandfather, Charles Schweitzer – Albert Schweitzer was a cousin – was an important influence. Schweitzer ran the Modern Language Institute in Paris, and had his grandson educated at home. Sartre has described his childhood in *The Words* (1964), a dark and brilliantly original auto-biography.

It was while teaching at Le Havre in 1938 that Sartre wrote *Nausea*. A claus-trophobic novel, about a young man who is overcome by the utter futility of life, *Nausea* is often cited as the source-book for those who want to understand the philosophy of existentialism. Sartre's most important philosophical work, *Being and Nothingness* (1943), inspired an entire generation of French students and philosophers. He had an enduring concern for the issues of freedom and moral responsibility.

Sartre's literary output was impres-sive: novels, plays, short stories, critical essays on literature and philosophy, biographies, journalism, political pamph-lets, and manifestos. He was one of the founders of *Les Tempes Modernes*, the literary and political review.

In the 1950s, Sartre became preoccu-pied with social problems and Marxism. While never a member of the Commu-nist Party, he was an admirer of the

His eyesight failing towards the end of his life, Sartre listens as Simone de Beauvoir, his lifelong companion, reads a newspaper to him.

Soviets until they cut short the Hungar-ian uprising in 1956. Sartre was an out-spoken opponent of the American presence in Vietnam, and headed a "commission" that found the Ameri-cans guilty of war crimes. In 1968 he spoke out in praise of the student riots, but gradually withdrew from political activism.

During his last years, Sartre was almost blind. He died in 1980. A French newspaper said in its obituary that "No French intellectual of this century, no Nobel Prize laureate, has exerted an influence as profound, as durable, as universal as Sartre's."

Man differs from other animals in one very important respect, and that is that he has some desires which are, so to speak, infinite, which can never be fully gratified, and which would keep him restless even in paradise.

BERTRAND RUSSELL, 1950

Above
During his activist days, Jean-Paul Sartre helped to unload newspapers. Sartre used his prestige to promote Socialism, and did not advocate nonviolence – he sought revolution and openly supported Marxism.

Right
Jean-Paul Sartre and Simone de Beauvoir had an enduring relationship. One contemporary French critic described Sartre as "our Jean Jacques Rousseau".

Yasunari Kawabata

Although the Nobel is an international prize, the Swedish Academy has not found it easy to choose a writer from the Orient. According to Kjell Espmark in his *Nobel Prize in Literature*, it took seven years before the Committee felt comfortable with the selection in 1968 of Yasunari Kawabata.

Their investigation was begun in 1961 by a Swedish critic who had read Kawabata in German, French, and English. His favourable impression was supported by leading literary critics and by a Japanese scholar, Sei Ito, who said that Kawabata was the only living writer worthy of representing Japanese literature.

Then the members of the Committee themselves read Kawabata in translation and were able to give him the award with some degree of confidence.

Kawabata was born in 1899, and in 1914 began writing *Diary of a Sixteen-Year-Old*, which was published in 1925. His first literary success, *Dancer at Izu City*, published in the same year, is about a student who falls in love with a virginal heroine. Similar characters appear in almost all his novels.

Among Kawabata's best-known works outside Japan is *Thousand Cranes*, a slender novel about a young man who attends a tea ceremony conducted by one of his late father's mistresses – a harsh, outspoken woman who wants to arrange a marriage for the hero. She introduces him to a young woman who is wearing a scarf printed with cranes. The young man, however, is distracted by another of his father's women. This older woman seduces him, commits suicide and leaves the young man feeling responsible for the woman's pass-ive daughter. The tea ceremony, with its precious, ancient bowls, is a recurring motif in a work which strikes most Westerners as mysterious, sensual, and uniquely Japanese.

In 1970, Kawabata's protégé, Yukio Mishima, the flamboyant actor and writer, committed *hara-kiri*. Two years later, Kawabata, who had been hospitalized for addiction to barbiturates, went to the apartment where he wrote and himself committed suicide. He left no note.

In his Nobel acceptance speech four years earlier, he had said, "However alienated one may be from the world, suicide is not a form of enlightenment. However admirable he may be, the man who commits suicide is far from the realm of the saint."

Right
The Japanese author Yukio Mishima, a close friend of Kawabata, is seen here at a Tokyo army barracks shortly before committing *hari-kiri*, ceremonial suicide, on 5 November 1970.

Far right
Kawabata was sixty-nine years old when he was awarded the Nobel Prize, the first Japanese writer to be so recognized. When he wanted to write, Kawabata went to an apartment he kept for that purpose and put on a kimono and wooden sandals.

Words may, through the devotion, the skill, the passion, and the luck of writers, prove to be the most powerful thing in the world. They may move men to speak to each other because some of those words somewhere express not just what the writer is thinking but what a huge segment of the world is thinking. They may allow man to speak to man, the man in the street to speak to his fellow until a ripple becomes a tide running through every nation – of common sense, of simple healthy caution, a tide that rulers and negotiators cannot ignore so that nation does truly speak unto nation. Then there is hope that we may learn to be temperate, provident, taking no more from nature's treasury than is our due. It may be by books, stories, poetry, lectures that we who have the ear of mankind can move man a little nearer the perilous safety of a warless and provident world.

WILLIAM GOLDING, 1983

Alexander Solzhenitsyn

1970   *"One Word of Truth"*

Alexander Solzhenitsyn is seen here chopping wood in Vermont. He was awarded the 1970 Nobel Prize "for the ethical force with which he has pursued the indispensable traditions of Russian literature". He ended his lecture with the sentence, "One word of truth shall outweigh the whole world."

A hammer is pounded on a rail, and its harsh ringing cracks the sub-zero air. The prisoners in a Soviet forced labour camp stir. It is 5 AM, the beginning of a day in the life of Ivan Denisovich Shukhow, the hero of Alexander Solzhenitsyn's first novel. Premier Nikita Khrushchev allowed the book to be published as part of a campaign to discredit Stalin, who had imprisoned or killed millions of Soviet citizens in the Russian Gulag. *One Day in the Life of Ivan Denisovich* is written in the vernacular, common curses and all, and its publication in 1962 created a sensation. Solzhenitsyn was a new literary force to be reckoned with.

Solzhenitsyn was born in 1918, a year after the Communists came to power. A brilliant student, he studied maths in college. He was a captain in the artillery during the Second World War when some anti-Stalin comments were found in a letter he had written to a friend. In 1945 Solzhenitsyn was sentenced to eight years and sent to a labour camp. *One Day* was written from that experience.

Because of his ability in maths, Solzhenitsyn eventually was transferred to a different kind of prison, a place that became the setting for *The First Circle* (1969) which developed the theme of a man having to make difficult moral choices. Khrushchev had died, however, and the book could not be published in the Soviet Union.

When Solzhenitsyn became ill with stomach cancer and underwent radiation treatment, his grim experience of the disease provided the material for *The Cancer Ward* (1968). In his books, it is made clear that in the Soviet Union those outside prison are no better off than those inside, and victims of cancer discover a freedom that healthy Soviet citizens have never known. When the books were smuggled out and published in the West, Solzhenitsyn's difficulties with the authorities increased. His Nobel Prize for Literature was awarded in 1970. Although he accepted the award, Solzhenitsyn was afraid that if he left the country he would not be permitted to return.

When the manuscript of *The Gulag Archipelago* – an exposé of the Soviet prison system – was seized, Solzhenitsyn sent word to Paris that a copy he had smuggled there should be published in the West. He was stripped of his citizenship and put on a plane with his family. After two years in Switzerland, he settled in a rural area of Vermont. He is working on an historical series, which began with *August 1914* (1971), to which he has given the title *The Red Wheel*.

Here, Solzhenitsyn's son shows a collection of flags to his father. Solzhenitsyn is working on a series of historical novels. He has said he expects the work to take twenty years, and that he will not live to finish it.

Each assumes the moral responsibility for his own story, and each must be allowed to tell it freely.

IVO ANDRIĆ, 1961

The whole of mankind is revealed in the peasant of our birthplace, every countryside of the world in the horizon seen through the eyes of our childhood. The novelist's gift consists precisely in his ability to reveal the universality of this narrow world into which we are born, where we have learned to love and to suffer.

FRANÇOIS MAURIAC, 1952

241

Isaac Bashevis Singer

Before he retired to Florida, the late Isaac Bashevis Singer was a familiar sight on Manhattan's upper West Side, not the most elegant area, but a substantial neighbourhood of solid apartment blocks and a vegetarian restaurant where he ate lunch every day.

Certainly it was a far cry from the village near Warsaw, where Singer spent his first four years. In 1908 the family moved to Warsaw and settled in the Jewish quarter, where Isaac's father was a judge in a Rabbinic court. Isaac became an insatiable reader of literary classics, especially the Russians. At thirteen he went with his mother to her village in eastern Poland, where they lived for four years. He recalled it as a period when time seemed to flow backwards: "I lived Jewish history", he said.

Many of Singer's stories reflect that period of his life. His stories are often magical, and have the quality of myth, of fairy and folk tale. Sexual folly is a favourite theme.

In 1935 Singer joined his older brother, the writer I. J. Singer, in the United States and wrote for the *Jewish Daily Forward*. He married Alma Wasserman, a German emigré, in 1940 and became an American citizen three years later. *The Family Moskat*, published in 1950, was the first of Singer's novels to be translated into English. *Satan in Goray* also received critical acclaim. Many of Singer's short stories have appeared in English, along with several novels, four volumes of autobiography, and a dozen books for children.

Singer said that he did not see any difference between his fiction and his memoirs. Among his translators is another Nobel laureate, Saul Bellow,

who translated *Gimpel the Fool*, a famous Singer story, into English.

Singer was an acknowledged master story-tellér. He once admitted that he did not read Faulkner, Beckett, or any number of other "notable" writers because he was not interested in studying literature. "I read it for enjoyment", he insisted.

On their selection of Singer for the 1978 Nobel Prize, the Committee noted "his impassioned narrative art which, with roots in a Polish-Jewish cultural tradition, brings universal human conditions to life". Singer himself said in his Nobel lecture that he thought the award was given in recognition of the Yiddish language, "a language of exile, without land, without frontiers". "Yiddish is", he said, "the wise and humble language of us all, the idiom of frightened and hopeful humanity."

I am an old man now. Like the lives of many others who inhabit our old Europe, my early life was no little disturbed. I witnessed a revolution. I went to war in singularly murderous circumstances (my regiment was one of those the general staffs coldly sacrificed in advance, so that a week later almost nothing remained of it). I have been taken prisoner. I've known hunger. Have been forced to exhaust myself with physical labour. Escaped. Been gravely ill, several times at the point of a violent or natural death. I've rubbed shoulders with all sorts and conditions of men, both clergy and incendiaries of churches, peaceable bourgeois and anarchists, philosophers and illiterates. I've shared my bread with tramps, in a word, I've been about the world . . . all, however, without finding any sense to all this, unless it should be the one assigned to it, I believe by Barthe, following Shakespeare: that "if the world signifies anything, it is that it signifies nothing – except that it exists."

CLAUDE SIMON, 1985

Gabriel García Márquez

The Maker of Macondo

"Folk culture . . . currents from Spanish baroque . . . influences from European surrealism and other modernism are blended into a spiced and life-giving brew." That was how the 1982 Nobel Prize presentation speech described the fiction of Gabriel García Márquez, leading figure of the renaissance in Latin American literature.

Unquestionably, Márquez's spiciest brew of all was his 1967 masterpiece *One Hundred Years of Solitude* (1970), which the Chilean poet and fellow Nobel laureate Pablo Neruda called the greatest Spanish-language novel since Cervantes's *Don Quixote*. The book traces the history of a family living in Macondo, a village where miracles are everyday events. Where, for example, a beautiful woman ascends to heaven with the sheets she is folding. It is a place so isolated, so solitary, that its inhabitants tell a priest he isn't necessary because they have lost the evil of original sin.

Macondo is modelled on the author's birthplace, Aracataca, a banana port on Colombia's Caribbean coast. Born in 1928, Gabriel was the eldest of sixteen children. From infancy until he was eight he was raised by his maternal grandparents; he was especially close to his grandmother, from whom flowed a seemingly endless stream of legends and myths. Discussing *One Hundred Years of Solitude* in a *Paris Review* interview, Márquez said: "It was based on the way my grandmother used to tell her stories. She told things that sounded supernatural and fantastic, but she told them with complete naturalness . . . with a brick face."

While granting that his grandmother was the single greatest force on Márquez's imagination, the novelist Salman Rushdie has pointed out that "the world of his fabulous Macondo is at least partly Yoknapatawpha County transported into the Colombia jungles". Indeed, Márquez has many times paid tribute to "my master William Faulkner", but insists that the haunting similarities between the two literary locations are coincidental. A writer who influenced him far more, he says, is Franz Kafka, who he first read while a student at a university near Bogotá. The first line of Kafka's story *Metamorphosis* "almost knocked me off the bed . . . I didn't know anyone was allowed to write things like that".

Although he studied law for several years, Márquez became a newspaper reporter while writing stories on the side. It was not until *One Hundred Years of Solitude* became an international best-seller that he could afford to devote himself to fiction full time. It was followed by *The Autobiography of the Patriarch* (1976), and *Chronicle of a Death Foretold* (1981), a classic murder story that has been highly praised. His latest book is *The General in His Labyrinth* (1991).

To the delight of all, Márquez showed up at the Nobel award ceremony wearing, instead of the traditional white tie and tails, the formal attire of Colombia: white trousers and a high-collared white shirt. In his lecture, as he eloquently conjured a utopia "where no one will be able to decide for others how they die", Márquez might have been the gypsy Melquiades in *One Hundred Years of Solitude* who, said, "Things have a life of their own. It's simply a matter of waking up their souls."

The born novelist recognizes himself by his passion to penetrate ever more deeply into the knowledge of man and to lay bare in each of his characters that individual element of his life which makes each being unique. It seems to me that any chance of survival which a novelist's work may have rests solely on the quantity and the quality of the individual lives that he has been able to create in his books. But that is not all. The novelist must also have a sense of life in general; his work must reveal a personal vision of the universe.

ROGER MARTIN DU GARD, 1937

William Golding

One day in 1983 William Golding heard his wife, in another part of the house, give a wild scream. He raced towards her, she raced towards him, and they collided. "You've won the Nobel Prize!" she gasped, and at that exact moment the back of Golding's hand accidentally slammed against a door, raising a huge blood blister. For the rest of the day friends poured into the house to offer congratulations and pump his hand, each putting a thumb right into the middle of his blister. "So my memory of winning the Nobel Prize," Golding said, "is having a delighted heart and a hand which every now and then was giving me absolute torture."

William Golding has been writing since he was seven years old. He published a collection of poems while still a student at Oxford University. After graduation, he worked for several years as a social worker in a settlement house, and in his spare time wrote plays for a small London theatre. Still in his twenties, he began teaching English and philosophy at a school in Salisbury.

In 1940 Golding joined the Royal Navy, and eventually, as commander of a rocket-launching ship, took part in the invasion of Normandy. He later attributed his relentless bleak view of human nature to his combat experiences: "Anyone who moved through those years without understanding that man produces evil as a bee produces honey must have been blind or wrong in the head."

In 1945 Golding resumed his teaching job, taught himself ancient Greek, and produced four novels, none of which were published. He then wrote a fifth

Above
Boys stranded on an island after a plane crash, go native in a recent film version, the second, of Golding's best-known novel, *Lord of the Flies*.

Left
William Golding has said, "I occasionally try to read my own books, but I find them distasteful to me. After all, writing them is quite a chore." Golding says that he believes that man will survive, "but I keep my fingers crossed".

novel in 1954, *Lord of the Flies*, about a group of adolescent boys who, marooned on a desert island, regress to a state of barbarism. Twenty-one publishers turned it down; the twenty-second was willing to gamble. The book became a bestseller on both sides of the Atlantic, and was made into a film.

Thirty years ago Golding left teaching to write full time. His output has included essays, short stories, plays, and several novels, among them *The Inheritors* (1955), *Pincher Martin* (1956), *Free Fall (1959)*, and *The Spire* (1964). Like *Lord of the Flies*, all could be characterized, in the words of the Nobel Prize presentation speech, as "sober moralities and dark myths about evil and treacherous, destructive forces". In his lecture to the Swedish Academy, Golding conceded being "a universal pessimist", but humorously insisted that his gloomy outlook was tempered by a certain "cosmic" optimism. The award

brought considerable protest. At the time the general consensus was that if the Nobel Prize for Literature were to be awarded to a Briton, the most deserving choice was Graham Greene.

Today, William Golding and his wife live near Salisbury. They have a son and a daughter. "I play the piano more than anything else," Golding says. He also continues to write, which he has always found extremely laborious, but as he himself once commented, "Genius is an infinite capacity for taking pains." He has recently completed a trilogy of novels: *Rites of Passage, Close Quarters,* and *Fire Down Below*.

Joseph Brodsky

When Joseph Brodsky was a boy, the city of Leningrad was his playground. In a well-known poem, "A Part of Speech", Brodsky wrote that he grew up in the Baltic marshland, where there was plenty of room for vision.

The world today seems allied with the side opposed to poetry. And for the world, the poet's very presence is an obstacle to be overcome. He must be annihilated. The force of poetry, on the other hand, fans out in every direction in organized societies; and if literary games escape the sensibilities of men everywhere, a poetic activity that is inspired by humanism does not.

SALVATORE QUASIMODO, 1959

The Nobel Committee awarded Brodsky the Nobel Prize "for an all-embracing authorship, imbued with clarity of thought and poetic intensity". He writes in Russian, and notable poets such as Anthony Hecht, Derek Walcott, and Richard Wilbur have translated his work. Brodsky is the first foreign-born American to be named US poet laureate.

The poet Joseph Brodsky made an appearance recently at the New York Public Library. Balding, a bit stout in rumpled grey trousers and even more rumpled tweed jacket, he stood at a podium before an audience of three hundred and read a paper on poetry he had prepared for the occasion.

He spoke so rapidly that his accented English was difficult to follow. Shortly after he began, a woman walked up to the podium and asked him to speak more slowly. For a sentence or two he tried, but as soon as he became absorbed in his reading, he speeded up again. He complained of today's poetry in which randomness and banality "belong together like hammer and sickle". He was unhappy about what he called the deflection school of poetry which is "all about *not* feeling. 'Look at me! I feel zilch!'"

Joseph Brodsky has never been short of feelings and the skill to express them. Born in 1940, his passion for poetry began when he was fifteen years old. "I read a most remarkable translation of Robert Burns into Russian. But he dropped out of school and worked in Leningrad in a hospital morgue "opening up corpses and that sort of thing, sewing them up and so forth. " That lasted only three months and then he became a milling machine operator, a photographer (as his father had been), a stoker, then a sailor on a tugboat. Gradually he turned into what he calls "a loafer". His poetry was being circulated throughout Leningrad and beyond; the authorities did not like what he was writing. "I was arrested two or three times," he recalls. The third time he was charged with "social parasitism" and sentenced to five years. Brodsky was exiled in March 1964, but allowed to return to Leningrad after two years of continuous pressure from intellectual circles. He continued to write, and in 1972 he emigrated, leaving the Soviet Union with a battered typewriter, a book of poems, and a bottle of vodka.

Once in Europe, he looked up W. H. Auden, whose poetry he had admired. Auden sent him to friends in England, and then to the United States, where he found a place for himself on a series of university campuses and became a citizen. His literary output has been small, and includes *Elegy to John Donne and Other Poems* (1967), and *Less Than One* (1986). He often does his own translations into English.

Brodsky has been described as "a lyricist of loss, of the slipping away of the past, loved ones, youth. His customary tone is one of passion tempered by hard-earned irony. His poems rely heavily on visual impressions . . . such concrete images can survive the translation from Russian to English with much of their freshness intact."

249

Naguib Mahfouz

1988   "The Real Winner"

A fellow Egyptian has likened Naguib Mahfouz to the sphinx, explaining that both are "silent but expressive". In 1988, when Mahfouz became the first Arab to win the Nobel Prize for Literature, there was a rejoicing throughout Egypt. As for the winner, a self-described introvert, he was so besieged by newspaper reporters and television crews that he was unable to write for a year.

Although his output has been prodigious – more than thirty novels, as many screenplays, and a dozen collections of short stories – Mahfouz is virtually unknown in the West. Arabic is particularly difficult to render into other languages, and the English translations of his work that exist tend to be clumsy approximations of the original.

Asked once what it was that propelled him to write, Mahfouz quipped, "I write because I have two daughters, and they need high-heeled shoes." Those same two young women went to Stockholm to receive Mahfouz's Nobel medal and diploma. The author, who has just entered his eighties, told an interviewer, "You know, at forty, fifty, even at sixty, a Nobel changes things, but at my age, at the end, a hundred Nobels would change nothing about the way I write."

Cairo, the setting for all his books, is also his birthplace. He lives there still with his wife – who, in keeping with Arab tradition, stays strictly out of the limelight – in an apartment overlooking the Nile. In the summer, to escape the heat, the couple go to a small apartment in Alexandria. Mahfouz's daily routine in both cities never varies. He rises at 5 AM, takes a long walk, and by 7 AM is seated in a favourite café where he sips Turkish coffee, smokes cigarettes, and reads the newspaper. Then he returns home, writes for several hours, eats lunch, takes a siesta, and in the evening watches television. On the street he is easily recognizable; not only does he wear wraparound dark glasses – his eyes are abnormally sensitive to light – but sports a straw hat and an ornate walking stick.

The youngest of seven children, Mahfouz was born to a low-ranking government functionary in the heart of the old city. He graduated from Cairo University with a degree in philosophy. At the age of twenty-five he became "plagued by a fearful struggle between literature and philosophy . . . I had to make up my mind or else lose my senses". He opted for literature, and immersed himself in the works of the great Western writers, such as Shaw, Galsworthy, Hemingway, Faulkner, O'Neill, Mauriac, Sartre, Camus, and Mann.

During the 1930s Mahfouz wrote nearly 150 short stories. His first three novels all take place 7,000 years ago, during the time of the Pharaohs; his depiction of the conquest of pharaonic Egypt by the Hittites has been seen by some as a condemnation of Egypt's colonization by the British. After the Second World War he began writing about contemporary Egypt. His fictional characters include a vast assortment of bureaucrats and minor civil servants, thieves and prostitutes, all trying desperately to survive in the economically blighted city. Some of his best-known works include *Midaq Alley* and *Children of Gebelawi*, both published in 1981.

Throughout his adult life Mahfouz has openly expressed his resentment at not being able to support his family by writing, being obliged instead to work at a variety of civil service jobs. Although long retired, for the last twenty years he has written a weekly political column for Egypt's biggest newspaper *al-Ahram*.

In his Nobel lecture, delivered by a colleague in both Arabic and English, Mahfouz called his native tongue "the real winner of the Prize". He thinks of the language of the *Koran* as holy, as "the Arab world's great gift to humanity". He himself often writes in a flowery, classical form of Arabic that is somewhat akin to Shakespearean English. There is something transcendent about the way he uses words. As the permanent secretary of the Swedish Academy said, "the poetic quality of your prose can be felt across the language barrier".

Mahfouz's latest works include *Palace Walk* (1990) and *Palace of Desire* (1991).

Camilo José Cela

When Camilo José Cela's first novel was published in 1942, the censor called it "nauseating" and banned it. *The Family of Pasqual Duarte* is in the form of a memoir written by a murderer, a peasant, as he awaits execution. Early in the novel, Duarte kills his dog and later murders his mother by slashing her throat. Cela vividly describes how her warm blood feels as it splashes on to the killer's face. Like the antihero Meursault in Camus's *The Stranger* – published in the same year – Cela's narrator is detached from life and free of any moral restraint. *Pasqual Duarte* is the most widely read book in Spanish since *Don Quixote*. When Cela accepted the Nobel Prize in 1989, he referred to Miguel de Cervantes as his teacher.

Cela, who is in his late seventies, has been described by a reporter as "pear-shaped of body and basset of face". In addition to his ten novels, Cela has published a collection of scatalogical and whorehouse terms in a *Secret Dictionary*. As a young man, he fought for Franco in the Spanish Civil War. His *Mazurka for Two Dead* (1983) is considered a masterpiece about that period.

Cela has also performed as a bullfighter, and on television in a series in which he rode around Spain in a Rolls Royce driven by a beautiful black woman in a white robe. Recently he left his wife of forty-four years for a radio reporter he calls "my dangerous blonde". The young woman accompanied him to the ceremonies in Stockholm. He said he planned to use the $463,000 award "to pay my debts – and, believe me, I've got a lot of them".

Cela said that because of the Nobel Award he received 37,310 telegrams and 110,109 letters. He wrote in a Madrid newspaper: "I also opened my doors to all the television and radio stations that asked me, and replied to as many questions as journalists wished to ask. I let them take hundreds of photographs and posed for a half a dozen portraits in oil and pastels, I was made an honorary professor of a non-Spanish university and received six or seven doctorates, *honoris causa*, none of them in Spanish."

After a year of indulging all this attention, Cela said he has shut his door because he believes he has another book in him, and must have solitude in order to write.

In the banquet hall during the 1989 Nobel celebration in Stockholm, Camilo José Cela drew a crowd of admirers as he took a turn around the dance floor. His dinner companion earlier that evening was Her Majesty Queen Silvia.

Cela's mastery of Castilian makes him one of the most original prose writers in that language since Cervantes. Cela, who began as a Surrealist poet, reflects the influence of Spain's picaresque tradition.

I write from solitude and I speak from solitude. Mateo Alemán in his Guzmán de Alfarache *and Francis Bacon in his essay* Of Solitude, *both writing more or less at the same period, said that the man who seeks solitude has much of the beast in him. However, I did not seek solitude. I found it. And from my solitude I think, work, and live – and I believe that I write and speak with almost infinite composure and resignation.*

CAMILO JOSÉ CELA, 1989

Nobel Laureates 1901–1990

Note: Titles, data and places given below refer to the time of the prize award.

Peace

1901 The prize was divided equally between:
DUNANT, JEAN HENRI, Switzerland, Founder International Committee of the Red Cross, Geneva, Originator Geneva Convention, 1828–1910; and
PASSY, FRÉDÉRIC, France, Founder and President first French peace society, 1822–1912.

1902 The prize was divided equally between:
DUCOMMUN, ÉLIE, Switzerland, Honorary Secretary Permanent International Peace Bureau, Berne, 1833–1906; and
GOBAT, CHARLES ALBERT, Switzerland, Secretary General Inter–Parliamentary Union, Berne, Honorary Secretary Permanent International Peace Bureau, Berne, 1843–1914.

1903 CREMER, Sir WILLIAM RANDAL, Great Britain, Member British Parliament, Secretary International Arbitration League, 1838–1908.

1904 INSTITUT DE DROIT INTERNATIONAL (INSTITUTE OF INTERNATIONAL LAW), Ghent, scientific society, founded in 1873.

1905 VON SUTTNER, Baroness BERTHA SOPHIE FELICITA, Austria, Writer, Honorary President Permanent International Peace Bureau, Berne, Author *Lay Down Your Arms*, 1843–1914.

1906 ROOSEVELT, THEODORE, USA, President United States of America,

collaborator various peace treaties, 1858–1919.

1907 The prize was divided equally between:
MONETA, ERNESTO TEODORO, Italy, President Lombard League of Peace, 1833–1918; and
RENAULT, LOUIS, France, Professor International Law, Sorbonne University, Paris, 1843–1918.

1908 The prize was divided equally between:
ARNOLDSON, KLAS PONTUS, Sweden, Writer, formerly Member Swedish Parliament, Founder Swedish Peace and Arbitration League, 1844–1916; and
BAJER, FREDRIK, Denmark, Member Danish Parliament, Honorary President Permanent International Peace Bureau, Berne, 1837–1922.

1909 The prize was divided equally between:
BEERNAERT, AUGUSTE MARIE FRANÇOIS, Belgium, ex–Prime Minister, Member Belgian Parliament, Member Cour internationale d'arbitrage at the Hague, 1829–1912; and
D'ESTOURNELLES DE CONSTANT, PAUL HENRI BENJAMIN BALLUET, Baron DE CONSTANT DE REBECQUE, France, Member French Parliament (Sénateur), Founder and President French parliamentary group for voluntary arbitration (Groupe parlimentaire de l'arbitrage international), Founder Comité de défense des intérets nationaux et de conciliation internationale (Committee for the Defence of National Interests and International Conciliation), 1852–1924.

1910 BUREAU INTERNATIONAL PERMANENT DE LA PAIX (PERMANENT INTERNATIONAL PEACE BUREAU), Berne, founded in 1891.

1911 The prize was divided equally between:
ASSER, TOBIAS MICHAEL CAREL, the Netherlands, Prime Minister, Member Privy Council, Originator International Conferences of Private Law at the Hague, 1838–1913; and
FRIED, ALFRED HERMANN, Austria, Journalist, Founder *Die Friedenswante* (a peace publication), 1864–1921.

1912 Reserved.

1913 The prize for 1912:
ROOT, ELIHU, USA, i.a. ex–Secretary of State, originator various treaties of arbitration, 1845–1937.
The prize for 1913:
LA FONTAINE, HENRI, Belgium, Member Belgian Parliament (Sénateur), President Permanent International Peace Bureau, Berne, 1854–1943.

1914 Reserved.

1915 The prize money for 1914 was allocated to the Special Fund of this prize section.
The prize for 1915: Reserved.

1916 The prize money for 1915 was allocated to the Special Fund of this prize section.
The prize for 1916: Reserved.

1917 The prize money for 1916 was allocated to the Special Fund of this prize section.
The prize for 1917:
COMITÉ INTERNATIONAL DE LA

CROIX ROUGE (International Committee of the Red Cross), Geneva, founded 1853.

1918 Reserved.

1919 The prize money for 1918 was allocated to the Special Fund of this prize section.
The prize for 1919: Reserved.

1920 The prize for 1919:
WILSON, THOMAS WOODROW, USA, President United States of America, Founder of Société des Nations (the League of Nations), 1856–1924.
The prize for 1920:
BOURGEOIS, LEON VICTOR AUGUSTE, France, i.a. ex–Secretary of State, President French Parliament (Sénat), President Conseil de la Société des Nations (Council of the League of Nations), 1851–1925.

1921 The prize was divided equally between:
BRANTING, KARL HJALMAR, Sweden, Prime Minister, Swedish Delegate Conseil de la Société des Nations (Council of the League of Nations), 1860–1925; and
LANGE, CHRISTIAN LOUIS, Norway, Secretary General Inter–Parliamentary Union, Brussels, 1869–1938.

1922 NANSEN, FRIDTJOF, Norway, Scientist, Explorer, Norwegian Delegate Société des Nations (League of Nations), Originator "Nansen passports" (for refugees), 1861–1930.

1923 Reserved.

1924 The prize money for 1923 was allocated to the Special Fund of this prize section.
The prize for 1924: Reserved.

1925 The prize money for 1924 was allocated to the Special Fund of this prize section.
The prize for 1925: Reserved.

1926 The prize for 1925 was awarded jointly to:
CHAMBERLAIN, Sir AUSTEN, Great Britain, Foreign Secretary, Part–originator Locarno Pact, 1863–1937; and
DAWES, CHARLES GATES, USA, Vice–President United States of America, Chairman Allied Reparation Commission (Originator "Dawes Plan"), 1865–1951.

The prize for 1926 was awarded jointly to:
BRIAND, ARISTIDE, France, Foreign Minister, Part–originator Locarno Pact, Briand–Kellogg Pact, 1862–1932; and
STRESEMANN, GUSTAV, Germany, ex–Lord High Chancellor (Riechskanzler), Foreign Minister, Part–originator Locarno Pact, 1878–1929.

1927 The prize was divided equally between:
BUISSON, FERDINAND, France, formerly Professor Sorbonne University, Paris, Founder and President Ligue des Droits de l'Homme (League for Human Rights), 1841–1932; and
QUIDDE, LUDWIG, Germany, Professor Berlin University, Member German Parliament, Participant various peace conferences, 1858–1941.

1928 Reserved.

1929 The prize money for 1928 was allocated to the Special Fund of this prize section.
The prize for 1929: Reserved.

1930 The prize for 1929:
KELLOGG, FRANK BILLINGS, USA, ex–Secretary of State, Part–originator Briand–Kellogg Pact, 1856–1937.
The prize for 1930:
SÖDERBLOM, LARS OLOF NATHAN (JONATHAN), Sweden, Archbishop, Leader in the ecumenical movement, 1866–1931.

1931 The prize was divided equally between:
ADDAMS, JANE, USA, Sociologist, International President Women's International League for Peace and Freedom, 1860–1935; and
BUTLER, NICHOLAS MURRAY, USA, President Columbia University, Promoter Briand–Kellogg Pact, 1862–1947.

1932 Reserved.

1933 The prize money for 1932 was allocated to the Special Fund of this prize section.
The prize for 1933: Reserved.

1934 The prize for 1933:
ANGELL (RALPH LANE) Sir NORMAN, Great Britain, Writer, Member Commission Exécutive de la Société des Nations (Executive Committee of the League of Nations)

and of National Peace Council, Author *The Great Illusion*, 1874–1967.
The prize for 1934:
HENDERSON, ARTHUR, Great Britain, ex–Foreign Secretary, President Disarmament Conference 1932, 1863–1935.

1935 Reserved.

1936 The prize for 1935:
VON OSSIETZKY, CARL, Germany, Journalist (i.a. *die Weltbühne*), Pacifist, 1889–1938.
The prize for 1936:
SAAVEDRA LAMAS, CARLOS, Argentine Secretary of State, President Société des Nations (League of Nations), Mediator in a conflict between Paraguay and Bolivia, 1878–1959.

1937 CECIL OF CHELWOOD, Viscount, (Lord EDGAR ALGERNON ROBERT GASCOYNE CECIL), Great Britain, writer, i.a. ex–Lord Privy Seal, Founder and President International Peace Campaign, 1864–1958.

1938 OFFICE INTERNATIONAL NANSEN POUR LES RÉFUGIÉS (Nansen International Office for Refugees), Geneva, an international relief organization, started by Fridtjof Nansen in 1921.

1939 – 1942 The prize money has been allocated with one–third to the Main Fund and with two–thirds to the Special Fund of this prize section.

1943 Reserved.

1944 The prize money for 1943 was allocated with one–third to the Main Fund and with two–thirds to the Special Fund of this prize section.
The prize for 1944: Reserved.

1945 The prize for 1944:
COMITÉ INTERNATIONAL DE LA CROIX–ROUGE (International Committee of the Red Cross), Geneva, founded 1863.
The prize for 1945:
HULL, CORDELL, USA, ex–Secretary of State, prominent part–taker in originating the United Nations, 1871–1955.

1946 The prize was divided equally between:
BALCH, EMILY GREENE, USA, formerly Professor of History and Sociology, Honorary International President Women's International

League for Peace and Freedom, 1867–1961; and
MOTT, JOHN RALEIGH, USA, Chairman International Missionary Council, President World Alliance of Young Men's Christian Associations, 1865–1955.

1947 The prize was awarded jointly to:
THE FRIENDS SERVICE COUNCIL (The Quakers), London, founded 1647; and
THE AMERICAN FRIENDS SERVICE COMMITTEE (The Quakers), Washington, first official meeting 1672.

1948 Reserved.

1949 The prize money for 1948 was allocated with one–third to the Main Fund and with two–thirds to the Special Fund of this prize section.
The prize for 1949:
BOYD ORR OF BRECHIN, Lord, JOHN, Great Britain, Physician, Alimentary Politician, prominent organizer and Director General Food and Agriculture Organization, President National Peace Council and World Union of Peace Organizations, 1880–1971.

1950 BUNCHE, RALPH, USA, Professor Harvard University, Cambridge, MA., Director division of Trusteeship UN, Acting Mediator in Palestine 1948, 1904–1971.

1951 JOUHAUX, LÉON, France, President Trade Union Confederation "CGT Force Ouvrière". President Conseil national économique and International Committee of the European Council, Vice President International Confederation of Free Trade Unions, Vice President Fédération syndicale mondiale, Member Council ILO (International Labour Organization), Delegate UN, 1879–1954.

1952 Reserved.

1953 The prize for 1952:
SCHWEITZER, ALBERT, France, Missionary surgeon. Founder Lambaréné Hospital (République du Gabon), 1875–1965.
The prize for 1953:
MARSHALL, GEORGE CATLETT, USA, General, President American Red Cross, ex–Secretary of State and of Defense, Delegate UN, Originator "Marshall Plan", 1880–1959.

1954 Reserved.

1955 The prize for 1954:
OFFICE OF THE UNITED NATIONS HIGH COMMISSIONER FOR REFUGEES, Geneva, an international relief organization, founded by UN in 1951.
The prize for 1955: Reserved.

1956 The prize money for 1955 was allocated with one–third to the Main Fund and with two–thirds to the Special Fund of this prize section.
The prize for 1956: Reserved.

1957 The prize money for 1956 was allocated with one–third to the Main Fund and with two–thirds to the Special Fund of this prize section.
The prize for 1957:
PEARSON, LESTER BOWLES, Canada, former Secretary of State for External Affairs of Canada, President 7th Session of the United Nations General Assembly, 1897–1972.

1958 PIRE, GEORGES, Belgium, Father of the Dominican Order, Leader of the relief organization for refugees, "L'Europe du Coeur au Service du Monde", 1910–1969.

1959 NOEL–BAKER, PHILIP J., Great Britain, Member of Parliament, life–long ardent worker for international peace and co–operation, 1889–1982.

1960 Reserved.

1961 The prize for 1960:
LUTHULI, ALBERT JOHN, South Africa, President of the African National Congress in SA, 1898–1967.
The prize for 1961:
HAMMARSKJÖLD, DAG HJALMAR AGNE CARL, Sweden, secretary general of the UN, 1905–1961.

1962 Reserved.

1963 The prize for 1962:
PAULING, LINUS CARL, USA, Pasadena, CA., 1901.
The prize for 1963 was divided equally between:
COMITÉ INTERNATIONAL DE LA CROIX–ROUGE (International Committee of the Red Cross), Geneva, founded 1863; and
LIGUE DES SOCIÉTÉS DE LA CROIX–ROUGE (League of Red Cross Societies), Geneva.

1964 KING, MARTIN LUTHER, JR, USA, Leader of Southern Christian Leadership Conference, 1929–1968.

1965 UNITED NATIONS CHILDREN'S FUND (UNICEF), New York, founded by UN in 1946.

1966 Reserved.

1967 The prize money for 1966 was allocated with one–third to the Main Fund and with two–thirds to the Special Fund of this prize section.
The prize for 1967: Reserved.

1968 The prize money for 1967 was allocated with one–third to the Main Fund and with two–thirds to the Special Fund of this prize section.
The prize for 1968:
CASSIN, RENÉ, France, President of the European Court for Human Rights, 1887–1976.

1969 INTERNATIONAL LABOUR ORGANIZATION (ILO), Geneva.

1970 BORLAUG, NORMAN E., USA, International Maize and Wheat Improvement Center, Mexico City, 1914.

1971 BRANDT, WILLY, Federal Republic of Germany, Chancellor of the Federal Republic of Germany, 1913.

1972 Reserved.

1973 The prize money for 1972 was allocated to the Main Fund.
The prize for 1973 was awarded jointly to:
KISSINGER, HENRY A., USA, Secretary of State, State Department, Washington, 1923; and
LE DUC THO, Democratic Republic of Viet Nam, 1910 (Declined the prize).

1974 The prize was divided equally between:
MACBRIDE, SEAN, Ireland, President of the International Peace Bureau, Geneva, and the Commission of Namibia, United Nations, New York, 1904–1988; and
SATO, EISAKU, Japan, Prime Minister of Japan, 1901–1975.

1975 SAKHAROV, ANDREI, USSR, Soviet nuclear physicist, 1921–1989.

1976 Reserved.

1977 The prize for 1976:
WILLIAMS, BETTY, Northern Ireland, Great Britain, 1943; and CORRIGAN, MAIREAD, Northern Ireland, Great Britain, 1944, Founders of the Northern Ireland Peace Movement (later renamed Community of Peace People).
The prize for 1977:
AMNESTY INTERNATIONAL, London, Great Britain.

1978 The prize for 1978 was divided equally between:
EL SADAT, MOHAMMED ANWAR, Egypt, President of the Arab Republic of Egypt, 1918–1981; and BEGIN, MENACHEM, Israel, Prime Minister of Israel, 1913 (in Brest Litovsk, then Poland).

1979 MOTHER TERESA, India, leader of Missionaries of Charities, Calcutta, 1910 (in Skoplje, then Serbia).

1980 PEREZ ESQUIVEL, ADOLFO, Argentina, architect, sculptor and human rights leader, 1931.

1981 OFFICE OF THE UNITED NATIONS HIGH COMMISSIONER FOR REFUGEES, Geneva, Switzerland.

1982 The prize was awarded jointly to:
MYRDAL, ALVA, Sweden, former Cabinet Minister, diplomat, writer, 1902–1986; and GARCÍA ROBLES, ALFONSO, Mexico, diplomat, delegate to the United Nations General Assembly on Disarmament, former Secretary for Foreign Affairs, 1911.

1983 WALESA, LECH, Poland, trade union leader (Solidarity), 1943.

1984 TUTU, DESMOND MPILO, South Africa, Bishop of Johannesburg, former Secretary General South African Council of Churches (SACC) 1931.

1985 INTERNATIONAL PHYSICIANS FOR THE PREVENTION OF NUCLEAR WAR Inc., Boston, MA., USA.

1986 WIESEL, ELIE, USA, Chairman of "The President's Commission on the Holocaust", 1928.

1987 ARIAS SANCHEZ, OSCAR, Costa Rica, President of Cost Rica, 1941.

1988 THE UNITED NATIONS PEACE–KEEPING FORCES, New York, NY., USA.

1989 THE 14TH DALAI LAMA (TENZIN GYATSO), Tibet, 1935.

1990 GORBACHEV, MIKHAIL, USSR, 1931, President of the Soviet Union.

Physics

1901 RÖNTGEN, WILHELM CONRAD, Germany, 1845–1923: "In recognition of the extraordinary services he has rendered by the discovery of the remarkable rays subsequently named after him."

1902 The prize was awarded jointly to:
LORENTZ, HENDRIK ANTOON, the Netherlands, 1853–1928; and ZEEMAN, PIETER, the Netherlands, 1865–1943: "In recognition of the extraordinary service they rendered by their researches into the influence of magnetism upon radiation phenomena."

1903 The prize was divided, one half being awarded to:
BECQUEREL, ANTOINE HENRI, France, 1852–1908: "In recognition of the extraordinary services he has rendered by his discovery of spontaneous radioactivity";
the other half jointly to:
CURIE, PIERRE, France, 1859–1906; and his wife
CURIE, MARIE, née SKLODOWSKA, France, 1867 (in Warsaw, Poland) – 1934: "In recognition of the extraordinary services they have rendered by their joint researches on the radiation phenomena discovered by Professor Henri Becquerel."

1904 RAYLEIGH, Lord (JOHN WILLIAM STRUTT), Great Britain, 1842–1919: "For his investigations of the densities of the most important gases and for his discovery of argon in connection with these studies."

1905 LENARD, PHILIPP EDUARD ANTON, Germany, 1862–1947: "For his work on cathode rays."

1906 THOMSON, Sir JOSEPH JOHN, Great Britain, 1856–1940: "In recognition of the great merits of his theoretical and experimental investigations on the conduction of electricity by gases."

1907 MICHELSON, ALBERT ABRAHAM, USA, 1852–1931: "For his optical precision instruments and the spectroscopic and metrological investigations carried out with their aid."

1908 LIPPMANN, GABRIEL, France, 1845 –1921: "For his method of reproducing colours photographically based on the phenomenon of interference."

1909 The prize was awarded jointly to:
MARCONI, GUGLIELMO, Italy, 1874 –1937; and BRAUN, CARL FERDINAND, Germany, 1850–1918: "In recognition of their contributions to the development of wireless telegraphy."

1910 VAN DER WAALS, JOHANNES DIDERIK, the Netherlands, 1837–1923: "For his work on the equation of state for gases and liquids."

1911 WIEN, WILHELM, Germany, 1864–1928: "For his discoveries regarding the laws governing the radiation of heat."

1912 DALÉN, NILS GUSTAF, Sweden, 1869–1937: "For his invention of automatic regulators for use in conjunction with gas accumulators for illuminating lighthouses and buoys."

1913 KAMERLINGH–ONNES, HEIKE, the Netherlands, 1853–1926: "For his investigations on the properties of matter at low temperatures which led, *inter alia*, to the production of liquid helium."

1914 VON LAUE, MAX, Germany, 1879–1960: "For his discovery of the diffraction of X–rays by crystals."

1915 The prize was awarded jointly to:
BRAGG, Sir WILLIAM HENRY, Great Britain, 1862–1942; and his son BRAGG, Sir WILLIAM LAWRENCE, Great Britain, 1890–1971: "For their services in the analysis of crystal structure by means of X–rays."

1916 Reserved.

1917 The prize money for 1916 was allocated to the Special Fund of this prize section.
The prize for 1917: Reserved.

1918 The prize for 1917:
BARKLA, CHARLES GLOVER, Great Britain, 1877–1944: "For his discovery of the characteristic Röntgen radiation of the elements.

The prize for 1918: Reserved.

1919 The prize for 1918:
PLANCK, MAX KARL ERNST
LUDWIG, Germany, 1858–1947: "In
recognition of the services he
rendered to the advancement of
Physics by his discovery of energy
quanta."
The prize for 1919:
STARK, JOHANNES, Germany, 1874
–1957: "For his discovery of the
Doppler effect in canal rays and the
splitting of spectral lines in electric
fields."

1920 GUILLAUME, CHARLES EDOUARD,
Switzerland, 1861–1938: "In
recognition of the service he has
rendered to precision measurements
in Physics by his discovery of
anomalies in nickel steel alloys."

1921 Reserved.

1922 The prize for 1921:
EINSTEIN, ALBERT, Germany and
Switzerland, 1879–1955: "For his
services to Theoretical Physics, and
especially for his discovery of the law
of the photoelectric effect."
The prize for 1922:
BOHR, NIELS, Denmark, 1885–1962:
"For his services in the investigation
of the structure of atoms and of the
radiation emanating from them."

1923 MILLIKAN, ROBERT ANDREWS,
USA, 1868–1953: "For his work on the
elementary charge of electricity and
on the photoelectric effect."

1924 Reserved.

1925 The prize for 1924:
SIEGBAHN, KARL MANNE GEORG,
Sweden, 1886–1978: "For his
discoveries and research in the field
of X–ray spectroscopy."
The prize for 1925: Reserved.

1926 The prize for 1925 was awarded
jointly to:
FRANCK, JAMES, Germany,
1882–1964; and
HERTZ, GUSTAV, Germany,
1887–1975: "For their discovery of the
laws governing the impact of an
electron upon an atom."
The prize for 1926:
PERRIN, JEAN BAPTISTE, France,
1870–1942: "For his work on the
discontinuous structure of matter,
and especially for his discovery of
sedimentation equilibrium."

1927 The prize was divided equally
between:
COMPTON, ARTHUR HOLLY, USA,
1892–1962: "For his discovery of the
effect named after him"; and
WILSON, CHARLES THOMSON
REES, Great Britain, 1869–1959: "For
his method of making the paths of
electrically charged particles visible
by condensation of vapour."

1928 Reserved.

1929 The prize for 1928:
RICHARDSON, Sir OWEN
WILLIAMS, Great Britain, 1879–1959:
"For his work on the thermionic
phenomenon and especially for the
discovery of the law named after
him."
The prize for 1929:
DE BROGLIE, Prince
LOUIS-VICTOR, France, 1892–1987:
"For his discovery of the wave nature
of electrons."

1930 RAMAN, Sir CHANDRASEKHARA
VENKATA, India, 1888–1970: "For his
work on the scattering of light and for
the discovery of the effect named
after him."

1931 Reserved.

1932 The prize money for 1931 was
allocated to the Special Fund of this
prize section.
The prize for 1932: Reserved.

1933 The prize for 1932:
HEISENBERG, WERNER, Germany,
1901–1976: "For the creation of
quantum mechanics, the application
of which has, *inter alia*, led to the
discovery of the allotropic forms of
hydrogen."
The prize for 1933 was awarded
jointly to:
SCHRÖDINGER, ERWIN, Austria,
1887–1961; and
DIRAC, PAUL ADRIEN MAURICE,
Great Britain, 1902–1984: "For the
discovery of new productive forms of
atomic theory."

1934 Reserved.

1935 One–third of the prize money for
1934 was allocated to the Main Fund,
and two–thirds to the Special Fund of
this prize section.
The prize for 1935:
CHADWICK, Sir JAMES, Great
Britain, 1891–1974: "For the discovery
of the neutron."

1936 The prize was divided equally
between:
HESS, VICTOR FRANZ, Austria, 1883
–1964: "For his discovery of cosmic
radiation"; and
ANDERSON, CARL DAVID, USA,
1905: "For his discovery of the
positron."

1937 The prize was awarded jointly to:
DAVISSON, CLINTON JOSEPH,
USA, 1881–1958; and
THOMSON Sir GEORGE PAGET,
Great Britain, 1892–1975: "For their
experimental discovery of the
diffraction of electrons by crystals."

1938 FERMI, ENRICO, Italy, 1901–1954:
"For his demonstrations of the
existence of new radioactive elements
produced by neutron irradiation, and
for his related discovery of nuclear
reactions brought about by slow
neutrons."

1939 LAWRENCE, ERNEST ORLANDO,
USA, 1901–1958: "For the invention
and development of the cyclotron
and for results obtained with it,
especially with regard to artificial
radioactive elements."

1940 – 1942 One–third of the prize money
was allocated to the Main Fund, and
two–thirds to the Special Fund of this
prize section.

1943 Reserved.

1944 The prize for 1943:
STERN, OTTO, USA, 1888–1969: "For
his contribution to the development
of the molecular ray method and his
discovery of the magnetic moment of
the proton."
The prize for 1944:
RABI, ISIDOR ISAAC, USA,
1898–1988: "For his resonance
method for recording the magnetic
properties of atomic nuclei."

1945 PAULI, WOLFGANG, Austria,
1900–1958: "For the discovery of the
Exclusion Principle, also called the
Pauli Principle."

1946 BRIDGMAN, PERCY WILLIAMS,
USA, 1882–1961: "For the invention of
an apparatus to produce extremely
high pressures, and for the
discoveries he made therewith in the
field of high pressure physics.

1947 APPLETON, Sir EDWARD VICTOR,
Great Britain, 1892–1965: "For his
investigations of the physics of the

upper atmosphere especially for the discovery of the so–called Appleton layer."

1948 BLACKETT, Lord PATRICK MAYNARD STUART, Great Britain, 1897–1974: "For his development of the Wilson cloud chamber method, and his discoveries therewith in the fields of nuclear physics and cosmic radiation."

1949 YUKAWA, HIDEKI, Japan, 1907–1981: "For his prediction of the existence of mesons on the basis of theoretical work on nuclear forces."

1950 POWELL, CECIL FRANK, Great Britain, 1903–1969: "For his development of the photographic method of studying nuclear processes and his discoveries regarding mesons made with this method."

1951 The prize was awarded jointly to: COCKCROFT, Sir JOHN DOUGLAS, Great Britain, 1897–1967; and WALTON, ERNEST THOMAS SINTON, Ireland, 1903: "For their pioneer work on the transmutation of atomic nuclei by artificially accelerated atomic particles."

1952 The prize was awarded jointly to: BLOCH, FELIX, USA, 1905–1983; and PURCELL, EDWARD MILLS, USA, 1912: "For their development of new methods for nuclear magnetic precision meaurements and discoveries in connection therewith."

1953 ZERNIKE, FRITS (FREDERIK), the Netherlands, 1888–1966: "For his demonstration of the phase contrast method, especially for his invention of the phase contrast microscope."

1954 The prize was divided equally between: BORN, MAX, Great Britain, 1882–1970: "For his fundamental research in quantum mechanics, especially for his statistical interpretation of the wave function"; and BOTHE, WALTHER, Germany, 1891–1957: "For the coincidence method and his discoveries made therewith."

1955 The prize was divided equally between: LAMB, WILLIS EUGENE, USA, 1913: "For his discoveries concerning the fine structure of the hydrogen spectrum"; and

KUSCH, POLYKARP, USA, 1911: "For his precision determination of the magnetic moment of the electron."

1956 The prize was awarded jointly, one–third each, to: SHOCKLEY, WILLIAM, USA, 1910–1989; BARDEEN, JOHN, USA, 1908–1991; and BRATTAIN, WALTER HOUSER, USA, 1902–1987: "For their researches on semiconductors and their discovery of the transistor effect."

1957 The prize was awarded jointly to: YANG, CHEN NING, China, 1922; and LEE, TSUNG–DAO, China, 1926: "For their penetrating investigation of the so–called parity laws which has led to important discoveries regarding the elementary particles."

1958 The prize was awarded jointly to: ČERENKOV, PAVEL ALEKSEJVIČ, USSR, 1904–1990; FRANK, IL'JA MICHAJLOVIČ, USSR, 1908–1990; and TAMM, IGOR JEVGEN'EVIC, USSR, 1895–1971: "For the discovery and the interpretation of the Cerenkov effect."

1959 The prize was awarded jointly to: SEGRÈ, EMILIO GINO, USA, 1905–1989; and CHAMBERLAIN, OWEN, USA, 1920: "For their discovery of the antiproton."

1960 GLASER, DONALD A., USA, 1926: "For the invention of the bubble chamber."

1961 The prize was divided equally between: HOFSTADTER, ROBERT, USA, 1915–1991: "For his pioneering studies of electron scattering in atomic nuclei and for his thereby achieved discoveries concerning the structure of the nucleons"; and MÖSSBAUER, RUDOLF LUDVIG, Germany, 1929: "For his researches concerning the resonance absorption of gamma radiation and his discovery in this connection of the effect which bears his name."

1962 LANDAU, LEV DAVIDOVIČ, USSR, 1908–1968: "For his pioneering theories for condensed matter, especially liquid helium."

1963 The prize was divided, one–half

being awarded to: WIGNER, EUGENE P., USA, 1902: "For his contributions to the theory of the atomic nucleus and the elementary particles, particularly through the discovery and application of fundamental symmetry principles."; and the other half jointly to: GOEPPERT–MAYER, MARIA, USA, 1906–1972; and JENSEN, J. HANS D., Germany, 1907–1973: "For their discoveries concerning nuclear shell structure."

1964 The prize was divided, one–half being awarded to: TOWNES, CHARLES H., USA, 1915; and the other half jointly to: BASOV, NICOLAI GENNADIEVIC, USSR, 1922; and PROKHOROV, ALEKSANDR MIKHAILOVIC, USSR, 1916: "For fundamental work in the field of quantum electronics, which has led to the construction of oscillators and amplifiers based on the maser–laser principle."

1965 The prize was awarded jointly to: TOMONAGA, SIN–ITIRO, Japan, 1906–1979; SCHWINGER, JULIAN, USA, 1918; and FEYNMAN, RICHARD P., USA, 1918–1988: "For their fundamental work in quantum electrodynamics, with deep–ploughing consequences for the physics of elementary particles."

1966 KASTLER, ALFRED, France, 1902–1984: "For the discovery and development of optical methods for studying hertzian resonances in atoms."

1967 BETHE, HANS ALBRECHT, USA, 1906: "For his contributions to the theory of nuclear reactions, especially his discoveries concerning the energy production in stars."

1968 ALVAREZ, LUIS W., USA, 1911–1988: "For his decisive contributions to elementary particle physics, in particular the discovery of a large number of resonance states, made possible through his development of the technique of using hydrogen bubble chamber and data analysis."

1969 GELL–MANN, MURRAY, USA, 1929: "For his contributions and discoveries concerning the classification of elementary particles and their interactions."

1970 The prize was divided equally between:
ALFVÉN, HANNES, Sweden, Royal Institute of Technology, Stockholm, 1908: "For fundamental work and discoveries in magneto–hydro-dynamics with fruitful applications in different parts of plasma physics"; and
NÉEL, LOUIS, France, 1904: "For fundamental work and discoveries concerning antiferromagnetism and ferrimagnetism which have led to important applications in solid state physics."

1971 GABOR, DENNIS, Great Britain, 1900–1979: "For his invention and development of the holographic method."

1972 The prize was awarded jointly to:
BARDEEN, JOHN, USA, 1908–1991;
COOPER, LEON N., USA, 1930; and
SCHRIEFFER, J. ROBERT, USA, 1931: "For their jointly developed theory of superconductivity, usually called the BCS–theory."

1973 The prize was divided, one–half being equally shared between:
ESAKI, LEO, Japan, 1925; and
GIAEVER, IVAR, USA, 1929: "For their experimental discoveries regarding tunnelling phenomena in semiconductors and superconductors, respectively."
and the other half to:
JOSEPHSON, BRIAN D., Great Britain, 1940: "For his theoretical predictions of the properties of a supercurrent through a tunnel barrier, in particular those phenomena which are generally known as the Josephson effects."

1974 The prize was awarded jointly to:
RYLE, Sir MARTIN, Great Britain, 1918–1984; and
HEWISH, ANTHONY, Great Britain, 1924: "For their pioneering research in radio astrophysics: Ryle for his observations and inventions, in particular of the aperture synthesis technique, and Hewish for his decisive role in the discovery of pulsars."

1975 The prize was awarded jointly to:
BOHR, AAGE, Denmark, 1922;
MOTTELSON, BEN, Denmark, 1926; and
RAINWATER, JAMES, USA,

1917–1986: "For the discovery of the connection between collective motion and particle motion in atomic nuclei and the development of the theory of the structure of the atomic nucleus based on this connection."

1976 The prize was divided equally between:
RICHTER, BURTON, USA, 1931; and
TING, SAMUEL C. C., USA, 1936: "For their pioneering work in the discovery of a heavy elementary particle of a new kind."

1977 The prize was divided equally between:
ANDERSON, PHILIP W., USA, 1923;
MOTT, Sir NEVILL F., Great Britain, 1905; and
VAN VLECK, JOHN H., USA, 1899–1980: "For their fundamental theoretical investigations of the

1978 The prize was divided, one–half being awarded to;
KAPITSA, PETER LEONIDOVITCH, USSR, 1894–1984: "For his basic inventions and discoveries in the area of low–temperature physics.";
and the other half divided equally between:
PENZIAS, ARNO A., USA, 1933; and
WILSON, ROBERT W., USA 1936: "For their discovery of cosmic microwave background radiation."

1979 The prize was divided equally between:
GLASHOW, SHELDON L., USA, 1932;
SALAM, ABDUS, 1926; and
WEINBERG, STEVEN, USA, 1933: "For their contributions to the theory of the unified weak and electromagnetic interaction between elementary particles, including *inter alia* the prediction of the weak neutral current."

1980 The prize was divided equally between:
CRONIN, JAMES W., USA 1931; and
FITCH, VAL L., USA, 1923: "For the discovery of violations of fundamental symmetry principles in the decay of neutral K–mesons."

1981 The prize was awarded by one half jointly to:
BLOEMBERGEN, NICOLAAS, USA, 1920; and
SCHAWLOW, ARTHUR L., USA, 1921: "For their contribution to the development of laser spectroscopy"; and the other half to:

SIEGBAHN, KAI M., Sweden, 1918: "For his contribution to the development of high–resolution electron spectroscopy."

1982 WILSON, KENNETH G., USA, 1936: "For his theory for critical phenomena in connection with phase transitions."

1983 The prize was awarded by one–half to:
CHANDRASEKHAR, SUBRAMANYAN, USA, 1910: "For his theoretical studies of the physical processes of importance to the structure and evolution of the stars."; and the other half to:
FOWLER, WILLIAM A., USA, 1911: "For his theoretical and experimental studies of the nuclear reactions of importance in the formation of the chemical elements in the universe."

1984 The prize was awarded jointly to:
RUBBIA, CARLO, Italy, 1934; and
VAN DER MEER, SIMON, the Netherlands, 1925: "For their decisive contributions to the large project, which led to the discovery of the field particles W and Z, communicators of weak interaction."

1985 VON KLITZING, KLAUS, Germany, 1943: "For the discovery of the quantized Hall efect."

1986 The prize was awarded by one–half to;
RUSKA, ERNST, Germany, 1906–1988: "For his fundamental work in electron optics, and for the design of the first electron microscope."
and the other half jointly to:
BINNIG, GERD, Germany, 1947; and
ROHRER, HEINRICH, Switzerland, 1933: "For their design of the scanning tunnelling microscope."

1987 The prize was awarded jointly to:
BEDNORZ, J. GEORG, Germany, 1950; and
MÜLLER, K. ALEXANDER, Switzerland, 1927: "For their important breakthrough in the discovery of superconductivity in ceramic materials."

1988 The prize was awarded jointly to:
LEDERMAN, LEON M., USA, 1922;
SCHWARTZ, MELVIN, USA, 1932; and
STEINBERGER, JACK, USA, 1921: "For the neutrino beam method and the demonstration of the doublet

structure of the leptons through the discovery of the muon neutrino."

1989 The prize was awarded one–half to:
RAMSEY, NORMAN F., USA, 1915: "For the invention of the separated oscillatory fields method and its use in the hydrogen maser and other atomic clocks."
and one–half jointly to:
DEHMELT, HANS G., USA, 1922; and PAUL, WOLFGANG, Germany, 1913: "For the development of the ion trap technique."

1990 The prize was awarded jointly to:
FRIEDMAN, JEROME I., USA, 1930; KENDALL, HENRY W., USA, 1926; TAYLOR, RICHARD E., Canada, 1929: "For their pioneering investigations concerning deep inelastic scattering of electrons on protons and bound neutrons, which have been of essential importance for the development of the quark model in particle physics."

Chemistry

1901 VAN'T HOFF, JACOBUS HENRICUS, the Netherlands, 1852–1911: "In recognition of the extraordinary services he has rendered by the discovery of the laws of chemical dynamics and osmotic pressure in solutions."

1902 FISCHER, HERMANN EMIL, Germany, 1852–1919: "In recognition of the extraordinary services he has rendered by his work on sugar and purine synthesis."

1903 ARRHENIUS, SVANTE AUGUST, Sweden, 1859–1927: "In recognition of the extraordinary services he has rendered to the advancement of chemistry by his electrolytic theory of dissociation."

1904 RAMSAY, Sir WILLIAM, Great Britain, 1852–1916: "In recognition of his services in the discovery of the inert gaseous elements in air, and his determination of their place in the periodic system."

1905 VON BAEYER, JOHANN FRIEDRICH WILHELM ADOLF, Germany, 1835–1917: "In recognition of his services in the advancement of organic chemistry and the chemical industry, through his work on organic dyes and hydro–aromatic compounds."

1906 MOISSAN, HENRI, France, 1852–1907: "In recognition of the great services rendered by him in his investigation and isolation of the element fluorine, and for the adoption in the service of science of the electric furnace called after him."

1907 BUCHNER, EDUARD, Germany, 1860–1917: "For his biochemical researches and his discovery of cell–free fermentation."

1908 RUTHERFORD, Lord ERNEST, Great Britain, 1871–1937: "For his investigations into the disintegration of the elements, and the chemistry of radioactive substances.

1909 OSTWALD, WILHELM, Germany, 1853–1932: "In recognition of his work on catalysis and for his investigations into the fundamental principles governing chemical equilibria and rates of reaction."

1910 WALLACH, OTTO, Germany, 1847–1931: "In recognition of his services to organic chemistry and the chemical industry by his pioneer work in the field of alicyclic compounds."

1911 CURIE, MARIE, née SKLODOWSKA, France, 1867–1934: "In recognition of her services to the advancement of chemistry by the discovery of the elements radium and polonium, by the isolation of radium and the study of the nature and compounds of this remarkable element."

1912 The prize was divided equally between:
GRIGNARD, VICTOR, France, 1871–1935: "For the discovery of the so–called Grignard reagent, which in recent years has greatly advanced the progress of organic chemistry"; and
SABATIER, PAUL, France, 1854–1941: "For his method of hydrogenating organic compounds in the presence of finely disintegrated metals whereby the progress of organic chemistry has been greatly advanced in recent years."

1913 WERNER, ALFRED, Switzerland, 1866–1919: "In recognition of his work on the linkage of atoms in molecules by which he has thrown new light on earlier investigations and opened up new fields of research especially in inorganic chemistry."

1914 Reserved.

1915 The prize for 1914:
RICHARDS, THEODORE WILLIAM, USA, 1868–1928: "In recognition of his accurate determinations of the atomic weight of a large number of chemical elements."
The prize for 1915:
WILLSTATTER, RICHARD MARTIN, Germany, 1872–1942: "For his researches on plant pigments, especially chlorophyll."

1916 Reserved.

1917 The prize money for 1916 was allocated to the Special Fund of this prize section.
The prize for 1917: Reserved.

1918 The prize money for 1917 was allocated to the Special Fund of this prize section.
The prize for 1918: Reserved.

1919 The prize for 1918:
HABER, FRITZ, Germany, 1868–1934: "For the synthesis of ammonia from its elements."

1920 The prize money for 1919 was allocated to the Special Fund of this prize section.
The prize for 1920: Reserved.

1921 The prize for 1920:
NERNST, WALTHER HERMANN, Germany, 1864–1941: "In recognition of his work in thermochemistry."
The prize for 1921: Reserved.

1922 The prize for 1921:
SODDY, FREDERICK, Great Britain, 1877–1956: "For his contributions to our knowledge of the chemistry of radioactive substances, and his investigations into the origin and nature of isotopes."
The prize for 1922:
ASTON, FRANCIS WILLIAM, Great Britain, 1877–1945: "For his discovery, by means of his mass spectrograph, of isotopes, in a large number of non–radioactive elements, and for his enunciation of the whole–number rule."

1923 PREGL, FRITZ, Austria, 1869–1930: "For his invention of the method of micro–analysis of organic substances."

1924 Reserved.

1925 The prize money for 1924 was allocated to the Special Fund of this prize section.
The prize for 1925: Reserved.

1926 The prize for 1925:
ZSIGMONDY, RICHARD ADOLF, Germany, 1865–1929: "For his demonstration of the heterogenous nature of colloid solutions and for the methods he used, which have since become fundamental in modern colloid chemistry."
The prize for 1926:
SVEDBERG, THE (THEODOR), Sweden, 1884–1971: "For his work on disperse systems."

1927 Reserved.

1928 The prize for 1927:
WIELAND, HEINRICH OTTO, Germany, 1877–1957: "For his investigations of the constitution of the bile acids and related substances."
The prize for 1928:
WINDAUS, ADOLF OTTO REINHOLD, Germany, 1876–1959: "For the services rendered through his research into the constitution of the sterols and their connection with the vitamins."

1929 The prize was divided equally between:
HARDEN, Sir ARTHUR, Great Britain, 1865–1940; and
VON EULER–CHELPIN, HANS KARL AUGUST SIMON, Sweden, 1873–1964: "For their investigations on the fermentation of sugar and fermentative enzymes."

1930 FISCHER, HANS, Germany, 1881–1945: "For his researches into the constitution of haemin and chlorophyll and especially for his synthesis of haemin."

1931 The prize was awarded jointly to:
BOSCH, CARL, Germany, 1874–1940; and
BERGIUS, FRIEDRICH, Germany, 1884–1949: "In recognition of their contributions to the invention and development of chemical high pressure methods."

1932 LANGMUIR, IRVING, USA, 1881–1957: "For his discoveries and investigations in surface chemistry."

1933 Reserved.

1934 The prize money for 1933 was with one–third allocated to the Main Fund and with two–thirds to the Special Fund of this prize section.
The prize for 1934:
UREY, HAROLD CLAYTON, USA, 1893–1981: "For his discovery of heavy hydrogen."

1935 The prize was awarded jointly to:
JOLIOT, FRÉDÉRIC, France, 1900–1958; and his wife
JOLIOT–CURIE, IRÈNE, France, 1897–1956: "In recognition of their synthesis of new radioactive elements."

1936 DEBYE, PETRUS (PETER) JOSEPHUS WILHELMUS, the Netherlands, 1884–1966: "For his contributions to our knowledge of molecular structure through his investigations on dipole moments and on the diffraction of X–rays and electrons in gases."

1937 The prize was divided equally between:
HAWORTH, Sir WALTER NORMAN, Great Britain, 1883–1950: "For his investigations on carbohydrates and vitamin C."
KARRER, PAUL, Switzerland, 1889–1971: "For his investigations on carotenoids, flavins and vitamins A and B2."

1938 Reserved.

1939 The prize for 1938:
KUHN, RICHARD, Germany, 1900–1967: "For his work on carotenoids and vitamins." (Caused by the authorities of his country to decline the award but later received the diploma and the medal.)
The prize for 1939 was divided equally between:
BUTENANDT, ADOLF FRIEDRICH JOHANN, Germany, 1903: "For his work on sex hormones." (Caused by the authorities of his country to decline the award but later received the diploma and the medal); and
RUŽIČKA, LEOPOLD, Switzerland, 1887–1976: "For his work on polymethylenes and higher terpenes."

1940 – 1942 The prize money was with one–third allocated to the Main Fund and with two–thirds to the Special Fund of this prize section.

1943 Reserved.

1944 The prize for 1943:
DE HEVESY, GEORG, Hungary,

1885–1966: "For his work on the use of isotopes as tracers in the study of chemical processes."
The prize for 1944: Reserved.

1945 The prize for 1944:
HAHN, OTTO, Germany, 1879–1968: "For his discovery of the fission of heavy nuclei."
The prize for 1945:
VIRTANEN, ARTTURI ILMARI, Finland, 1895–1973: "For his research and inventions in agricultural and nutrition chemistry, especially for his fodder preservation method."

1946 The prize was divided, one half being awarded to:
SUMNER, JAMES BATCHELLER, USA, 1887–1955: "For his discovery that enzymes can be crystallized."
and the other half jointly to:
NORTHROP, JOHN HOWARD, USA, 1891–1987; and
STANLEY, WENDELL MEREDITH, USA, 1904–1971: "For their preparation of enzymes and virus proteins in a pure form."

1947 ROBINSON, Sir ROBERT, Great Britain, 1886–1975: "For his investigations on plant products of biological importance, especially the alkaloids."

1948 TISELIUS, ARNE WILHELM KAURIN, Sweden, 1902–1971: "For his research on electrophoresis and adsorption analysis, especially for his discoveries concerning the complex nature of the serum proteins."

1949 GIAUQUE, WILLIAM FRANCIS, USA, 1895–1982: "For his contributions in the field of chemical thermodynamics, particularly concerning the behaviour of substances at extremely low temperatures."

1950 The prize was awarded jointly to:
DIELS, OTTO PAUL HERMANN, Germany, 1876–1954; and
ALDER, KURT, Germany, 1902–1958: "For their discovery and development of the diene synthesis."

1951 The prize was awarded jointly to:
McMILLAN, EDWIN MATTISON, USA, 1907, and
SEABORG, GLENN THEODORE, USA, 1912: "For their discoveries in the chemistry of the transuranium elements."

1952 The prize was awarded jointly to:

MARTIN, ARCHER JOHN PORTER, Great Britain, 1910; and SYNGE, RICHARD LAURENCE MILLINGTON, Great Britain, 1914: "For their invention of partition chromatography."

1953 STAUDINGER, HERMANN, Germany, 1881–1965: "For his discoveries in the field of macromolecular chemistry."

1954 PAULING, LINUS CARL, USA, 1901: "For his research into the nature of the chemical bond and its application to the elucidation of the structure of complex substances."

1955 DU VIGNEAUD, VINCENT, USA, 1901–1978: "For his work on biochemically important sulphur compounds, especially for the first synthesis of a polypeptide hormone."

1956 The prize was awarded jointly to: HINSHELWOOD, Sir CYRIL NORMAN, Great Britain, 1897–1967; and SEMENOV, NIKOLAJ NIKOLAJEVIČ, USSR, 1896–1986: "For their researches into the mechanism of chemical reactions."

1957 TODD, Lord ALEXANDER R., Great Britain, 1907: "For his work on nucleotides and nucleotide co–enzymes."

1958 SANGER, FREDERICK, Great Britain, 1918: "For his work on the structure of proteins, especially that of insulin."

1959 HEYROVSKY, JAROSLAV, Czechoslovakia, 1890–1967: "For his discovery and development of the polarographic methods of analysis."

1960 LIBBY, WILLARD FRANK, USA, 1908–1980: "For his method to use carbon–14 for age determination in archaeology, geology, geophysics, and other branches of science."

1961 CALVIN, MELVIN, USA, 1911: "For his research on the carbon dioxide assimilation in plants."

1962 The prize was divided equally between: PERUTZ, MAX FERDINAND, Great Britain, 1914; and KENDREW, Sir JOHN COWDERY, Great Britain, 1917: "For their studies of the structures of globular proteins."

1963 The prize was divided equally between: ZIEGLER, KARL, Germany, 1898–1973; and NATTA, GIULIO, Italy, 1903–1979: "For their discoveries in the field of the chemistry and technology of high polymers."

1964 HODGKIN, DOROTHY MAY CROWFOOT, Great Britain, 1910: "For her determinations by X–ray techniques of the structures of important biochemical substances."

1965 WOODWARD, ROBERT BURNS, USA, 1917–1979: "For his outstanding achievements in the art of organic synthesis."

1966 MULLIKEN, ROBERT S., USA, 1896–1986: "For his fundamental work concerning chemical bonds and the electronic structure of molecules by the molecular orbital method."

1967 The prize was divided, one–half being awarded to: EIGEN, MANFRED, Germany, 1927; and the other half jointly to: NORRISH, RONALD GEORGE WREYFORD, Great Britain, 1897–1978; and PORTER, Sir GEORGE, Great Britain, 1920: "For their studies of extremely fast chemical reactions, effected by disturbing the equilibrium by means of very short pulses of energy."

1968 ONSAGER, LARS, USA, 1903–1976: "For the discovery of the reciprocal relations bearing his name, which are fundamental for the thermodynamics of irreversible processes."

1969 The prize was divided equally between: BARTON, Sir DEREK H. R., Great Britain, 1918, and HASSEL, ODD, Norway, 1897–1981: "For their contributions to the development of the concept of conformation and its application in chemistry."

1970 LELOIR, LUIS F., Argentina, 1906–1987: "For his discovery of sugar nucleotides and their role in the biosynthesis of carbohydrates."

1971 HERZBERG, GERHARD, Canada, 1904: "For his contributions to the knowledge of electronic structure and geometry of molecules, particularly free radicals."

1972 The prize was divided, one–half being awarded to: ANFINSEN, CHRISTIAN B., USA, 1916: "For his work on ribonuclease, especially concerning the connection between the amino acid sequence and the biologically active confirmation"; and the other half jointly to: MOORE, STANFORD, USA, 1913–1982; and STEIN, WILLIAM H., USA, 1911–1980: "For their contribution to the understanding of the connection between chemical structure and catalytic activity of the active centre of the ribonuclease molecule."

1973 The prize was divided equally between: FISCHER, ERNST OTTO, Germany, 1918; and WILKINSON, Sir GEOFFREY, Great Britain, 1921: "For their pioneering work, performed independently, on the chemistry of the organometallic, so called sandwich compounds."

1974 FLORY, PAUL J., USA, 1910–1985: "For his fundamental achievements, both theoretical and experimental, in the physical chemistry of the macromolecules."

1975 The prize was divided equally between: CORNFORTH, Sir JOHN WARCUP, Australia and Great Britain, 1917: "For his work on the stereochemistry of enzyme–catalyzed reactions"; and PRELOG, VLADIMIR, Switzerland, 1906: "For his research into the stereochemistry of organic molecules and reactions."

1976 LIPSCOMB, WILLIAM N., USA, 1919: "For his studies on the structure of boranes illuminating problems of chemical bonding."

1977 PIRGOGINE, ILYA, Belgium, 1917: "For his contributions to non–equilibrium thermodynamics, particularly the theory of dissipative structures."

1978 MITCHELL, PETER D., Great Britain, 1920: "For his contribution to the understanding of biological energy transfer through the formulation of the chemiosmotic theory."

1979 The prize was divided equally between: BROWN, HERBERT C., USA, 1912; and WITTIG, GEORG, Germany,

1897–1987: "For their development of the use of boron– and phosphorus–containing compounds, respectively, into important reagents in organic synthesis."

1980 The prize was divided, one–half being awarded to:
BERG, PAUL, USA, 1926: "For his fundamental studies of the biochemistry of nucleic acids, with particular regard to recombinant–DNA";
and the other half jointly to:
GILBERT, WALTER, USA 1932; and
SANGER, FREDERICK, USA, Great Britain, 1918: "For their contributions concerning the determination of base sequences in nucleic acids."

1981 The prize was awarded jointly to:
FUKUI, KENICHI, Japan, 1918; and
HOFFMANN, ROALD, USA, 1937: "For their theories, developed independently, concerning the course of chemical reactions."

1982 KLUG, AARON, Great Britain, 1926: "For his development of crystallographic electron microscopy and his structural elucidation of biologically important nuclei acid–protein complexes."

1983 TAUBE, HENRY, USA, 1915: "For his work on the mechanisms of electron transfer reactions, especially in metal complexes."

1984 MERRIFIELD, ROBERT BRUCE, USA, 1921: "For his development of methodology for chemical synthesis on a solid matrix."

1985 The prize was awarded jointly to:
HAUPTMAN, HERBERT A., USA, 1917; and
KARLE, JEROME, USA, 1918: "For their outstanding achievements in the development of direct methods for the determination of crystal structures."

1986 The prize was awarded jointly to:
HERSCHBACH, DUDLEY R., USA, 1932;
LEE, YUAN T., USA, 1936; and
POLYANI, JOHN C., Canada, 1929: "For their contributions concerning the dynamics of chemical elementary processes."

1987 The prize was awarded jointly to:
CRAM, DONALD J., USA, 1919;
LEHN, JEAN–MARIE, France, 1939; and

PEDERSEN, CHARLES J., USA, 1904–1989: "For their development and use of molecules with structure–specific interactions of high selectivity."

1988 DEISENHOFER, JOHANN, Germany, 1943;
HUBER, ROBERT, Germany, 1937; and
MICHEL, HARTMUT, Germany, 1948: "For the determination of the three–dimensional structure of a photosynthetic reaction centre."

1989 ALTMAN, SIDNEY, USA, 1939; and
CECH, THOMAS R., USA, 1947: "For their discovery of catalytic properties of RNA."

1990 COREY, ELIAS JAMES, USA, 1928: "For his development of the theory and methodology of organic synthesis."

Physiology or Medicine

1901 VON BEHRING, EMIL ADOLF, Germany, 1854–1917: "For his work on serum therapy, especially its application against diphtheria, by which he has opened a new road in the domain of medical science and thereby placed in the hands of the physician a victorious weapon against illness and deaths."

1902 ROSS, Sir RONALD, Great Britain, 1857–1932: "For his work on malaria, by which he has shown how it enters the organism and thereby has laid the foundation for successful research on this disease and methods of combating it."

1903 FINSEN, NIELS RYBERG, Denmark, 1860–1904: "In recognition of his contribution to the treatment of diseases, especially lupus vulgaris, with concentrated light radiation, whereby he has opened a new avenue for medical science."

1904 PAVLOV, IVAN PETROVIČ, Russia, 1849–1936: "In recognition of his work on the physiology of digestion, through which knowledge on vital aspects of the subject has been transformed and enlarged."

1905 KOCH, ROBERT, Germany, 1843–1910: "For his investigations and discoveries in relation to tuberculosis."

1906 The prize was awarded jointly to:
GOLGI, CAMILLO, Italy, 1843–1926; and
RAMON Y CAJAL, SANTIAGO, Spain, 1852–1934: "In recognition of their work on the structure of the nervous system."

1907 LAVERAN, CHARLES LOUIS ALPHONSE, France, 1845–1922: "In recognition of his work on the role played by protozoa in causing diseases."

1908 The prize was awarded jointly to:
METCHNIKOFF, ELIE, Russia, 1845–1916; and
EHRLICH, PAUL, Germany, 1854–1915: "In recognition of their work on immunity."

1909 KOCHER, EMIL THEODOR, Switzerland, 1841–1917: "For his work on the physiology, pathology and surgery of the thyroid gland."

1910 KOSSEL, ALBRECHT, Germany, 1853–1927: "In recognition of the contributions to our knowledge of cell chemistry made through his work on proteins, including the nucleic substances."

1911 GULLSTRAND, ALLVAR, Sweden, 1862–1930: "For his work on the dioptrics of the eye."

1912 CARREL, ALEXIS, France, 1873–1944: "In recognition of his work on vascular suture and the transplantation of blood–vessels and organs."

1913 RICHET, CHARLES ROBERT, France, 1850–1935: "In recognition of his work on anaphylaxis."

1914 BÁRÁNY, ROBERT, Austria, 1876–1936: "For his work on the physiology and pathology of the vestibular apparatus."

1915 Reserved.

1916 The prize money for 1915 was allocated to the Special Fund of this prize section.
The prize for 1916: Reserved.

1917 The prize money for 1916 was allocated to the Special Fund of this prize section.
The prize for 1917: Reserved.

1918 The prize money for 1917 was allocated to the Special Fund of this

prize section.
The prize for 1918: Reserved.

1919 The prize money for 1918 was allocated to the Special Fund of this prize section.
The prize for 1919: Reserved.

1920 The prize for 1919:
BORDET, JULES, Belgium, 1870–1961: "For his discoveries relating to immunity."
The prize for 1920:
KROGH, SCHACK AUGUST STEENBERGER, Denmark, 1874–1943: "For his discovery of the capillary motor regulating mechanism."

1921 Reserved.

1922 The prize money for 1921 was allocated to the Special Fund of this prize section.
The prize for 1922: Reserved.

1923 The prize for 1922 was divided equally between:
HILL, Sir ARCHIBALD VIVIAN, Great Britain, 1886–1977: "For his discovery relating to the production of heat in the muscle"; and
MEYERHOF, OTTO FRITZ, Germany, 1884–1951: "For his discovery of the fixed relationship between the consumption of oxygen and the metabolism of lactid acid in the muscle."
The prize for 1923 was awarded jointly to:
BANTING, Sir FREDERICK GRANT, Canada, 1891–1941; and
MACLEOD, JOHN JAMES RICHARD, Canada, 1876–1935: "For the discovery of insulin."

1924 EINTHOVEN, WILLEM, the Netherlands, 1860–1927: "For his discovery of the mechanism of the electrocardiogram."

1925 Reserved.

1926 The prize money for 1925 was allocated to the Special Fund of this prize section.
The prize for 1926: Reserved.

1927 The prize for 1926:
FIBIGER, JOHANNES ANDREAS GRIB, Denmark, 1867–1928: "For his discovery of the spiroptera carcinoma."
The prize for 1927:
WAGNER–JAUREGG, JULIUS, Austria, 1857–1940: "For his discovery

of the therapeutic value of malaria inoculation in the treatment of dementia paralytica."

1928 NICOLLE, CHARLES JULES HENRI, France, 1866–1936: "For his work on typhus."

1929 The prize was divided equally between:
EIJKMAN, CHRISTIAAN, the Netherlands, 1858–1930: "For his discovery of the anti–neuritic vitamin"; and
HOPKINS, Sir FREDERICK GOWLAND, Great Britain, 1861–1947: "For his discovery of the growth–stimulating vitamins."

1930 LANDSTEINER, KARL, Austria, 1868–1943: "For his discovery of human blood groups."

1931 WARBURG, OTTO HEINRICH, Germany, 1883–1970: "For his discovery of the nature and mode of action of the respiratory enzyme."

1932 The prize was awarded jointly to:
SHERRINGTON, Sir CHARLES SCOTT, Great Britain, 1857–1952; and
ADRIAN, Lord EDGAR DOUGLAS, Great Britain, 1889–1977: "For their discoveries regarding the functions of neurons."

1933 MORGAN, THOMAS HUNT, USA, 1866–1945: "For his discoveries concerning the role played by the chromosome in heredity."

1934 The prize was awarded jointly to:
WHIPPLE, GEORGE HOYT, USA, 1878–1976;
MINOT, GEORGE RICHARDS, USA, 1885–1950; and
MURPHY, WILLIAM PARRY, USA, 1892–1987: "For their discoveries concerning liver therapy in cases of anaemia."

1935 SPEMANN, HANS, Germany, 1869–1941: "For his discovery of the organizer effect in embryonic development."

1936 The prize was awarded jointly to:
DALE, Sir HENRY HALLETT, Great Britain, 1875–1968; and
LOEWI, OTTO, Austria, 1873–1961: "For their discoveries relating to chemical transmission of nerve impulses."

1937 SZENT–GYÖRGYI VON NAGYRAPOLT, ALBERT, Hungary,

1893–1986: "For his discoveries in connection with the biological combustion processes, with special reference to vitamin C and the catalysis of fumaric acid."

1938 Reserved.

1939 The prize for 1938:
HEYMANS, CORNEILLE JEAN FRANÇOISE, Belgium, 1892–1968: "For the discovery of the role played by the sinus and aortic mechanisms in the regulation of respiration."
The prize for 1939:
DOMAGK,GERHARD, Germany, 1895–1964: "For the discovery of the antibacterial effects of prontosil." (Caused by the authorities of his country to decline the award, but later received the diploma and the medal.)

1940 – 1942 The prize money was with one–third allocated to the Main Fund and with two–thirds to the Special Fund of this prize section.

1943 Reserved.

1944 The prize for 1943 was divided equally between:
DAM, HENRIK CARL PETER, Denmark, 1895–1976: "For his discovery of vitamin K"; and
DOISY, EDWARD ADELBERT, USA, 1893–1986: "For his discovery of the chemical nature of vitamin K."
The prize for 1944 was awarded jointly to:
ERLANGER, JOSEPH, USA, 1874–1965; and
GASSER, HERBERT SPENCER, USA, 1888–1963: "For their discoveries relating to the highly differentiated functions of single nerve fibres."

1945 The prize was awarded jointly to:
FLEMING, Sir ALEXANDER, Great Britain, 1881–1955;
CHAIN, Sir ERNST BORIS, Great Britain, 1906–1979; and
FLOREY, Lord HOWARD WALTER, Great Britain, 1898–1968: "For the discovery of penicillin and its curative effect in various infectious diseases."

1946 MULLER, HERMANN JOSEPH, USA, 1890–1967: "For the discovery of the production of mutations by means of X–ray irradiation."

1947 The prize was divided, one–half being awarded jointly to:
CORI, CARL FERDINAND, USA, 1896–1984; and his wife

CORI, GERTY THERESA, née RADNITZ, USA, 1896–1957: "For their discovery of the course of the catalytic conversion of glycogen"; the other half being awarded to: HOUSSAY, BERNARDO ALBERTO, Argentina, 1887–1971: "For his discovery of the part played by the hormone of the anterior pituitary lobe in the metabolism of sugar."

1948 MÜLLER, PAUL HERMANN, Switzerland, 1899–1965: "For his discovery of the high efficiency of DDT as a contact poison against several arthropods."

1949 The prize was divided equally between: HESS, WALTER RUDOLF, Switzerland, 1881–1973: "For his discovery of the functional organization of the interbrain as a co–ordinator of the activities of the internal organs"; and EGAS MONIZ, ANTONIO CAETANO DE ABREU FREIRE, Portugal, 1874–1955: "For his discovery of the therapeutic value of leucotomy in certain psychoses."

1950 The prize was awarded jointly to: KENDALL, EDWARD CALVIN, USA, 1886–1972; REICHSTEIN, TADEUS, Switzerland, 1897; and HENCH, PHILIP SHOWALTER, USA, 1896–1965: "For their discoveries relating to the hormones of the adrenal cortex, their structure and biological effects."

1951 THEILER, MAX, Union of South Arica, 1899–1972: "For his discoveries concerning yellow fever and how to combat it."

1952 WAKSMAN, SELMAN ABRAHAM, USA, 1888–1973: "For his discovery of streptomycin, the first antibiotic effective against tuberculosis."

1953 The prize was divided equally between: KREBS, Sir HANS ADOLF, Great Britain, 1900–1981: "For his discovery of the citric acid cycle"; and LIPMANN, FRITZ ALBERT, USA, 1899–1986: "For his discovery of co–enzyme A and its importance for intermediary metabolism."

1954 The prize was awarded jointly to: ENDERS, JOHN FRANKLIN, USA, 1915–1985; WELLER, THOMAS HUCKLE, USA,

1915; and ROBBINS, FREDERICK CHAPMAN, USA, 1916: "For their discovery of the ability of poliomyelitis viruses to grow in cultures of various types of tissue."

1955 THEORELL, AXEL HUGO THEODOR, Sweden, 1903–1982: "For his discoveries concerning the nature and mode of action of oxidation enzymes."

1956 The prize was awarded jointly to: COURNAND, ANDRÉ FRÉDÉRIC, USA, 1895–1988; FORSSMANN, WERNER, Germany, 1904–1979; and RICHARDS, DICKINSON W., USA, 1895–1973: "For their discoveries concerning heart catherization and pathological changes in the circulatory system."

1957 BOVET, DANIEL, Italy, 1907: "For his discoveries relating to synthetic compounds that inhibit the action of certain body substances, and especially their action on the vascular system and the skeletal muscles."

1958 The prize was divided, one–half being awarded jointly to: BEADLE, GEORGE WELLS, USA, 1903–1989; and TATUM, EDWARD LAWRIE, USA, 1909–1975: "For their discovery that genes act by regulating definite chemical events"; and the other half to: LEDERBERG, JOSHUA, USA, 1925: "For his discoveries concerning genetic recombination and the organization of the genetic material of bacteria."

1959 The prize was awarded jointly to: OCHOA, SEVERO, USA, 1905; and KORNBERG, ARTHUR, USA, 1918: "For their discovery of the mechanisms in the biological synthesis of ribonucleic acid and deoxiribonucleic acid."

1960 The prize was awarded jointly to: BURNET, Sir FRANK MACFARLANE, Australia, 1899–1985; and MEDAWAR, Sir PETER BRIAN, Great Britain, 1915–1987: "For discovery of acquired immunological tolerance."

1961 VON BÉKÉSY, GEORG, USA, 1899–1972: "For his discoveries of the physical mechanism of stimulation within the cochlea."

1962 The prize was awarded jointly to: CRICK, FRANCIS HARRY COMPTON, Great Britain, 1916; WATSON, JAMES DEWEY, USA, 1928; and WILKINS, MAURICE HUGH FREDERICK, Great Britain, 1916: "For their discoveries concerning the molecular structure of nuclear acids and its significance for information transfer in living material."

1963 The prize was awarded jointly to: ECCLES, Sir JOHN CAREW, Australia, 1903; HODGKIN, Sir ALAN LLOYD, Great Britain, 1914; and HUXLEY, Sir ANDREW FIELDING, Great Britain, 1917: "For their discoveries concerning the ionic mechanisms involved in excitation and inhibition in the peripheral and central portions of the nerve cell membrane."

1964 The prize was awarded jointly to: BLOCH, KONRAD, USA, 1912; and LYNEN, FEODOR, Germany, 1911–1979: "For their discoveries concerning the mechanism and regulation of the cholesterol and fatty acid metabolism."

1965 The prize was awarded jointly to: JACOB, FRANCOIS, France, 1920; LWOFF, ANDRÉ, France, 1902; and MONOD, JACQUES, France, 1910–1976: "For their discoveries concerning genetic control of enzyme and virus synthesis."

1966 The prize was divided equally between: ROUS, PEYTON, USA, 1879–1970: "For his discovery of tumor–inducing viruses"; and HUGGINS, CHARLES BRENTON, USA, 1901: "For his discoveries concerning hormonal treatment of prostatic cancer."

1967 The prize was awarded jointly to: GRANIT, RAGNAR, Sweden, 1900–1991; HARTLINE, HALDAN KEFFER, USA, 1903–1983; and WALD, GEORGE, USA, 1906: "For their discoveries concerning the primary physiological and chemical visual processes in the eye."

1968 The prize was awarded jointly to: HOLLEY, ROBERT W., USA, 1922; KHORANA, HAR GOBIND, USA, 1922; and NIRENBERG, MARSHALL W., USA,

1927: "For their interpretation of the genetic code and its function in protein synthesis."

1969 The prize was awarded jointly to: DELBRÜCK, MAX, USA, 1906–1981; HERSHEY, ALFRED D., USA, 1908; and LURIA, SALVADOR E., USA, 1912–1991: "For their discoveries concerning the replication mechanism and the genetic structure of viruses."

1970 The prize was awarded jointly to: KATZ, Sir BERNARD, Great Britain, 1911; VON EULER, ULF, Sweden, 1905–1983; and AXELROD, JULIUS, USA, 1912: "For their discoveries concerning the humoral transmittors in the nerve terminals and the mechanism for their storage, release and inactivation."

1971 SUTHERLAND, EARL W., JR, USA, 1915–1974: "For his discoveries concerning the mechanisms of the action of hormones."

1972 The prize was awarded jointly to: EDELMAN, GERALD M., USA, 1929; and PORTER, RODNEY R., Great Britain, 1917–1985: "For their discoveries concerning the chemical structure of antibodies."

1973 The prize was awarded jointly to: VON FRISCH, KARL, Germany, 1886–1982; LORENZ, KONRAD, Austria, 1903–1989, and TINBERGEN, NIKOLAAS, Great Britain, 1907–1988: "For their discoveries concerning organization and elicitation of individual and social behaviour patterns."

1974 The prize was awarded jointly to: CLAUDE, ALBERT, Belgium, 1899–1983; DE DUVE, CHRISTIAN, Belgium, 1917; and PALADE, GEORGE E., USA, 1912: "For their discoveries concerning the structural and functional organization of the cell."

1975 The prize was awarded jointly to: BALTIMORE, DAVID, USA, 1938; DULBECCO, RENATO, USA, 1914; and TEMIN, HOWARD MARTIN, USA, 1934: "For their discoveries concerning the interaction between tumour viruses and the genetic material of the cell."

1976 The prize was awarded jointly to: BLUMBERG, BARUCH S., USA, 1925; and GAJDUSEK, D. CARLETON, USA, 1923: "For their discoveries concerning new mechanisms for the origin and dissemination of infectious diseases."

1977 The prize was divided, one–half being awarded jointly to: GUILLEMIN, ROGER, USA, 1924; and SCHALLY, ANDREW V., USA, 1926: "For their discoveries concerning the peptide hormone production of the brain"; and the other half being awarded to: YALOW, ROSALYN S., USA, 1921: "For the development of radioimmunoassays of peptide hormones."

1978 The prize was awarded jointly to: ARBER, WERNER, Switzerland, 1929; NATHANS, DANIEL, USA, 1928; and SMITH, HAMILTON O., USA, 1931: "For the discovery of restriction enzymes and their application to problems of molecular genetics."

1979 The prize was awarded jointly to: CORMACK, ALAN M., USA, 1924; and HOUNSFIELD, Sir GODFREY N., Great Britain, 1919: "For the development of computer assisted tomography."

1980 The prize was awarded jointly to: BENACERRAF, BARUJ, USA, 1920; DAUSSET, JEAN, France, 1916; and SNELL, GEORGE D., USA, 1903: "For their discoveries concerning genetically determined structures on the cell surface that regulate immunological reactions."

1981 The prize was awarded by one–half to: SPERRY, ROGER W., USA, 1913: "For his discoveries concerning the functional specialization of the cerebral hemispheres." and the other half jointly to: HUBEL, DAVID H., USA, 1926; and WIESEL, TORSTEN, Sweden, 1924: "For their discoveries concerning information processing in the visual system."

1982 The prize was awarded jointly to: BERGSRÖM, SUNE K., Sweden, 1916; SAMUELSSON, BENGT I., Sweden, 1934; and VANE, Sir JOHN R., Great Britain, 1927: "For their discoveries concerning prostaglandins and related biologically active substances."

1983 McCLINTOCK, BARBARA, USA, 1902: "For her discovery of mobile genetic elements."

1984 The prize was awarded jointly to: JERNE, NIELS K.,Denmark, 1911; KÖHLER, GEORGES J. F., Germany, 1946; and MILSTEIN, CÉSAR, Great Britain and Argentina, 1927: "For theories conerning the specificity in development and control of the immune system and the discovery of the principle for production of monoclonal antibodies."

1985 The prize was awarded jointly to: BROWN, MICHAEL S., USA, 1941; and GOLDSTEIN, JOSEPH L., USA, 1940: "For their discoveries concerning the regulation of cholesterol metabolism."

1986 The prize was awarded jointly to: COHEN, STANLEY, USA, 1922; and LEVI–MONTALCINI, RITA, Italy and USA, 1909: "For their discoveries of growth factors."

1987 TONEGAWA, SUSUMU, Japan, 1939: "For his discovery of the 'genetic principle for generation of antibody diversity'."

1988 The prize was awarded jointly to: BLACK, Sir JAMES W., Great Britain, 1924; ELION, GERTRUDE B., USA, 1918; and HITCHINGS, GEORGE H., USA, 1905: "For their discoveries of important principles for drug treatment."

1989 The prize was awarded jointly to: BISHOP, J. MICHAEL, USA, 1936; and VARMUS, HAROLD E., USA, 1939: "For their discovery of the cellular origin of retroviral oncogenes."

1990 The prize was awarded jointly to: MURRAY, JOSEPH E., USA, 1919, and THOMAS, E. DONNALL, USA, 1920: "For their discoveries concerning organ and cell transplantation in the treatment of human disease."

267

Economic Sciences

1969 The prize was awarded jointly to:
FRISCH, RAGNAR, Norway, 1895–1973; and
TINBERGEN, JAN, The Netherlands, 1903: "For having developed and applied dynamic models for the analysis of economic processes."

1970 SAMUELSON, PAUL A., USA, 1915: "For the scientific work through which he has developed static and dynamic economic theory and actively contributed to raising the level of analysis in economic science."

1971 KUZNETS, SIMON, USA, 1901–1985: "For his empirically founded interpretation of economic growth which has led to new and deepened insight into the economic and social structure and process of development."

1972 The prize was awarded jointly to:
HICKS, Sir JOHN R., Great Britain, 1904–1989; and
ARROW, KENNETH J., USA, 1921: "For their pioneering contributions to general economic equilibrium theory and welfare theory."

1973 LEONTIEF, WASSILY, USA, 1906: "For the development of the input–output method and for its application to important economic problems."

1974 The prize was divided equally between:
MYRDAL, GUNNAR, Sweden, 1898–1987; and
VON HAYEK, FRIEDRICH AUGUST, Great Britain, 1899: "For their pioneering work in the theory of money and economic fluctuations and for their penetrating analysis of the interdependence of economic, social and institutional phenomena."

1975 The prize was awarded jointly to:
KANTOROVICH, LEONID, USSR, Academy of Sciences, Moscow, 1912–1986; and
KOOPMANS, TJALLING C., USA, 1910–1986: "For their contributions to the theory of optimum allocation of resources."

1976 FRIEDMAN, MILTON, USA, 1912: "For his achievements in the fields of consumption analysis, monetary history and theory and for his demonstration of the complexity of stabilization policy."

1977 The prize was divided equally between:
OHLIN, BERTIL, Sweden, 1899–1979; and
MEADE, JAMES, Great Britain, 1907: "For their pathbreaking contribution to the theory of international trade and international capital movements."

1978 SIMON, HERBERT A., USA, 1916: "For his pioneering research into the decision–making process within economic organizations."

1979 The prize was divided equally between:
SCHULTZ, THEODORE W., USA, 1902; and
LEWIS, Sir ARTHUR, United Kingdom, 1915: "For their pioneering research into economic development research with particular consideration of the problems of developing countries."

1980 KLEIN, LAWRENCE R., USA, 1920: "For the creation of econometric models and their application to the analysis of economic fluctuations and economic policies."

1981 TOBIN, JAMES, USA, 1918: "For his analysis of financial markets and their relations to expenditure decisions, employment, production and prices."

1982 STIGLER, GEORGE J., USA, 1911: "For his seminal studies of industrial structures, functioning of markets and causes and effects of public regulation."

1983 DEBREU, GERARD, USA, 1921: "For having incorporated new analytical methods into economic theory and for his rigorous reformulation of the theory of general equilibrium."

1984 STONE, Sir RICHARD, Great Britain, 1913: "For having made fundamental contributions to the development of systems of national accounts and hence greatly improved the basis for empirical economic analysis."

1985 MODIGLIANI, FRANCO, USA, 1918: "For his pioneering analyses of saving and of financial markets."

1986 BUCHANAN, JAMES M., JR, USA, 1919: "For his development of the contractual and constitutional bases for the theory of economic and political decision–making."

1987 SOLOW, ROBERT M., USA, 1924: "For his contributions to the theory of economic growth."

1988 ALLAIS, MAURICE, France, 1911: "For his pioneering contributions to the theory of markets and efficient utilization of resources."

1989 HAAVELMO, TYGVE, Norway, 1911: "For his clarification of the probility theory foundations of econometrics and his analyses of simultaneous economic structures."

1990 The prize was divided equally between:
MARKOWITZ, HARRY M., USA, 1927;
MILLER, MERTON H., USA, 1923; and
SHARPE, WILLIAM F., USA, 1934: "For their pioneering work in the theory of financial economics."

Literature

1901 PRUDHOMME, SULLY, France, 1839–1907: "In special recognition of his poetic composition, which gives evidence of lofty idealism, artistic perfection and a rare combination of the qualities of both heart and intellect."

1902 MOMMSEN, CHRISTIAN MATTHIAS THEODOR, Germany, 1817–1903: "The greatest living master of the art of historical writing, with special reference to his monumental work, *A History of Rome*."

1903 BJORNSON, BJORNSTJERNE MARTINUS, Norway, 1832–1910: "As a tribute to his noble, magnificent and versatile poetry, which has always been distinguished by both the freshness of its inspiration and the rare purity of its spirit."

1904 The prize was divided equally between:
MISTRAL, FRÉDÉRIC, France, 1830–1914: "In recognition of the fresh originality and true inspiration of his poetic production, which faithfully reflects the natural scenery and native spirit of his people, and, in addition, his significant work as a Provençal philologist"; and
ECHEGARAY Y EIZAGUIRRE, JOSÉ, Spain, 1832–1916: "In recognition of the numerous and brilliant compositions which, in an individual and original manner, have revived the great traditions of the Spanish drama."

1905 SIENKIEWICZ, HENRYK, Poland, 1846–1916: "Because of his outstanding merits as an epic writer."

1906 CARDUCCI, GIOSUE, Italy, 1835–1907: "Not only in consideration of his deep learning and critical research, but above all as a tribute to the creative energy, freshness of style, and lyrical force which characterize his poetic masterpieces."

1907 KIPLING, RUDYARD, Great Britain, 1865–1936: "In consideration of the power of observation, originality of imagination, virility of ideas and remarkable talent for narration which characterize the creations of this world–famous author."

1908 EUCKEN, RUDOLF CHRISTOPH, Germany, 1846–1926: "In recognition of his earnest search for truth, his penetrating power of thought, his wide range of vision, and the warmth and strength in presentation with which in his numerous works he has vindicated and developed an idealistic philosophy of life."

1909 LAGERLÖF, SELMA OTTILIANA LOVISA, Sweden, 1858–1940: "In appreciation of the lofty idealism, vivid imagination and spiritual perception that characterize her writings."

1910 HEYSE, PAUL JOHANN LUDWIG, Germany, 1830–1914: "As a tribute to the consummate artistry, permeated with idealism, which he has demonstrated during his long productive career as a lyric poet, dramatist, novelist and writer of world–renowned short stories."

1911 MAETERLINCK, Count MAURICE, Belgium 1862–1949: "In appreciation of his many–sided literary activities, and especially of his dramatic works, which are distinguished by a wealth of imagination and by a poetic fancy, which reveals, sometimes in the guise of a fairy tale, a deep inspiration, while in a mysterious way they appeal to the readers' own feelings and stimulate their imaginations."

1912 HAUPTMANN, GERHART JOHANN ROBERT, Germany, 1862–1946: "Primarily in recognition of his fruitful, varied and outstanding production in the realm of dramatic art."

1913 TAGORE, RABINDRANATH, India, 1861–1941: "Because of his profoundly sensitive, fresh and beautiful verse, by which, with comsummate skill, he has made his poetic thought, expressed in his own English words, a part of the literature of the West."

1914 Reserved.

1915 The prize money for 1914 was allocated to the Special Fund of this prize section.
The prize for 1915: Reserved.

1916 The prize for 1915:
ROLLAND, ROMAIN, France, 1866–1944: "As a tribute to the lofty idealism of his literary production and to the sympathy and love of truth with which he has described different types of human beings."
The prize for 1916:
VON HEIDENSTAM, CARL GUSTAF VERNER, Sweden, 1859–1940: "In recognition of his significance as the leading representative of a new era in our literature."

1917 The prize was divided equally between:

GELLERUP, KARL ADOLPH, Denmark, 1857–1919: "For his varied and rich poetry, which is inspired by lofty ideals."
PONTOPPIDAN, HENRIK, Denmark, 1857–1943; "For his authentic descriptions of present–day life in Denmark."

1918 Reserved.

1919 The prize money for 1918 was allocated to the Special Fund of this prize section.
The prize for 1919: Reserved.

1920 The prize for 1919:
SPITTELER, CARL FRIEDRICH GEORG, Switzerland, 1845–1924: "In special appreciation of his epic, *Olympian Spring.*"
The prize for 1920:
HAMSUN, KNUT PEDERSEN, Norway, 1859–1952: "For his monumental work, *Growth of the Soil.*"

1921 FRANCE, ANATOLE, France, 1844–1924: "In recognition of his brilliant literary achievements, characterized as they are by a nobility of style, a profound human sympathy, grace, and a true Gallic temperament."

1922 BENAVENTE, JACINTO, Spain, 1866–1954: "For the happy manner in which he has continued the illustrious traditions of the Spanish drama."

1923 YEATS, WILLIAM BUTLER, Ireland, 1865–1939: "For his always inspired poetry, which in a highly artistic form gives expression to the spirit of a whole nation."

1924 REYMONT, WLADYSLAW STANISLAW, Poland, 1867–1925: "For his great national epic, *The Peasants.*"

1925 Reserved.

1926 The prize for 1925:
SHAW, GEORGE BERNARD, Great Britain, 1856–1950: "For his work which is marked by both idealism and humanity, its stimulating satire often being infused with a singular poetic beauty."
The prize for 1926: Reserved.

1927 The prize for 1926:
GRAZIA, DELEDDA, Italy, 1871–1936: "For her idealistically inspired writings which with plastic clarity picture the life on her native island and with depth and sympathy deal with human problems in general."
The prize for 1927: Reserved.

1928 The prize for 1927:
BERGSON, HENRI, France, 1859–1941: "In recognition of his rich and vitalizing ideas and the brilliant skill with which they have been presented."
The prize for 1928:
UNDSET, SIGRID, Norway, 1882–1949: "Principally for her powerful descriptions of Northern life during the Middle Ages."

1929 MANN, THOMAS, Germany, 1875–1955: "Principally for his great novel, *Buddenbrooks*, which has won steadily increased recognition as one of the classic works of contemporary literature."

1930 LEWIS, SINCLAIR, USA, 1885–1951: "For his vigorous and graphic art of description and his ability to create, with wit and humour, new types of characters."

1931 KARLFELDT, ERIK AXEL, Sweden, 1864–1931: "The poetry of Erik Axel Karlfeldt."

1932 GALSWORTHY, JOHN, Great Britain, 1867–1933: "For his distinguished art of narration which takes its highest form in *The Forsythe Saga*."

1933 BUNIN, IVAN ALEKSEJEVIC, stateless domicile in France, 1870–1953: "For the strict artistry with which he has carried on the classical Russian traditions in prose writing."

1934 PIRANDELLO, LUIGI, Italy, 1867–1936: "For his bold and ingenious revival of dramatic scenic art."

1935 Reserved.

1936 The prize money for 1935 was with one–third allocated to the Main Fund and with two–thirds to the Special Fund of this prize section.
The prize for 1936:
O'NEILL, EUGENE GLADSTONE, USA, 1888–1953: "For the power, honesty and deep–felt emotions of his dramatic works, which embody an original concept of tragedy."

1937 MARTIN DU GARD, ROGER, France, 1881–1958: "For the artistic power and truth with which he has depicted human conflict as well as some fundamental aspects of contemporary life in his novel cycle *Les Thibault*."

1938 BUCK, PEARL, USA, 1892–1973: "For her rich and truly epic descriptions of peasant life in China and for her biographical masterpieces."

1939 SILLANPÄÄ, FRANS EEMIL, Finland, 1888–1964: "For his deep understanding of his country's peasantry and the exquisite art with which he has portrayed their way of life and their relationship with Nature."

1940 – 1943 The prize money was with one–third allocated to the Main Fund and with two–thirds to the Special Fund of this prize section.

1944 JENSEN, JOHANNES VILHELM, Denmark, 1873–1950: "For the rare strength and fertility of his poetic imagination with which is combined an intellectual curiosity of wide scope and a bold, freshly creative style."

1945 GABRIELA MISTRAL, Chile, 1889–1957: "For her lyric poetry which, inspired by powerful emotions, has made her name a symbol of the idealistic aspirations of the entire Latin American world."

1946 HESSE, HERMANN, Switzerland, 1877–1962: "For his inspired writings which, while growing in boldness and penetration, exemplify the classical humanitarian ideals and high qualities of style."

1947 GIDE, ANDRÉ PAUL GUILLAUME, France, 1869–1951: "For his comprehensive and artistically significant writings, in which human problems and conditions have been presented with a fearless love of truth and keen psychological insight."

1948 ELIOT, THOMAS STEARNS, Great Britain, 1888–1965: "For his outstanding, pioneer contribution to present–day poetry."

1949 Reserved.

1950 The prize for 1949:
FAULKNER, WILLIAM, USA, 1897–1962: "For his powerful and artistically unique contribution to the modern American novel."
The prize for 1950:
RUSSELL, BERTRAND, Great Britain, 1872–1970: "In recognition of his varied and significant writings in which he champions humanitarian ideals and freedom of thought.

1951 LAGERKVIST, PÄR FABIAN, Sweden, 1891–1974: "For the artistic vigour and true independence of mind with which he endeavours in his poetry to find answers to the eternal questions confronting mankind."

1952 MAURIAC, FRANÇOIS, France, 1885–1970: "For the deep spiritual insight and the artistic intensity with which he has in his novels penetrated the drama of human life."

1953 CHURCHILL, Sir WINSTON LEONARD SPENCER, Great Britain, 1874–1965: "For his mastery of historical and biographical description as well as for brilliant oratory in defending exalted human values."

1954 HEMINGWAY, ERNEST MILLER, USA, 1899–1961: "For his mastery of the art of narrative, most recently demonstrated in *The Old Man and the Sea*, and for the influence that he has exerted on contemporary style."

1955 LAXNESS, HALLDOR KILJAN, Iceland, 1902: "For his vivid epic power which has renewed the great narrative art of Iceland."

1956 JIMÉNEZ, JUAN RAMON, Spain, 1881–1958: "For his lyrical poetry, which in Spanish language constitutes an example of high spirit and artistical purity."

1957 CAMUS, ALBERT, France, 1913–1960: "For his important literary production, which with clear–sighted earnestness illuminates the problems of the human conscience in our times."

1958 PASTERNAK, BORIS LEONIDOVIC, USSR, 1890–1960: "For his important achievement both in contemporary lyrical poetry and in the field of the great Russian epic tradition." (Accepted first, later caused by the authorities of his country to decline the prize.)

1959 QUASIMODO, SALVATORE, Italy, 1901–1968: "For his lyrical poetry, which with classical fire expresses the tragic experience of life in our own times."

1960 SAINT–JOHN PERSE, France, 1887–1975: "For the soaring flight and the evocative imagery of his poetry which in a visionary fashion reflects the conditions of our time."

1961 ANDRIĆ, IVO, Yugoslavia, 1892–1975: "For the epic force with which he has traced themes and depicted human destinies drawn from the history of his country."

1962 STEINBECK, JOHN, USA, 1902–1968: "For his realistic and imaginative writings, combining as they do sympathetic humour and keen social perception."

1963 SEFERIS, GIORGOS, Greece, 1900–1971: "For his eminent lyrical writing, inspired by a deep feeling for the Hellenic world of culture."

1964 SARTRE, JEAN–PAUL, France, 1905–1980: "For his work which, rich in ideas and filled with the spirit of freedom and the quest for truth, has exerted a far–reaching influence on our age." (Declined the prize.)

1965 SHOLOKHOV, MIKHAIL ALEKSANDROVICH, USSR, 1905–1984: "For the artistic power and integrity with which, in his epic of the Don, he has given expression to a historic phase in the life of the Russian people."

1966 The prize was divided equally between:
AGNON, SHMUEL YOSEF, Israel, 1888–1970: "For his profoundly characteristic narrative art with motifs from the life of the Jewish people"; and
SACHS, NELLY, Germany, domiciled in Sweden since 1940, 1891–1970: "For her outstanding lyrical and dramatic writing, which interprets Israel's destiny with touching strength."

1967 ASTURIAS, MIGUEL ANGEL, Guatemala, 1899–1974: "For his vivid literary achievement, deep–rooted in the national traits and traditions of Indian peoples of Latin America."

1968 KAWABATA, YASUNARI, Japan, 1899–1972: "For his narrative mastery, which with great sensibility expresses the essence of the Japanese mind."

1969 BECKETT, SAMUEL, Ireland, 1906–1989: "For his writing, which – in new forms for the novel and drama – in the destitution of modern man acquires its elevation."

1970 SOLZHENITSYN, ALEXANDER, USSR, 1918 : "For the ethical force with which he has pursued the indispensable traditions of Russian literature."

1971 NERUDA, PABLO, Chile, 1904–1973: "For a poetry that with the action of an elemental force brings alive a continent's destiny and dreams."

1972 BÖLL, HEINRICH, Germany, 1917–1985: "For his writing which through its combination of a broad perspective on his time and a sensitive skill in characterization has contributed to a renewal of German literature."

1973 WHITE, PATRICK, Australia, 1912–1990: "For an epic and psychological narrative art which has introduced a new continent into literature."

1974 The prize was divided equally between:
JOHNSON, EYVIND, Sweden, 1900–1976: "For a narrative art, far–seeing in lands and ages, in the service of freedom"; and
MARTINSON, HARRY, Sweden, 1904–1978: "For writings that catch the dewdrop and reflect the cosmos."

1975 MONTALE, EUGENIO, Italy, 1896–1981: "For his distinctive poetry which, with great artistic sensitivity, has interpreted human values under the sign of an outlook on life with no illusions."

1976 BELLOW, SAUL, USA, 1915: "For the human understanding and subtle analysis of contemporary culture that are combined in his work."

1977 ALEIXANDRE, VICENTE, Spain, 1898–1984: "For a creative poetic writing which illuminates man's condition in the cosmos and in present–day society, at the same time representing the great renewal of the traditions of Spanish poetry between the wars."

1978 SINGER, ISAAC BASHEVIS, USA, 1904–1991: "For his impassioned narrative art which, with roots in a Polish–Jewish cultural tradition, brings universal human conditions to life."

1979 ELYTIS, ODYSSEUS, Greece, 1911: "For his poetry, which, against the background of Greek tradition, depicts with sensuous strength and intellectual clear–sightedness modern man's struggle for freedom and creativeness."

1980 MILOSZ, CZESLAW, USA, and Poland, 1911: "Who with uncompromising clear–sightedness voices man's exposed condition in a world of severe conflicts.

1981 CANETTI, ELIAS, Great Britain, 1905: "For writings marked by a broad outlook, a wealth of ideas and artistic power."

1982 GARCÍA MÁRQUEZ, GABRIEL, Colombia, 1928: "For his novels and short stories in which the fantastic and the realistic are combined in a richly composed world of imagination, reflecting a continent's life and conflicts."

1983 GOLDING, Sir WILLIAM, Great Britain, 1911: "For his novels which, with the perspicuity of realistic narrative art and the diversity and universality of myth, illuminate the human condition in the world of today."

1984 SEIFERT, JAROSLAV, Czechoslovakia, 1901–1986: "For his poetry which endowed with freshness, sensuality and rich inventiveness provides a liberating image of the indomitable spirit and versality of man."

1985 SIMON, CLAUDE, France, 1913: "Who in his novel combines the poet's and the painter's creativeness with a deepened awareness of time in the depiction of the human condition."

1986 SOYINKA, WOLE, Nigeria, 1934: "Who in a wide cultural perspective and with poetic overtones fashions the drama of existence."

1987 BRODSKY, JOSEPH, USA, 1940: "For an all–embracing authorship, imbued with clarity of thought and poetic intensity."

1988 MAHFOUZ, NAGUIB, Egypt, 1911: "Who, through works rich in nuance – now clear–sightedly realistic, now evocatively ambiguous – has formed an Arabian narrative art that applies to all mankind."

1989 CELA, CAMILO JOSÉ, Spain, 1916: "For a rich and intensive prose, which with restrained compassion forms a challenging vision of man's vulnerability."

1990 PAZ, OCTAVIO, Mexico, 1914: "For impassioned writing with wide horizons, characterized by sensuous intelligence and humanistic integrity."

About the Contributors

In addition to the Preface by Stig Ramel of the Nobel Foundation and the Introduction by Lord Briggs, Provost of Worcester College, Oxford, the following writers contributed to *The Nobel Century*:

Irwin Abrams, author of *The Nobel Peace Prize and the Laureates*, is the world's foremost historian of the Nobel Peace Prize. He is a distinguished university professor emeritus at Antioch University.

Frank Kendig has been editor of *The Saturday Review of Science* and was founding editor of *Omni*. He served as writer-consultant on the television series, *The Brain*.

Richard Wolkomir is a recipient of the American Association for the Advancement of Science/Westinghouse Award for Distinguished Science Writing. He contributes to many American magazines, including *Smithsonian, Air & Space* and *Reader's Digest*.

Douglas Gasner is the former editor of *Psychology Today* and *Science Digest*. He is co-author of *Heartcare*.

Charles C. Mann, a journalist, and Mark L. Plummer, a consultant on economics, are co-authors of *Marketing a Miracle*, to be published in September 1991.

Emmanuel Le Roy Ladurie, a leading historian and Administrateur Général of the Bibliothèque Nationale in Paris, is the author of many historical works, among them the best-selling study *Montaillou*.

Selected Bibliography

The primary source for information about the Nobel Awards is *Les Prix Nobel*, published each year by the Nobel Foundation. These volumes include the opening addresses, the introductions of the laureates, their acceptance speeches, biographical information supplied by the laureates, and their lectures. The material is copyrighted by the Nobel Foundation.

Each year since 1988, IMG Publishing, with the assistance of the Nobel Foundation, has published *The Nobel Prize Annual*, with interviews, articles, and photographs about the laureates.

As a quick reference, *Nobel Prize Winners*, edited by Tyler Wasson, was published by H. W. Wilson Company of New York. For more details on the Peace laureates, *The Nobel Peace Prize and the Laureates*, by Irwin Abrams, was published in 1987 by G. K. Hall & Co. of Boston. Dr Abrams also served as a consultant on this book.

Many other books were consulted while researching this volume. The following are listed for those who would like to read more about the most accomplished men and women of this century.

Bettinson, Christopher, *André Gide: A Study* (Heinemann, London, 1977)

Blaug, Mark, *Great Economists Since Keynes* (Barnes & Noble, Totowa, NJ, 1986)

Braun, Ernest, and MacDonald, Stuart, *Revolution in Miniature* (Cambridge Univ. Cambridge, 1978)

Brodsky, Joseph, *Less Than One* (Farrar Straus Giroux, NY, 1986)

Caldwell, Mark, *The Last Crusade* (Atheneum, NY, 1988)

Churchill, Randolph, and Gernsheim, Helmut, eds, *Churchill, His Life in Photographs* (Rinehart and Company, NY 1955)

Coote, Colin R., ed., *A Churchill Reader* (Houghton Mifflin, Boston, 1954)

Craig, Mary, *Lech Walesa and His Poland* (Continuum, NY, 1986)

Crick, Francis, *What Mad Pursuit* (Basic, NY, 1988)

DuBoulay, Shirley, *Tutu: Voice of the Voiceless* (Erdmans, Grand Rapids, MI, 1988)

Espmark, Kjell, *Nobel Prize in Literature* (G. K. Hall, Boston, 1991)

Farber, Eduard, *Nobel Prize Winners in Chemistry* (Abelard-Schuman, NY, 1963)

Fermi, Laura, *Atoms in the Family: My Life with Enrico Fermi* (Univ. Chicago Press, Chicago, 1958)

Feuer, Lewis S., *Einstein and the Generations of Science* (Basic, NY, 1974)

Freeman, E., *The Theatre of Albert Camus* (Methuen, London, 1971)

French, A. P., ed., *Albert Einstein: A Centenary Volume* (Harvard, Cambridge, MA, 1979)

Hammarskjöld, Dag, *Markings* (Knopf, NY, 1964)

Heathcote, Neils, H. deV., *Nobel Prize Winners in Physics* (Schuman NY, 1953)

Holroyd, Michael, ed., *The Genius of Shaw* (Holt, Rinehart and Winston, NY, 1979)

Johnson, Emily Cooper, ed. *Jane Addams: A Centennial Reader* (Macmillan, NY, 1960)

Le Joly, Edward, *Mother Teresa of Calcutta* (Harper and Row, San Francisco, 1983)

Levitan, Tina, *The Laureates: Jewish Winners of the Nobel Prize* (Twayne, NY, 1960)

Lewis, David L., *King: A Biography* (Univ. Illinois, Urbana, 1978)

Magill, Frank N., ed., *Masterpieces of World Literature* (Harper, NY, 1952)

Marconi, Degna, *My Father Marconi* (McGraw-Hill, NY, 1962)

Marriott, Henry J. L., *Medical Milestones* (Williams and Wilkins, Baltimore, 1952)

Nitske, W. Robert, *The Life of Wilhelm Conrad Röntgen* (Ariz. Univ. Press, AZ, 1971)

Pasternak, Boris, *Safe Conduct and Other Writings* (New Directions, NY, 1958)

Schulke, Flip, ed., *Martin Luther King, Jr., A Documentary – Montgomery to Memphis* (Norton, NY, 1976)

Schweitzer, Albert, *Out of My Life and Thought* (Holt, Rinehart and Winston, NY, 1949)

Sencourt, Robert, *T. S. Eliot: A Memoir* (Dodd, Mead & Company, NY, 1971)

Silk, Joseph, *The Big Bang* (Freeman, NY, 1989)

Spiegel, H., and Samuels, W. J., eds, *Contemporary Economists in Perspective* (JAI Press, Greenwich, CTT, 1984)

Walesa, Lech, *A Path of Hope* (Collins Harvill, London, 1987)

Watson, James D., *The Double Helix* (New American Library, NY, 1968)

Weinstein, Edwin A., *Woodrow Wilson: A Medical and Psychological Biography* (Princeton Univ. Press, Princeton, NJ, 1981)

Wilson, David, *In Search of Penicillin* (Knopf, NY, 1976)

Picture Credits

The illustrations, listed by page number, are reproduced courtesy of:

1 Lars Aström; 2 Lawrence Berkeley Laboratory/Science Photo Library; 14, 15 Mary Evans Picture Library, London; 16, 17, 18, 19 (both), 20 Lars Aström; 21 A. Nogues/Sygma; 23, 24, 25, 27 (both), 29, 30, 31 Lars Aström; 34 Popperfoto; 37 (both) Lars Aström; 39 Mary Evans Picture Library, London; 40–41 The United Nations; 43 Crown copyright © reproduced by permission of The Trustees of The Imperial War Museum; 44 Thierry Chesnot/Sipa Press; 47 The Nobel Foundation; 48 Historical Pictures Service, Chicago; 49 (both) The Granger Collection; 50 (both), 51 (bottom) Culver Pictures; 51 (top) The Hulton Picture Company; 52 Culver Pictures; 53 (top) AP/Wide World Photos; 53 (bottom) Historical Pictures Service, Chicago; 55 (left) Sir Norman Angell Collection, Ball State University Libraries; 55 (right) Jane Bown/Camera Press/Globe Photos; 56 © ADN-Zentralbild; 57 AP/Wide World Photos; 58, 59 (both) © Erica Anderson, Albert Schweitzer Center, Great Barrington, Massachusetts, USA; 60, 61 (top) Culver Pictures; 61 (bottom) Crown copyright © reproduced by permission of The Trustees of The Imperial War Museum; 62 Pictorial Parade; 63 Mohamed Youssef/Black Star; 65 Fred Ward/Black Star; 66 Flip Schulke/Black Star; 67 (top) Joseph Louw, Life Magazine © Time Warner Inc.; 67 (bottom) Charles Moore/Black Star; 68 Jasmin/Gamma-Liaison; 69 Shone-Blanche/Gamma-Liaison; 70 Giansanti/Sygma; 71 (top) Gornaciari/Gamma-Liaison; 71 (bottom) J.P. Laffont/Sygma; 72 Pictorial Parade; 73 (top) G. Merillon/Gamma-Liaison; 73 (bottom) Francois Lochon/Gamma-Liaison; 74 Chris Niedenthal/Black Star; 75 deWildenberg/Sygma; 76 Dhladhla/Gamma-Liaison; 77 David Turnley/Black Star; 79 J.K. Isaac/The United Nations; 80–81 Custom Medical Stock Photo; 83 Culver Pictures; 84 NASA; 86 The Bettmann Archive; 87 (top) courtesy AIP Niels Bohr Library; 87 (bottom left) AP/Wide World Photos; 87 (bottom right) The Bettmann Archive; 88 Movie Star News; 89, 90 The Bettmann Archive; 91 (top) Peter Bradford; 91 (bottom) courtesy Philip L. Dondax/International Museum of Photography at George Eastman House; 92 Culver Pictures; 93 (top) National Radio Astronomy Observatory/AUI; 93 (bottom) The Bettmann Archive; 94 UPI/Bettmann; 95 (top) AP/Wide World Photos; 95 (bottom) courtesy The Archives, California Institute of Technology; 96 Culver Pictures; 97 Bob Citron/AllStock; 98 UPI/Bettmann; 99 Jerry Mason/Science Photo Library; 100 NASA; 101 The Bettmann Archive; 101 (inset), 102 AP/Wide World Photos; 103 (top) courtesy Bell Laboratories; 103 (bottom) Michael Davidson/Custom Medical Stock Photo; 104 courtesy AIP Niels Bohr Library; 105 Patrice Loiez, Cern/Science Photo Library; 107 Michael Freeman; 108 Malcolm S. Kirk/Peter Arnold, Inc.; 109 Dr Fred Espenak/Science Photo Library; 110 © Patrick Boye/courtesy Museum of Holography; 111 (left) Lawrence Manning/Physical Optics Corporation, Torrance, Calif.; 111 (right) UPI/Bettmann; 113 AP/Wide World Photos; 114, 115, 116, 117 courtesy IBM; 118–119 Jack Novak/SuperStock; 122 Lars Aström; 124 Brown Brothers; 125 Harold Sund/The Image Bank; 126 Brown Brothers; 127 courtesy Levi Strauss & Co.; 128 (left) Culver Pictures; 128 (right) AP/Wide World Photos; 129 Peter Berndt, M.D./Custom Medical Stock Photo; 130 Brown Brothers; 131 Pamla Toler/Impact Photos; 132 AP/Wide World Photos; 133 David Scharf/Peter Arnold, Inc.; 135 (top, left and right) Brown Brothers; 135 (bottom) Davidson/Custom Medical Stock Photo; 136 UPI/Bettmann; 137 Frank Whitney/The Image Bank; 139 AP/Wide World Photos; 140 UPI/Bettmann; 141 UPI/Bettmann; 142 (left, centre) AP/Wide World Photos; 142 (right) UPI/Bettmann; 143 Charlotte Raymond/Science Photo Library; 145 courtesy Roald Hoffmann; 147 courtesy State University of New York at Buffalo; 149 (left) UPI/Bettmann; 149 (right) Will & Deni McIntyre/Science Photo Library; 150 Lars Aström; 151 CNRI/Science Photo Library; 152–153 CDC/RG/Peter Arnold, Inc.; 155 The Hulton Picture Company; 156 The Bettmann Archive; 158 Brown Brothers; 159 (left) The Bettmann Archive; 159 (top) Manfred Kage/Peter Arnold, Inc.; 159 (bottom) Shell Photographic Library, London, © Shell International; 160 AP/Wide World Photos; 161 (top) The Bettmann Archive; 161 (bottom), 162 Culver Pictures; 163 Brown Brothers; 164 The Bettmann Archive; 165 Culver Pictures; 167 (left) P. Barber/Custom Medical Stock Photo; 167 (right) The Bettmann Archive; 168 (left) AP/Wide World Photos; 168 (right) Pictorial Parade; 169 (top) UPI/Bettmann; 169 (bottom) UPI/Bettmann Newsphotos; 170 (both) UPI/Bettmann; 171 David Leah/Science Photo Library/Custom Medical Stock Photo; 172 UPI/Bettmann; 173 Frans Lanting/Zefa Picture Library (UK) Ltd; 175 (left) Larry Fried/The Image Bank; 175 (right) Prof. Luc Montagnier, Institut Pasteur/CNRI/Science Photo Library; 177 Georgianna Silk; 178 AP/Wide World Photos; 179 courtesy Marjorie Bhavnani; 181 (left) Lars Aström; 181 (right) NIBSC/Science Photo Library; 182–183 Pictor Uniphoto, London, © MCMXCI; 187 Joe McNally; 190 UPI/Bettmann Newsphotos; 191 Brown Brothers; 193 (top) UPI/Bettmann; 193 (bottom) Christopher Morris/Black Star; 194 Popperfoto; 195 (left) George Rose/Gamma Liaison; 195 (right) AP/Wide World Photos; 196 UPI/Bettmann; 197 Bill Varie/The Image Bank; 198 AP/Wide World Photos; 199 Dennis Brack/Black Star; 200–201 reproduced by permission of the Syndics of the Fitzwilliam Museum, Cambridge; 204 The Bettmann Archive; 206 Punch; 207 The Hulton Picture Company; 208 (top) The National Trust/The University of Sussex Library; 208 (bottom) The Bettmann Archive; 209 The Illustrated London News; 210 The Hulton Picture Company; 211 Pictorial Parade; 212 Photofest; 213 (left) Martha Swope; 213 (right) Brown Brothers; 214 UPI/Bettmann; 215 (top) Culver Pictures; 215 (bottom) Photofest; 217 (top) Culver Pictures; 217 (bottom) The Kobal Collection/SuperStock; 218 The Hulton Picture Company; 219 Brown Brothers; 220 Mary Evans Picture Library; 221 The National Portrait Gallery, London; 222 UPI/Bettmann; 223 Photofest; 224 Brown Brothers; 225 Spink & Son Ltd, London/Bridgeman Art Library; 226 (top) The Bettmann Archive; 226 (bottom) UPI/Bettmann; 227 Carl Mydans/Black Star; 228 Brown Brothers; 229 (top) Photofest; 229 (bottom) Ken Heyman/Black Star; 230 The Hulton Picture Company; 231 The Bettmann Archive; 232 UPI/Bettmann; 233 Musée d'Orsay, Paris/Bridgeman Art Library; 234 Culver Pictures; 235 (top) Peter Cunningham; 235 (bottom) AP/Wide World Photos; 236 Guy LeQuerrec/Magnum Photos; 237 (top) Bruno Barbey/Magnum Photos; 237 (bottom) The Hulton Picture Company; 238 Popperfoto; 239 Burt Glinn/Magnum Photos; 240, 241 Richard Howard; 242 Bruce Davidson/Magnum Photos; 243 Abe Frajndlich/Sygma; 245 (top) Photofest; 245 (bottom) Peter Jordon/Gamma-Liaison; 246 Pictorial Parade; 247 The Kobal Collection/SuperStock; 248 courtesy The Nobel Foundation; 249 Andrew Sacks/Black Star; 251 (left) Eric Brissaud/Gamma-Liaison; 251 (right) The Hulton Picture Company; 252 Lars Aström; 253 Raphael Gaillarde/Gamma-Liaison.

Index

Page references in *italic* type indicate illustrations.